D0845873

Imagining Characters

also by A. S. Byatt

FICTION

The Shadow of the Sun

The Game

The Virgin in the Garden

Still Life

Sugar and Other Stories

Possession: A Romance

Angels and Insects

The Matisse Stories

The Djinn in the Nightingale's Eye

CRITICISM

Degrees of Freedom:
The Novels of Iris Murdoch

Unruly Times: Wordsworth and Coleridge

Passions of the Mind: Selected Writings

Imagining Characters

Six Conversations about Women Writers

A. S. Byatt and Ignês Sodré

Edited by Rebecca Swift

Chatto & Windus

LONDON

First published in 1995

1 3 5 7 9 10 8 6 4 2

First published in Great Britain in 1995 by
Chatto & Windus Limited
Random House, 20 Vauxhall Bridge Road,
London SW1V 2SA

Random House Australia (Pty) Limited
20 Alfred Street, Milsons Point, Sydney
New South Wales 2061, Australia

Random House New Zealand Limited
18 Poland Road, Glenfield
Auckland 10, New Zealand

Random House South Africa (Pty) Limited
PO Box 337, Bergvlei, South Africa

Random House UK Limited Reg. No. 954009

Papers used by Random House UK Limited are natural, recyclable products made from wood grown in sustainable forests. The manufacturing processes conform to the environmental regulations of the country of origin.

A CIP catalogue record for this book is available from the British Library.

ISBN 0 7011 6500 6

Typeset by Deltatype Ltd, Ellesmere Port, Cheshire
Printed and bound in Great Britain by
Mackays of Chatham PLC, Chatham, Kent

For Antonio Augusto de Azevedo Sodré
and Maria Thereza de Azevedo Sodré

and

In memory of
John Frederick Drabble
and Kathleen Marie Drabble

Contents

Acknowledgements

The authors are grateful to Richard Cohen, organiser of the Cheltenham Literary Festival 1992, and to Caroline Garland for suggesting Ignês Sodré to him for the *Middlemarch* discussion. Of the many people who have been helpful in the preparation of the manuscript, we would especially like to thank Gill Marsden, Daniel Hahn, Jeri Johnson, Gabriel Palma and Priscilla Roth. We are also very grateful to Michael Sissons of Peters Fraser & Dunlop.

Above all, our thanks go to Jenny Uglow.

Preface

A. S. Byatt met Ignês Sodré when they came together to discuss *Middlemarch* at the Cheltenham Festival of Literature in October 1992, one of the chief themes of which was psychoanalysis and literature. A. S. Byatt is one of Britain's leading novelists and critics and for many years she taught literature at university. Ignês Sodré, a Brazilian psychoanalyst who has practised in England for over twenty years, participates in a poetry reading group for psychoanalysts and has written papers on literature, and in particular on George Eliot. George Eliot brought them together, and they quickly discovered that they shared the writer's view of art, expressed in her essay 'The Natural History of German Life', as a mode of amplifying experience and extending our contact with our fellow men beyond the bounds of our personal lot.

A. S. Byatt opened the *Middlemarch* conversation in Cheltenham by saying that while she did not in general like psychoanalytic criticism – because it tended to analyse the writer rather than the writing and be generally reductive – she had warmed to Ignês Sodré's work, which was unusually illuminating, passionate and generous. The conversation that followed was electrifying, informed not only by a mutual knowledge and love of literature but also by a deep interest in human development. Each speaker sparked the other with a challenging blend of sympathy and difference. It was soon after this that I approached them to see if there might be the possibility of a book. Delighted at the thought of working together again they readily agreed.

It was thought that, by choosing six major texts from different periods in history, starting with the early nineteenth century and Jane Austen's *Mansfield Park*, running through Charlotte Brontë, George Eliot, Willa Cather and Iris Murdoch to Toni Morrison's *Beloved*, one could not only discuss the individuality of each work – what effect it has on the reader and an attempt to understand how it achieves that effect – but also look at the interesting relationship between the books, and think about what that has to say about the development of the novel up to the present day. As a result of this, despite obvious and tremendous differences, it became clear that really successful novels have elements in common, such as underlying archetypal structure, which echo the fairy stories with which we are all familiar. Some of the elements that the works have in common, along with an important discussion as to why stories and reading are so vital to us, are considered in the invaluable final chapter. This was recorded some months after the main discussions, with distance and some hindsight.

For the next two years A. S. Byatt and Ignês Sodré read and re-read their texts, and around the texts, contacting one another regularly about their thoughts, and in May 1994 recording began in earnest. Despite worked-out plans, conversations take on a life of their own, and, while it was important to edit, it was thought that to leave a certain amount of ebb and flow would be the most exciting way of presenting the material, recreating the atmosphere of spontaneity and the pleasure of joining in a live debate. The dialogue form is not, of course, new. Famously, it was a favourite of Greek philosophers, who used it as a means of making complex debate accessible, and of using dialectic to get to the core of a problem, providing opposing arguments in order to stretch the mind and enable it to think for itself. Here, likewise, one feels encouraged to think for oneself as a result of 'listening', not merely to the theories of an individual, but to the animated and original ideas that fly when two informed minds come together. As they testify in their conclusion, A. S. Byatt and Ignês Sodré were continually learning from one another during the course of their conversations.

The consideration that 'art' is the nearest thing to life, as asserted by George Eliot and as broadly accepted by A. S. Byatt and Ignês Sodré for the duration of this book, has been hotly contested in recent theoretical literary debate about language, subjectivity, representation – arguments in which George Eliot herself would surely have been interested and engaged. These academic debates have not been forgotten, but have been set aside here. Philosophically complex literary theories such as deconstruction and structuralism have taught that we must take nothing for granted: all well and good – but a troubling side effect is that some readers now feel inhibited in their response to writing. If Ignês Sodré is right, and we actually need stories as we need to dream – to function successfully as human beings – then surely we should be able, as we are with our dreams, to possess the material with confidence in a way that is both personal and of value, if communicated beyond ourselves.

It goes without saying that each of the novels discussed could have provoked a book by itself: many thoughts, observations and inspirations remain, of necessity, unsaid. There are probably also many which as yet remain unthought: for there is no end to the process of responding to a truly cherished novel. These six books were chosen because they are works that the authors have found themselves going back and back to in life; finding them infinitely rich and complex.

I hope the reader shares in the deep pleasure I had in listening to these conversations as they took place. *Imagining Characters* is a celebration of reading. It hopes to provoke, suggest, stimulate and ignite or re-ignite that love of the written word which so many people share and which, despite increasingly abundant alternative forms of communication, remains so vital and unique.

Rebecca Swift, 1995

Chapter 1

Jane Austen: *Mansfield Park*

Mansfield Park, the backdrop to this, Jane Austen's third novel (1814), is an estate in Northamptonshire owned by Sir Thomas Bertram: Lady Bertram was originally one of three Ward sisters. Sir Thomas takes into his family the young heroine, Fanny Price, who is one of too many children belonging to his sister-in-law who made a bad match. Deeply unhappy at first, largely because she is to be separated from her beloved older brother William, Fanny is coldly received by her cousins, uncle and aunts, particularly by cruel Mrs Norris, the third Ward sister, whose sense of Fanny's inferiority is articulated at every opportunity.

Only Edmund, Sir Thomas's sensitive younger son, is kind to her, and with him, Fanny falls secretly in love. Edmund, however, falls for the charms of the pretty, flirtatious Mary Crawford, a sister by a first marriage of Mrs Grant, who lives at the parsonage. It is agonising for Fanny to watch as he is seduced by the charms of Mary, whom she considers to be an unworthy match. Mary also has a dashing brother, Henry, who upsets the apple cart by flirting outrageously with Edmund's sisters, Julia and Maria, particularly with the latter, who is betrothed to the well-off but foppish Mr Rushworth. Mr Rushworth is the owner of Sotherton, a fine house and estate that Henry wants to 'improve' and modernise. In a famous scene during a visit to Sotherton, Fanny, who has unusually been included, quietly witnesses the complicated undercurrent of feeling in the young people around her.

Things come to a head when, in Sir Thomas's long absence as he attends to the problems on his estates in the West Indies, the young people decide to act in a play, choosing, after some deliberation, the risqué *Lovers' Vows*, which fuels 'romantic' feeling among them. Urged on by the interfering and disingenuous Mrs Norris, and ignored by their lethargic mother, Fanny unpopularly refuses to take a part in the play; she is again the observer as they descend into confused excitement. Sir Thomas returns unexpectedly during rehearsals, is appalled, and puts an end to the theatricals. Henry's flirtation comes to nothing, and in the absence of advice to the contrary from her father, Maria marries Mr Rushworth. Henry decides to turn his attention to Fanny, partly because she herself has by now grown attractive, as Sir Thomas was quick to notice, and partly for sport.

William, now a midshipman, much to Fanny's delight, comes to stay at Mansfield, and becomes a firm favourite. Sir Thomas arranges a ball, despite the absence of his daughters, for Fanny and her brother. Crawford persists with Fanny, wooing her brilliantly and with energy. She, however, refuses his offer of marriage, much to the irritation of Sir Thomas who cannot understand her reticence. With the desire that she should learn the error of her ways, and see what she is missing if she refuses Crawford, he arranges for her to go back to her original family in Portsmouth. Fanny does indeed find the chaotic and impoverished life with her original family very disturbing: her siblings and mother unruly, her father drunken. Only Susan, despite surface disturbance, shows promise. Henry Crawford pays a visit, and is courteous and attentive. He offers to convey her back to Mansfield, her love of which has been intensely fortified. Meanwhile, Edmund's older brother, Tom, has fallen ill and Lady Bertram begins to long for Fanny's company and good sense. Just as we think that Fanny may have to accept at last that Edmund will marry Mary, and it is suggested that Henry may have persuaded her of a degree of constancy, she hears news from Mary that he has eloped, with Mrs Maria Rushworth. The frivolous way in which Mary responds to her brother's misdemeanour shocks Edmund, who is to become a clergyman, out of his infatuation with Mary once and for all. The Crawfords are disgraced, and the path ahead open for Edmund and Fanny, who will now marry. Susan returns to Mansfield and takes up Fanny's redundant position as 'stationary niece'.

BYATT: *Mansfield Park* has been described as one of the great works of Western European literature, and has also been described as a novel in which nobody can manage to like the heroine. Modern criticism has picked on it from all sorts of angles. It's been used to prove that Jane Austen was secretly concerned to make a point about slavery; it's been used to illustrate her involvement with Tory high politics. Feminist critics see it as a critique of patriarchy. What I want to talk about here is the novel I read as a child, and the novel I now read as an adult, as a writer.

SODRE: I think we read novels primarily for the pleasure of being told a story and being able to imagine new worlds, and the different ways in which we relate to these very 'real' imaginary people, the characters in fiction. The first time we met, you joked about reinstating 'the pleasure principle' in novel reading!

BYATT: I think it struck both of us that in this novel the family structure is at the centre. We both felt, didn't we, that this is clear from that very first paragraph about Lady Bertram?

SODRE: Yes, I think it is interesting that Jane Austen starts with the three Ward sisters, because sibling relationships are going to be of central importance throughout the novel: definitely one of the things she wanted to explore, and we want to explore.

BYATT: 'About thirty years ago Miss Maria Ward of Huntingdon, with only seven thousand pounds, had the good luck to captivate Sir Thomas Bertram, of Mansfield Park, in the county of Northampton, and to be thereby raised to the rank of a baronet's lady, with all the comforts and consequences of an handsome house and large income' (Ch. I). The structure's like a fairy story, there are three sisters, and the word 'captivate' suggests things we shall be talking about – enclosure and imprisonment – although at the superficial level it just means to charm and to attract.

SODRE: In the case of Miss Maria Ward we soon feel it must have been to captivate in the first way you imply, because there isn't anything tremendously charming about her personality at all! She had only external beauty and an extreme passivity which, it is implied, was pleasing to men, or to that man, Sir Thomas. But immediately after that Jane Austen brings in the world, everybody's opinion on this marriage: 'All Huntingdon exclaimed . . .' – she brings the satirical point of view.

> All Huntingdon exclaimed on the greatness of the match, and her uncle, the lawyer, himself, allowed her to be at least three thousand pounds short of any equitable claim to it. She had two sisters to be benefited by her elevation; and such of their acquaintance as thought Miss Ward and Miss Frances quite as handsome as Miss Maria, did not scruple to predict their marrying with almost equal advantage. But there certainly are not so many men of large fortune in the world, as there are pretty women to deserve them. Miss Ward, at the end of half a dozen years, found

> herself obliged to be attached to the Rev. Mr Norris, a friend of her brother-in-law, with scarcely any private fortune, and Miss Frances fared yet worse. (Ch. 1)

BYATT: How do you think the structure of the Ward family relates to the structure of the Bertram family and the Price family – and for that matter the Norris family – with which we then become concerned, which the three sisters build?

SODRE: Well, the three Ward sisters together create a new set of three sisters when Fanny, through being adopted at the suggestion of Mrs Norris, becomes the third Bertram sister: the child of the poorest, least successful Ward sister eventually becomes the favourite, and by far the most successful of the three new sisters. But Jane Austen makes it clear that in this world most marriages are built on a false basis; this is going to be explored in much greater depth in the generation of the children, in terms of their choice of partners and their mistakes.

BYATT: Yes, it's as though the narrator of the first paragraph and the first chapter is a kind of gossiping social commentator speaking from a distance, and then she moves into the emotions of people after she's set out this satirical portrait of a society. It interests me very greatly, when we get into Lady Bertram's own family, just how much and how little we are told about what is quite an extensive group of people. Fanny is adopted from the Price family into the Bertram family as you say and becomes automatically in a sense the fairy princess. She's number three, and she's the stepsister; it's not that she's got ugly stepsisters, it's that she's the pretty or the good stepsister. And her first relationships that are described, her first intense relationships are with the brother she's left behind, and with Edmund, the second brother of the two sisters she's joined, with whom she falls in love. When Edmund finds her crying and says to her 'You are sorry to leave Mamma', she doesn't correct him, but makes it clear that what she really wants is to write to her brother. And from that point he becomes her brother but also at that point becomes the hero of the novel, because of brotherly affection – because of noticing her feelings. The whole novel in a way is about people who don't notice other people's feelings, and the extraordinary rarity of people who do notice other people's feelings, or who can act on this noticing. And in that sense Edmund's first act of kindness is a central act that reverberates throughout the whole book.

SODRE: And this establishes what their love is based on, which is kindness and interest in the feelings of the other person. But of course, as you say, he thinks she's missing her mother when in fact she's missing her brother. This is important because it sets the scene for what I think is one of the central themes of the novel – the question of constancy. Fanny remains forever constant to what you might call an original love object – her brother. She declares her love for William, and at that moment, which is also when Edmund begins to appear to her as a kind brother, she starts transferring her love to him. In her choice of sexual partner, she moves only from William to Edmund – from a real brother to an adopted one. This is a very small step: she does not choose a partner from outside the family. On the other hand, the beginning of her own story is deeply concerned with a lack of constancy: she is given away to another family. Her parents were not constant to her. Indeed, Fanny herself is expected to be *in*constant, she is expected to cease to love her original family and to adopt a new one. This she has enormous trouble in doing because the Bertrams aren't very nice!

BYATT: And the motivation of the people who propose the transfer of this child from one family to another is suspect. It's an idle idea of Mrs Norris's, who is apparently offering to be a mother to one of her poor sister's children because she is childless, but in fact she proposes to do no such thing.

> When the subject was brought forward again, her views were more fully explained; and, in reply to Lady Bertram's calm enquiry of 'Where shall the child come to first, sister, to you or to us?' Sir Thomas heard, with some surprise, that it would be totally out of Mrs Norris's power to take any share in the personal charge of her. (Ch. I)

She makes it perfectly clear that it's really Sir Thomas and Lady Bertram who will have the child. And Lady Bertram is a person almost incapable of deep feeling or deep affection, who simply lies on her sofa. So Sir Thomas, who is a man of principle, simply takes over providing for, if not loving, this child.

It's interesting that Jane Austen's second brother was given away in exactly this way. He attracted Mr and Mrs Knight, who asked if they might adopt him and left the whole of their fortune to him. As far as I can see from the biographies, nobody seems to have felt that this was an odd thing to do, and this seems, in fact, in the case of Jane Austen's family, not to have soured relations between the family of origin and the family of adoption. Which may cast some light on why in the end it seems to have been good for Fanny to move from a poorer household to a richer one, even if at first it seems rather frightening.

SODRE: Yes, I also get the feeling from the biographies that there weren't tremendous difficulties about this adoption, that relations between the families remained very friendly; Jane Austen's knowledge of a great house like Mansfield Park came at least partly from her intimate knowledge of her brother's rather grand home with the Knights. It is interesting that in the novel it is a girl that is adopted, not a boy. Mrs Price herself doesn't understand why they should want a girl, when she has so many fine boys. But it is clear that a girl is needed for Mrs Norris, who is a witch, to torment; she's adopted in a very different spirit. The Knights adopted because they needed a child . . .

BYATT: They needed an heir, yes.

SODRE: The Knights gave Edward Austen everything, whereas I think the spirit of Fanny's adoption is that she shouldn't be given almost anything; as far as Mrs Norris, the *oldest* daughter in her family, is concerned, Fanny is brought into the family to take the role of the poor, inferior *youngest* one – in contrast to the wonderfulness of her other *older* nieces, Maria and Julia.

BYATT: Yes, very clever of Jane Austen to divide the adopting women into the very actively malevolent and the very passively neglecting without leaving anything in between, so that there is a gap where there should be an adult woman who cares. And there's a gap where there should be an adult man who cares, simply because Sir Thomas goes away or doesn't look. It raises the whole question of upbringing, which is one of the things people always say *Mansfield Park* is about. If Maria and Julia have been taught to think of themselves as very wonderful and have been taught to behave well without being taught principles, how does it come about that Edmund is so full of good principles? Who has taught them to him?

SODRE: One could just say that Jane Austen is being realistic: children make different use of what's happening in the family; although in fairytales there is often only one 'good' child, usually the youngest. But you are right, it does make one wonder, how could Edmund be all right, in this horrible family? William, who is the first person who loves Fanny, was his mother's favourite; it is therefore possible to imagine that he knows how to be a good 'parent' to Fanny through identification with his own loving mother.

BYATT: You can in a way pick this out by observing *Mansfield Park* as though you were a real human being observing a real world. Towards the end of the book it becomes quite clear that Sir Thomas is in the habit of talking to Edmund, whereas he's completely incapable of talking to his son Tom, because Tom is perfectly incapable of listening to anything anybody says and just flies about being dissipated and has been a great disappointment. Sir Thomas's life consists of being disappointed by people who might expect to be first in his love and admiration, and finding substitutes and secondary people whom he loves much more. So that in the end he ends up with a family that consists of two substitute nieces – having lost (more or less) two daughters – and a satisfactory son and a less satisfactory son. And William of course, the good nephew. It's as though those people capable of affection are finally congregated into a rather narrow space which excludes all those who have been found incapable of responding with real warmth or kindness. Which includes the Crawfords, who are the intruders into this static world where Mrs Norris hurts people and Lady Bertram ignores them.

SODRE: I think this separating out of 'good' and 'bad' qualities is important also in the way Mansfield itself is modified. Mansfield as a place is always idealised ('Mansfield will cure you,' Mrs Grant tells Mary Crawford) – but there is a sense in which it only remains that way if 'good' people get in whilst the 'bad' are let out. It improves with the presence of Fanny; in her passivity she is capable of transforming the home where she lives. Whereas in fact the innovators, supposedly the improvers, who are Henry and Mary, cause havoc.

BYATT: That's very interesting, because it's Fanny's love for William and Edmund's observing that she loves William and communicating this to Sir Thomas, who then invites William to Mansfield Park, that is instrumental in all sorts of changes. And his coming changes their perception of her. I'd never thought of it quite that way before, because you always think of the people who come into Mansfield as being the Crawfords. But of course William is very important, he too comes into Mansfield and is rather robust, and does things like announce that he likes dancing. So Sir Thomas responds by suggesting the ball. Here we have the fairy story again – this is the ball, at which the prince is to be met. Mrs Norris feels violently that the ball ought to be for Maria or Julia, and she actually interrupts Sir Thomas to announce that of course he couldn't hold one because they're away, she tells him she knows what he's going to say – but he brushes her aside:

> 'My daughters,' replied Sir Thomas, gravely interposing, 'have their pleasures at Brighton, and I hope are very happy; but the

> dance which I think of giving at Mansfield, will be for their cousins.' (Ch. 26)

William's delight in dancing perhaps modifies some of the things that are usually said about the static nature of the people held up for admiration, and the extreme busybodiness and activity of the people whom we are meant not to like.

SODRE: I think there is something important about the transforming quality of Fanny's inner life – and this gets communicated almost without her making any external sign that it exists.

BYATT: I remember when I first read this book when I was really quite a little girl. Jane Austen was almost the first author in whom I met the convention that a woman couldn't speak if a man didn't ask her to marry him. They were the first women's novels I read in which the story was about waiting to see whether the man would speak, and silence was an essential part of being a woman no matter how violently you felt. Not only Fanny, but the much more active heroines such as Emma couldn't speak once they had realised what their feelings were. They simply had to be passive. I remember as a little girl thinking, is this my fate, is this the nature of being female? This kind of silence, this kind of waiting? It was a terrible shock to me. I think the convention certainly still existed when I was a young woman, you would never have asked a man to marry you, though you might by then have told him you loved him. Fanny, in a sense, is very purely bound by those conventions. You may see everything, but you must never speak. So your inner life becomes all your life and is lived with an intensity that is the greater because it can have no outside expression.

SODRE: This conventional behaviour is also clearly built into Fanny's personality. Emma is completely different: she is quite forthright and only silent when bound by convention. Fanny, however, says almost nothing: she is bound not merely by convention, but by her psychological difficulties as well. Fanny's psychological make-up is the extreme opposite of Maria's and Julia's – she was brought up to think nothing of herself, even in her original family, so her self-esteem is extremely low; clearly Jane Austen feels that not enough attention is almost as bad as too much! Fanny is not only a virtuous heroine, thoughtful and unselfish, unlike her narcissistic, rather grandiose, cousins; she is also terrified of everybody and everything – a very neurotic heroine! She is very different from all the other Austen heroines; her excessive modesty can be irritating to readers, but Austen does see it as a sign of psychological weakness. Fanny is passive to an unhealthy degree, and it is clear in the end that she gets her 'prince' only because there is no one else around.

BYATT: One moment of psychological truthfulness is when Fanny returns to Portsmouth and observes her sister Susan to be in a perpetual rage, fighting her mother and complaining about the servants. The awful battle between the siblings about the little silver knife that was left by the little girl who died, made my hair stand on end with misery and grief when I first read it.

> Betsey, at a small distance, was holding out something to catch her eyes, meaning to screen it from Susan's.
>
> 'What have you got there, my love?' said Fanny, 'come and shew it to me.'
>
> It was a silver knife. Up jumped Susan, claiming it as her own, and trying to get it away; but the child ran to her mother's protection, and Susan could only reproach, which she did very warmly, and evidently hoping to interest Fanny on her side. 'It was very hard that she was not to have her *own* knife; it was her own knife; little sister Mary had left it to her upon her death-bed, and she ought to have had it to keep herself long ago. But mamma kept it from her, and was always letting Betsey get hold of it; and the end of it would be that Betsey would spoil it, and get it for her own, though mamma had *promised* her that Betsey should not have it in her own hands.'
>
> Fanny was quite shocked. Every feeling of duty, honour, and tenderness was wounded by her sister's speech and her mother's reply.
>
> 'Now, Susan,' cried Mrs Price in a complaining voice, 'now, how can you be so cross?' (Ch. 38)

Fanny does then reflect that her own nature had always been quieter and that she could never have thought as Susan did. And she broods away about how to teach Susan to behave better and to be more decorous. At that point Jane Austen has a little fun with Fanny, which Fanny herself is almost prepared to join in, about how difficult this is for her, how hard it is for her to think how to teach Susan how to behave better, since Susan is braver than she herself is. It is a moment of separation between Jane Austen and Fanny. I think they are very very close in the sense that almost everything Jane Austen says that Fanny feels, she also implicitly or explicitly expresses approval of.

SODRE: Fanny the silent heroine is portrayed as extremely fearful and diffident: 'she crept about in constant terror of something or other' (Ch. 2). Fanny feels and thinks very intensely, but finds it very difficult to communicate. If you have strong needs but you don't express them ever, either there is a kind of permanent desperation, or a more passive giving up – as, for instance, when Jane Austen says that Fanny could take pleasure in hearing about Maria's and Julia's going to balls because it never had occurred to her that she might have been invited too. Here Fanny seems to think that she will be a little girl for ever; sometimes she seems masochistic. But for this silent, self-effacing heroine, any hope of having her needs satisfied depends on a relationship with a very particular, very special person: somebody who will listen to her when she hasn't said anything. Which is what Edmund does. She has this desire for Sir Thomas to respond to her, and he doesn't. She thinks, if only he said 'My dear Fanny' – but he never says it – until the end, when he has finally learned from his experience, from all the terrible things that happened because of his neglect; then he becomes somebody who can be sensitive to needs that are not put into words.

BYATT: Yes, one of the most wonderful moments in the book every time you read it, is when although very angry with Fanny, Sir Thomas causes a fire to be put in her room:

> She was struck, quite struck, when on returning from her walk, and going into the east room again, the first thing which caught her eye was a fire lighted and burning. A fire! it seemed too much; just at that time to be giving her such an indulgence, was exciting even painful gratitude. She wondered that Sir Thomas could have leisure to think of such a trifle again; but she soon found, from the voluntary information of the housemaid, who came in to attend it, that so it was to be every day. Sir Thomas had given orders for it. (Ch. 32)

Sir Thomas produces warmth, that is, both really and figuratively. Warmth which Mrs Norris has prevented her having throughout the book. Every time Mrs Norris has anything to do with a fire, it's a disaster. There's a wonderful comic scene where she disarranges the fire that the butler has beautifully set up before the return of Sir Thomas. Just in order to have something to do she destroys the beautiful shape of it. Fanny is looking forward to the ball:

> . . . and was actually practising her steps about the drawing-room

> as long as she could be safe from the notice of her aunt Norris, who was entirely taken up at first in fresh arranging and injuring the noble fire which the butler had prepared. (Ch. 28)

We ought to talk about Maria and Julia here. We share so much in Fanny's feelings and her inner life, and her perception of the movement of the house, but very occasionally we're also told what *they* feel. We're told what they feel when they're battling to be with Henry Crawford on the seat of the barouche. We are told what Julia feels particularly, but also a little of what Maria feels, when they are both trying to get cast as Agatha in *Lovers' Vows*. But on the whole they are rather like silhouettes or counters. We're told very early on by a narrative voice that they were a kind of simulacrum, they had been taught good manners so they knew better than to behave badly, but they hadn't been taught good feelings so they never actually noticed what anybody felt. Mrs Norris's favouritism has simply reinforced their sense of their own special superiority.

> it is not very wonderful that with all their promising talents and early information, they should be entirely deficient in the less common acquirements of self-knowledge, generosity and humility. In every thing but disposition, they were admirably taught. (Ch. 2)

But they wouldn't make a vulgar scene at a party or anything because they were too well-bred. And yet there is one sharply moving moment, which is when Maria, in the little wilderness at Sotherton, says 'I cannot get out, as the starling said'. Because one has had the feeling again and again all the way through *Mansfield Park* of 'I cannot get out, I cannot get out' – the whole world is restrictive and encircling. And Maria is almost never offered as an object of our sympathy. And yet here she is uttering one terrible phrase, and suddenly she is opened up. She has made the mistake of agreeing to marry Mr Rushworth. For a moment you share her total panic at being confined. And also you know exactly – Jane Austen tells you exactly – by what degree of lack of self-knowledge she got into this mess.

SODRE: And also to what tremendous extent she has been abandoned by her parents – because even Sir Thomas, who ought to have known better, allowed her to marry Mr Rushworth; he feels guilty about that in the end, because he knows that it was through his neglect that he allowed the marriage to take place. Fanny (who wants as desperately to get *in* as Maria wants to get *out*) is aware of his neglect; she says about Sir Thomas that 'somebody who allowed a daughter to marry Mr Rushworth', has no delicacy of feeling.

BYATT: The novel is about intelligence, it's about persistent failures in intelligence. Sir Thomas was just not paying enough attention and was also not quite clever enough. And also is a bit reluctant to interfere, and so he lets Maria marry Mr Rushworth. He did ask Maria the right questions, but accepted her answers too easily. He discovers the truth too late.

> In this quarter, indeed, disappointment was impending over Sir Thomas. Not all his good-will for Mr Rushworth, not all Mr Rushworth's deference for him, could prevent him from soon discerning some part of the truth – that Mr Rushworth was an inferior young man, as ignorant in business as in books, with opinions in general unfixed, and without seeming much aware of it himself.
>
> He had expected a different son-in-law; and beginning to feel grave on Maria's account, tried to understand *her* feelings. (Ch. 21)

SODRE: In the novel he goes through a process of emotional education. As you said, Sir Thomas can talk to Edmund but not to Tom. It is as if Sir Thomas needs a special child so that he can be a good father: he has to have his goodness brought out through contact with somebody who is more in touch; he couldn't be a good father to ordinary children, he needed some special contribution from the outside to be able to function – which is of course what Fanny provides. This reminds me of what you said about Fanny's cold room and his providing her with a fire (after years of not having noticed anything wrong in Mrs Norris's treatment of Fanny!): presumably, at a symbolic level, that is the moment when he finally realises he has always been cold to Fanny.

BYATT: He presumably (and it's interesting that we can talk about them in this speculative manner as though they were real people – I think it's one of Jane Austen's greatnesses that you don't feel you are doing anything wrong if you speculate about her people) – Sir Thomas was presumably not emotionally educated or he wouldn't have picked Lady Bertram to be his wife.

BYATT: Let's talk about the active destroyers in this novel. Mrs Norris is a total destroyer, she is both active and negative. The narrator says once, she hated Fanny because she had neglected her. She is 'bitterly angry' with Fanny over Mr Crawford's offer:

> but she was more angry with Fanny for having received such an offer, than for refusing it. It was an injury and affront to Julia, who ought to have been Mr Crawford's choice; and, independently of that, she disliked Fanny, because she had neglected her; and she would have grudged such an elevation to one whom she had been always trying to depress. (Ch.33)

That is beautifully moving. At no point ever does Mrs Norris see what anybody feels correctly, and she retells any story she is told – for instance the whole story of Mr and Mrs Grant in the parsonage, so that it's not that they have improved what she left but that they have messed up what she left perfect. I think she's an absolutely wonderful creation. The sentences in which her behaviour is described are very very funny, but if you stop at perceiving that she's funny you're only a tiny bit of the way there, because she's actually wicked. She is a wicked fairy. If Sir Thomas hadn't had her in his household, it is quite possible that Maria and Julia and indeed Tom would not have been spoilt, because Lady Bertram was not going to exert herself to spoil them, but only to neglect them, and they might have grown up much better, as Fanny grew up better being neglected.

SODRE: Yes, and they might have made use of other people around them, other influences, instead of being dominated by Mrs Norris. The thing about Mrs Norris is that she doesn't only not understand herself – she lacks self-knowledge, like almost everybody else in the novel – but she also perverts the truth. She constantly invents a different version of reality. So whilst the other people are not in touch with their hearts and minds, they are just ignorant and unthinking, Mrs Norris does a *lot* of thinking, of a completely distorting kind: she lies to herself as much as to everybody else.

BYATT: She is a monstrous egoist, who precedes all George Eliot's monstrous egoists, and could be said to descend from Milton's Satan, I think, who is a very active principle. She rushes around finding things for herself to do which (a) concentrate on herself, and (b) are intensely destructive. I think if she didn't exist, the Crawfords would be more of a principle of evil than they are. As it is, the Crawfords, who are the intruders, in a sense, into paradise, are simply intruding human beings, because the snake is already there. *Mansfield Park* is a closed garden, but something has already got in. The stepmother has got in.

SODRE: Her wickedness is compounded by the insistence on absolutely, at every moment, perverting the truth. The image you brought up, where she undoes the fire and rearranges it to have something to do, illustrates what she does in her mind with her thoughts: after organising the adoption in an entirely selfish way, cleverly manoeuvring everything to avoid any inconvenience for herself, she walks home 'in the happy belief of being the most liberal-minded sister and aunt in the world' (Ch. 1). Milton's Satan was better than that: he could sometimes be truthful to himself.

BYATT: In this book goodness goes almost entirely with intelligence, educated intelligence. Fanny watches very carefully, and although she appears to be a little nobody, she actually thinks very justly. Maria and Julia are completely incapable of thinking, they only feel egoistic feelings. And Jane Austen herself, not Fanny, remarks rather contemptuously that Julia was slightly better than Maria because she'd always been accustomed to think less well of herself because she was the second and had had less attention from Mrs Norris. We're not told that by Fanny, this is not an observation of Fanny's. But Fanny does observe things like that, she never stops thinking. There is almost nothing that Fanny thinks that Jane Austen tells us was wrong or silly. And if you think of the general run of Jane Austen's novels, this is unusual because all Jane Austen's other heroines (except possibly Anne in *Persuasion*), have histories of having thought wrongly, of having made mistakes. Fanny doesn't actually make a slip or a mistake. She is afraid, and at some gut level I believe we experience her fear, which is why I don't hate her as most critics do, I am too involved with her fear to be able to detach myself enough to think she's a mouse. But her judgements are always right. A lot of modern critics, I think, have judged Fanny adversely because they dislike her judgements being right, but I don't think the book allows you to do that. The form of the book is such that you have to take her judgements and say yes of course, this is how it is.

SODRE: I think that's true, and Jane Austen makes it clear that knowledge of others and self-knowledge go together. Fanny knows more about what is going on in other people's minds than anybody else in the novel. But there are moments where Fanny doesn't think entirely correctly, and then Edmund comes in and corrects her judgement; this tends to happen when she is over-censorious in relation to Mary. Edmund corrects her partly because he is falling in love with Mary, but he is also right, and we are given to believe he is right. For instance, at the dinner party when Mary speaks meanly about her uncle, Admiral Crawford, with whom she and Henry lived, Fanny says she thought that Mary was being ungrateful. But Edmund says:

> 'Ungrateful is a strong word. I do not know that her uncle has any claim to her *gratitude*; his wife certainly had; and it is the warmth of her respect for her aunt's memory which misleads her here. She is awkwardly circumstanced . . . I do not censure her *opinions*; but there certainly *is* impropriety in making them public.' (Ch. 7)

Which slightly changes it. And of course he is right: there is no reason why Mary should be grateful, since Admiral Crawford has been a complete monster, but she is being disrespectful when making those puns about . . .

BYATT: – rears and vices, when speaking of the 'circle of admirals' (Ch. 6). What is so beautiful about that, of course, is that it reflects back on to Fanny, who does feel deep gratitude and is also required to feel gratitude to people who treat her abominably. Such as Mrs Norris who sends her trotting endlessly up and down the garden as though she were an animal, and Lady Bertram.

SODRE: But I think the reader sometimes feels unsympathetic to Fanny, when she is too judgmental, and when her goodness is excessive. Then I think one feels, I do at least, that she is being too strict or prim or righteous.

Going back to the scene where Mary is being disrespectful: I think the Admiral is to Mary what Mr Price, her own father, is to Fanny. Mr Price would have given her a very bad home, almost as vile as Admiral Crawford: he drinks and doesn't look after his family. I think, if it's possible to say this, that in Fanny's unconscious there's also a dilemma about whether she needs to respect her father or not. This is why she is so outraged at Mary's lack of respect for her own 'father', the Admiral. And of course when she goes to Portsmouth she doesn't respect him, she's horrified by her family. She has little compassion for them, because she is so shocked. In connection to her father, then, it is psychologically right that she would be over-censorious with Mary, as the issue of having to be grateful to people who are vile, just because they happen to be relatives, must touch her deeply – she projects her own sense of guilt into Mary. Her father is also a sailor, like Admiral Crawford.

BYATT: Fanny is possibly the only Jane Austen heroine who has a whole life story, whom we see from being a child to being married and continuing in happiness after her marriage. Nevertheless, that childhood, the revelation of what it really was, is delayed until very late in the

book, because Portsmouth, which could well have come first, comes last. This is very interesting as a structural device. The visit, the experience of what it would have been like to stay with her real parents, is offered to her by Sir Thomas as a kind of educative punishment to make her love Mr Crawford. And it is a kind of educative punishment, but it only makes her love Mansfield in a way she hadn't quite known she did, although Mansfield is the centre of her value system.
SODRE: I think that's right; and so interesting, that Portsmouth comes towards the end of the novel. So we see her whole development from the age of ten without knowing clearly enough what came before; and yet, as you say, she is the only Jane Austen heroine whom we see as a child, and whose childhood is portrayed entirely realistically. There is nothing at all like Portsmouth – the chaos, poverty, misery – in any of her other novels. When we get to Portsmouth, almost at the end, we also go back to pre-Mansfield, and we can completely imagine what happened before Fanny left her original family. This then deepens our understanding of Fanny's personality. There are infantile conflicts in Portsmouth – the sisters fighting for the knife, for example – that we have seen in modified form in the adult relationships throughout the novel. We have seen the dynamics of the knife episode in the rivalry between Maria and Julia, and more subtly between Fanny and Mary Crawford. We understand Fanny's jealousy better when we get some insight into what she must have experienced at home. Jealousy in Fanny is what makes her most human and alive, most sympathetic, because we can experience the depth of her feeling, the intensity which appears as that furious fight between Betsey and Susan.
BYATT: You see it in complete crudity and in a very confined space and with a great deal of noise. And this again makes you realise that quietness, and the possibility of taking yourself away and having a quiet room, make those emotions more bearable, which is not the first thing you would think of when considering those emotions and putting them into a novel. Fanny's own little space and own little room into which Edmund and Mary intrude with their emotional problems, which they tell her, making her jealous and unhappy, is nevertheless *her space*. Whereas in Portsmouth there isn't any space, and this is very moving.

It's interesting that the Crawfords too are siblings, and the precise degree of affection and distance between those two is very well done. I think the first time I met them I felt that Mary's actual real passion was Henry. She does care very deeply for Henry. And I didn't want to believe the first time I read it that Mary really had attached herself to Edmund; it was surprising.

SODRE: And yet Jane Austen shows us that her attachment is for good reasons; Mary herself thinks that she ought to prefer Tom: 'She had felt an early presentiment that she *should* like the eldest best. She knew it was her way'. Mary is aware of Edmund's qualities, even though she doesn't entirely understand them. For instance, in the same dinner party scene, she notices, and is impressed by, Edmund's kindness to the idiotic Mr Rushworth, his 'good breeding'; she is capable of perceiving his concern for others, and yet, later on, is totally baffled when she discovers he wants to be a priest – she can't make the right connection, because she is emotionally uneducated. Jane Austen tells us this directly, quite sympathetically, when she mentions 'the really good feelings by which she was almost purely governed'.

BYATT: Yes, she has a kind of undeveloped intelligence. You can feel the whole weight of Jane Austen's knowledge of her world as you talk about this. If one goes back a step, you were saying that Fanny is unattractive because she always judges and she always presents the very highest possible line of conduct for anybody as the way they should behave. Whereas Mary doesn't do that, she has a genuine warmth, and is ready to excuse failings and follies and lack of perfection in other human beings. And one immediately finds that more attractive. And yet in a sense Fanny represents the moral centre of a book which really believes it is possible to make moral judgements. Mary's conversation with Edmund after Henry has run off with Mrs Rushworth is quite as horrible as Edmund thinks it is, though at first this is obscured for a modern reader by a dislike, perhaps, of Edmund's expressions of horror.

> After a little reflection, he went on with a sort of desperate calmness – 'I will tell you every thing, and then have done for ever. She saw it only as folly, and that folly stamped only by exposure. The want of common discretion, of caution – his going down to Richmond for the whole time of her being at Twickenham – her putting herself in the power of a servant; – it was the detection in short – Oh! Fanny, it was the detection, not the offence which she reprobated. It was the imprudence which had brought things to extremity, and obliged her brother to give up every dearer plan, in order to fly with her.' (Ch. 47)

In fact these expressions of horror are justified. Mary's reactions are flippant and egocentric.

SODRE: I agree that this scene is as horrible as it is supposed to be, and it shows Mary's ignorance as to who Edmund is. She should have been able to guess that his way of thinking would be entirely different from hers. In fact Edmund says so to Fanny, when she accuses Mary of cruelty: 'I do not consider her as meaning to wound my feelings. The evil lies yet deeper; in her total ignorance, unsuspiciousness of there being such feelings, in a perversion of mind which made it natural to her to treat the subject as she did' (Ch. 47).

But, to go back to Fanny, I don't think she's always judgmental, but I don't like her when she is. She is most judgmental when she's stirred up by her jealousy of Mary. But she is also capable of real self-doubt; for instance when, after deciding not to act in the play, she questions her motives:

> Was she *right* in refusing what was so warmly asked, so strongly wished for? What might be so essential to a scheme on which some of those to whom she owed the greatest complaisance, had set their hearts? Was it not ill-nature – selfishness – and a fear of exposing herself? (Ch. 16)

I think Mary's story is a rather tragic one, because she becomes worse and worse for lack of somebody who can help her with her better feelings: for lack of a good parent. Mary's chosen 'parent' is Henry, again a brother, but one whose influence is of the wrong kind; she doesn't make use of Mrs Grant as she perhaps could have, because although Mrs Grant is a kind, loving woman she is weak, and not really able to understand Mary.

BYATT: In a way Henry and Mary move around rather like a married couple. They're not within a family structure. As a man and a woman who travel together, they come and go. Which brings us back to a sort of incestuous closeness of everybody to their siblings rather than to anybody from the outside world. Which I suppose at one realistic level was a characteristic of a society which was small like that, in which your group was your extended family. People were much less mobile.

SODRE: But this also brings a parallel between Fanny and Mary, who are so completely opposite in character, but who in this respect share some biographical circumstances: their central relationship is with a brother. If Mary had married Edmund, she would have moved from a relationship with a 'bad' brother to a relationship with a 'good' non-brother.

BYATT: Yes, with a stranger.

SODRE: With a stranger, exactly. Whereas if Fanny had moved from William to Henry, she would have made exactly the opposite journey, wouldn't she, from a good reliable brother to a bad stranger. There is an interesting symmetry between the two of them, which I think is quite important.

BYATT: And it's a symmetry that's also brought out by their relationship to Amelia in *Lovers' Vows*, who in a way represents both of them. It's interesting that Lionel Trilling – whose essay on *Mansfield Park* I do admire – obviously dislikes Mary very much more than he dislikes Henry, whereas you obviously feel the opposite.

SODRE: Well, I think that Jane Austen probably liked Mary too much, had made her too attractive, and then has a problem with the ending of the novel; to make it a happy ending she has to side with Fanny's wishes and therefore to turn against Mary, and make her worse than she is. So, although I believe Mary would have talked to Edmund as frivolously as she did in relation to Maria's adultery, I don't believe she could have been as stupid and as cruel as to write to Fanny that she wished Tom dead when he was so desperately ill. I think the author turns against her character at this point because she needs her to be a villain, so that her virtuous heroine can triumph.

BYATT: Jane Austen is one of the masters in the portrayal of embarrassment, and I think Mary is one of those women who start saying something outside the pale and can't stop. Like her long speech in the chapel against the clergy. She's making the wrong kind of noise for the place she's in. She persists, even when it's clear that it's the wrong kind of noise. She tries to redeem herself by muttering later on that had she known that Edmund was destined for the Church she wouldn't have said all this. But it's interesting to know where the embarrassment is located. When Emma insults Miss Bates, Emma has done something appallingly vulgar, and the reader is struck through with knives when Mr Knightley corrects her. And Emma herself immediately sees that she has been both vulgar and morally indefensible. You don't exactly get the same feeling about Mary, because I don't know that you actually really are ever told by Jane Austen that Mary understands how awful some of the things she has said are. And I think Jane Austen is more ready to condemn her than I would be for not understanding, for example, that country people cannot spare a cart to get a harp. Mary genuinely thinks the harp matters more than the harvest. This is clearly wrong, but I think it's also funnier than Jane Austen thinks it is. Just as long as she doesn't get the cart.

SODRE Yes, I think Mary could be forgiven for that. What is 'unforgivable' (within the moral context of the novel) is that she allows herself to be seduced and corrupted by the more 'evil' side of life – London society – when she should have known better, after having had the Mansfield experience. She says about the Mansfield people, 'you have all so much more *heart*'; she has had contact with something better, but she allows herself to be seduced into the world of Mrs Fraser and Lady Webb. Mary is punished for being unable to value her good experiences enough to be guided by them.

BYATT: This is equally true of Henry, if you suppose that he really does come to love Fanny under the influence of Mansfield. In many ways this is the most incredible and most fairytale-like part of the whole novel. That Henry should ever come to want to have Fanny is not wholly plausible, because Fanny has been presented as so invisible. And Jane Austen uses all the tricks of a novelist to make it plausible, by making him annoyed that *she* doesn't see *him*. She keeps it comic by pointing out that it's very unlikely he even remembers seeing Fanny earlier. And you can believe he's the sort of man who will pursue any woman who refuses him until she gives in, because he says that's what he intends to do. You then have to think quite hard about what the influence of Mansfield is, if it renders Henry good in terms of Fanny. I think of when he comes to Portsmouth and notices that she needs to sit down when they are walking, although this is also very convenient for him because it means he can detach her from her family and talk to her. But when I read this as a young girl, I was so relieved for her to have been rescued from Portsmouth by the glamorous Henry Crawford. I did put the kind of stock romantic scenario into action in my own head: virtuous woman reforms wicked rake, and they live happy ever after because virtue is always stronger than vice. Then you come back to Jane Austen's extraordinary inexorable moral realism. It wouldn't have worked. Fanny knows it wouldn't have worked, and is alone in the world in saying 'This isn't going to work, I can't love him, I won't love him.' And Jane Austen then piles it on by pointing out that if Henry had only – and this is where the narrator speaks again – if Henry had only kept it up, if Mary had managed to remain virtuous and marry Edmund, the marriage of Henry and Fanny must have followed quite soon after. It's so deep, really, because Jane Austen lets you know that it would not have worked. You cannot really believe that Henry would have stayed much longer with Fanny than he stayed with Maria, unless he had been trapped in some magic atmosphere in Mansfield, which obviously half works, in so far as it's magic, on people like the Crawfords. It isn't a question of country against city. It has been pointed out that Henry has a perfectly good estate of his own. Mansfield Park does cause Henry briefly to think he'll go back to his own estate in the country and run it and make it good.

SODRE: I suppose this makes one think about how much is evil in Henry's character. Because he is so attractive, one tends to think that there must be something good in Henry that gets corrupted. This seems to be Austen's own opinion, as she wrote to her sister Cassandra that 'Henry [Austen] is going on with Mansfield Park; He admires H. Crawford – I mean properly, as a clever, pleasant man.' But Mary's is a more tragic fate, because Mary is entirely aware of her loss. We don't know what's going to happen. Will she marry an older brother? But she suffers from having lost her love. To a very small degree, so does Henry. But we also believe that Henry's motivation to fall in love with Fanny is mainly that she is out of reach. There are two different ways of thinking about his losing Fanny because of his affair with Maria: one is that he cannot bear not to be loved by Fanny, tries hard to conquer her, and then can't bear to wait and gives her up; the other possibility is that he is simply doing what he plans to do in the beginning: to pierce a little hole in her heart, just out of cruelty.

BYATT: Yes, in a way Henry and Mary come out of a kind of Byronic world, a society world of Lady Caroline Lamb, where the last thing you could admit to was a good impulse and it's fashionable to claim that you do everything for the worst motives and then everybody laughs. It is actually quite hard to admit to wishing to be good or admit to wishing to be virtuous. And the whole tone of that world – it doesn't occur very often in *Mansfield Park* – is most beautifully caught. It's caught perfectly in Mary's speech about the valuelessness of clergymen, which is the kind of satirical speech anybody might make, it's a completely recognisable image of eighteenth-century clergymen, and early nineteenth-century clergymen, it's the one we ourselves now hold. They did very little and just sat about and ate a lot. She just happens to be saying it in the wrong place to the wrong man. And Henry in a way, you could argue, was saying 'I have to make a little hole in her heart, this is how the world works.' And he's playing with something that never does work quite as simply as that. Though whatever it is he's playing with is not sexuality, because the people in the whole of this novel apart from Maria don't feel any physical passion that you can feel. Do you not think?

SODRE: Henry is excited by his power over women. Maria has unbridled passions; her sexuality is seen as destructive because she has no control over it.

BYATT: You know that Emma has very strong physical feelings for Mr Knightley and physical repulsion to Mr Elton, and you know that Anne worships the ground Captain Wentworth walks on and feels his presence in a room from wherever she happens to be sitting.

SODRE: Even though she doesn't see him.

BYATT: Even if she can't see him. She knows he's there. So it isn't a question of Jane Austen having written about sexual passion in youth and having stopped with the novels of her maturity. It is a question of *Mansfield Park* being a curiously passionless book. It's a moral book, and there are moral passions in it and there's terrible pain, the pain of jealousy. Talking of passion brings me back to your point that the loves are all part-incestuous. Which of course could produce physical passion, but there is so little difference between Fanny's love for William and Fanny's love for Edmund. There is this wonderful symbolic moment where she has chains round her neck given to her to hold William's little topaz cross, and one is given by Henry that won't fit into the hole, and one is given by Edmund, that will. But both are around her neck, and both are confining her in a way, bringing us back to one of the very central images of the novel; her neck is held in these two chains.

> All went well – she did not dislike her own looks; and when she came to the necklaces again, her good fortune seemed complete, for upon trial the one given her by Miss Crawford would by no means go through the ring of the cross. She had, to oblige Edmund, resolved to wear it – but it was too large for the purpose. His therefore must be worn; and having, with delightful feelings, joined the chain and the cross, those memorials of the two most beloved of her heart, those dearest tokens so formed for each other by every thing real and imaginary – and put them round her neck, and seen and felt how full of William and Edmund they were, she was able, without an effort, to resolve on wearing Miss Crawford's necklace too. (Ch. 27)

The image of the chain works like the word captivate in the sentence about Lady Bertram at the beginning of the book, at a purely practical level and much deeper. It is as though some kind of rejection was going on, rejection of sexuality, rejection of spontaneous passion, in favour of what you call constancy – or fidelity or a kind of stationary virtue. Because when one identifies with Fanny one doesn't feel desire for

Edmund, one feels jealousy of Mary and pain of concealment. And one feels terribly oppressed by the sexual presence of Henry Crawford, which is unwanted. I think that's the first time in fiction I had ever met that emotion. It doesn't happen in run-of-the-mill fiction, to want to reject an extremely attractive, charming, active sexual man, and to be endorsed in that.

SODRE: I like your phrase, 'stationary virtue', because 'constant' in *Mansfield Park* means both 'faithful' and 'unchanging'; these two meanings are equated to the extent that it would seem impossible to be simultaneously faithful in one's affections and in favour of progress and development!

It is interesting that Henry and Mary (the faithless innovators) are both described as dark, but Mary is dark in a sexy, attractive way, whereas Henry, to start with, is seen as 'plain and black': it is his personality that makes him attractive, his cleverness and his rakishness.

BYATT: And then he becomes glamorous and you forget that they had ever said he was plain, as they forget it. But it has been stated.

SODRE: His sexuality is seen as destructive, because it is used to seduce and to corrupt.

BYATT: And to play power games. In a sense it therefore connects to Mrs Norris, because both of them are playing power games with other people.

SODRE: This duality links to another point I thought we should discuss: that Mary and Fanny may represent different aspects of Jane Austen. Obviously she's not either of them, but she seems to be leaving all the gossip and liveliness with Mary and all the seriousness with Fanny; Fanny doesn't have any sense of humour. There's only one moment in the novel where Fanny spontaneously laughs, at a potentially embarrassing situation. Tom is making a sly face and saying something wicked about Dr Grant: that Mrs Grant needs a lover, because Dr Grant is so repulsive – and he suddenly notices Dr Grant just behind him, and looks completely disconcerted. And Fanny laughs at Tom's face, and doesn't say, 'How can you say such a terrible thing!' But the rest of the time Mary has all the fun. This is interesting, because this aspect of Mary is also linked with her 'immorality' – she is so critical, she mocks people, that she is cynical about marriage and cynical about the Church – and yet she sounds so much more like the Jane Austen of the letters than the morally superior Fanny does. At a deeper level, I think Jane Austen must be examining, via her characters, the relationship between different aspects of herself. The 'gossip', the character who is witty and even cynical, can be quite helpful in terms of understanding the world. It is very different from another aspect of the personality, which is much more serious or preoccupied with what it means to be good. You can't simultaneously gossip about somebody and be sympathetic to them, but you can gossip now and be sympathetic in five minutes' time, and gossip again in ten minutes. These different attitudes of the same person can be explored in two different characters.

BYATT: One of the deep and intense pleasures of writing novels is this possibility of dividing yourself up and pushing aspects of yourself out to see where they would go if they were the most important aspect. I remember Iris Murdoch once said to me, 'I have a certain number of kinds of people I can do and I move them around and make them slightly different and do them again differently.' Jane Austen has done so many wonderful satirically slicing, judging sorts of people. Then she has this satirical, slicing, judging narrator. Because in the early chapters of *Mansfield Park* the voice of the narrator is very close to the voice of Mary. For instance – this is quite a bit of the way in – the narrator observes: 'Maria was more to be pitied when Sir Thomas came back than Julia, for to her the father brought a husband and the return of the friend most solicitous for her happiness would unite her to the lover on whom she had chosen that happiness should depend'. Well, that's sharp, and it's the sort of thing that Mary could have said.

SODRE: Shall we discuss *Lovers' Vows* and theatricals now?

BYATT: It's surprising how many people in the early days of Jane Austen criticism wrote about the theatricals without actually taking a good look at the play that was being acted. Although as Marilyn Butler (who has done a lot of very useful research on *Lovers' Vows* and the private theatricals in the Austen family, which were many) has pointed out, Kotzebue's *Lovers' Vows*, in Mrs Inchbald's translation, was extremely well known at the time and was a kind of point of reference among people's discussions of German Romantic feeling and theatrical licence. The thing that struck me is just how many correspondences of varying kinds there are between the plot and characters of *Lovers' Vows* and the plot and characters of *Mansfield Park*.

SODRE: Yes, I think that's tremendously interesting and clever, the way it all works out. I suppose she was assuming that her reader would know the play, because she doesn't tell you enough about it in the novel. To be able to understand all the correspondences you have to know the play. The novel works without it, but there's a lot of depth, and a lot of fun, in knowing who's who and what they're doing. (Very briefly, the plot is this: Frederick, the hero, comes back from the war to an emotional reunion with his weak and impoverished mother Agatha, and discovers he is the natural son of Baron Wildenheim. The Baron wants his daughter Amelia to marry the silly Count Cassel, but she declares her love for her tutor, Anhalt; in the end the Baron marries Agatha, and Amelia marries Anhalt. The subtlety of Austen's use comes in her cast list: Frederick – Henry Crawford; Agatha – Maria Bertram; Baron Wildenheim – Mr Yates; Amelia – Mary Crawford; Anhalt – Edmund Bertram; Count Cassel – Mr Rushworth.)

I think it's important to make the point that although Jane Austen may have felt emotionally ambivalent about theatricals (one of Austen's biographers, Park Honan, suggests a possible rivalry with her extrovert and flirtatious cousin Eliza de Feuillide, a theatrical 'star' in the family, who Mary Crawford may resemble) they were an accepted and important part of the Austen family life. The theatricals in the novel, set up to be strongly disapproved of, relate essentially to the characters and the plot, and not to Austen's own life. She is making the point that for that family, at that moment, in the particular circumstances of the absence of Sir Thomas, the father, the theatricals were destructive. Nor I think does it have to do with her dislike for this particular play. Sometimes critics say she hated the play, but I don't see any evidence. What one sees is Austen making extremely good use of the play to enrich the novel. I'm struck by the fact that she never says explicitly that Agatha is Frederick's mother, and we only know that because Mary eventually says jokingly that Maria looks so maternal. When you understand what the play is about, you realise the extraordinary meaning of the scene Sir Thomas nearly falls upon when he comes back. The scene he would have seen on his arrival, had he gone straight into the theatre, would have been the endlessly rehearsed one between Agatha-Maria and Frederick-Henry. Maria and Henry had chosen to play mother and son (rather than the romantic young lovers Anhalt and Amelia) because of the possibility of being in close physical contact – the long separation between mother and son, and her fragile state, making this necessary in the scene. So what Sir Thomas would actually see would be a mother and a son touching each other like lovers: an incestuous relationship!

BYATT: It's a beautiful reversal of the situation of Oedipus, really. You can make love to a man who is neither your father nor your fiancé because you are pretending to be his mother. It has a sort of wit to it.

SODRE: Tremendous. But one can't see it immediately, because one isn't quite told that. It's obviously funny because Sir Thomas would see his child Maria dressed up as a mother (so symbolically being Lady Maria) making love to the son, and that's the result of his (Father's) having been away for three months . . .

BYATT: And of course the son is played by an intruder, Henry Crawford, a young man who has got into his family while he wasn't looking, in an illegitimate way acting in fact the illegitimate son of Baron Wildenheim, who is a repentant seducer, who is played by another intruder, Mr Yates. I've seen several comments on *Lovers' Vows*, but none of them have pointed out that what Sir Thomas meets is Mr Yates doing a ghastly parody of Sir Thomas himself, as a sort of owner of the house in his own library ranting and raving. And all sorts of other delicious parallels – there is a moment when Baron Wildenheim summons the clergyman Anhalt and asks him to find out if his daughter Amelia's affections are engaged or not, because he doesn't want her to marry Count Cassel, the frightful fop; Count Cassel of course is being played by Mr Rushworth, who is going to marry Maria. And Sir Thomas subsequently enacts that scene. He does ask Maria if she wants to marry Mr Rushworth, and he doesn't press her as Baron Wildenheim does. And Amelia in the play says 'No I don't want to marry him, he seduces young women, he's just stupid, he's a fop, I know what true love is.' Previously the Baron has said to Anhalt, 'Her affections cannot be engaged elsewhere', and Anhalt agrees with him. Which is of course Sir Thomas's opinion both about Maria and later about Fanny when he's trying to push her into marrying Henry Crawford, and he's wrong about both of them, their affections *are* actually engaged elsewhere. And so in a way Sir Thomas bears a very peculiar relationship to the central figure in *Lovers' Vows*. I think the most moving parallel is the parallel between Amelia and the Fanny/Mary character we've been discussing. It's Mary who gets to act Amelia, and Amelia is a woman who breaks that law of silence which is imposed upon Fanny. Fanny is in love with Edmund, who is both her adviser and a clergyman or about to be; Amelia is in love with Anhalt, who is her spiritual adviser and a clergyman and lives in her house. But when Anhalt says 'Can you bring yourself to love Baron Cassel?' Amelia simply says 'No, I love *you*, will you marry me?', which a woman may not do, and which is obviously what Fanny's deepest soul must want to say, but she can't. Mary on the other hand can, or at least can go further. Mary loves playing this part, because she can ask Edmund to marry her in this scene. I think they never actually get round to doing it together, do they, they keep practising it at Fanny, perpetuating the triangle.

SODRE: They do it together only when rehearsing in front of Fanny, but we don't see it. We see it from the point of view of Fanny, who's feeling tortured by having to watch them proposing to each other.

BYATT: It does prove the point that in many ways dramatic enactments and powerful emotions are extremely dangerous to spectators, and indeed to participants, and the more you know the story of *Lovers' Vows,* the more it does make this point in its subtle and cruel and witty way. The question I ask myself as a writer is – when Jane Austen decided to use *Lovers' Vows* as the play which Mr Yates had been in and which he as an outsider brought into Mansfield Park, did she *right from the beginning* create Mary and Fanny and Edmund and Sir Thomas partly in terms of their parallelisms and their differences from the characters in the play? Because I can't see how she could not have done, unless she only thought of *Lovers' Vows* very late on.

SODRE: Yes, I agree, it's difficult to imagine that she would have researched until she found a play that would fit in with her plan so extremely well. I think that would have been difficult.

BYATT: No, I think she must have had the play in mind from the beginning. What I emotionally feel (and I say this because I don't think it can be provable) is that in many ways the centre of *Lovers' Vows* for Jane Austen was what Marilyn Butler says the general public did find most shocking, which was the indecorous behaviour of Amelia in saying who it was she loved and in actually proposing to a man. And I think buried in the centre of *Mansfield Park* and all the events that take place is the prohibition, like a fairytale, but it's also convention in society, the prohibition that Fanny wouldn't break: she couldn't speak to Edmund, because she was a woman. Also, of course, a poor relation. Mary could get round it because if she was in the position of acting 'I love you' she could make him feel it. But Fanny is completely stuck in silence, which is a moment of pure horror. There in a way is the sexual/emotional centre that we were saying was missing, in our earlier discussion of the characters. There, in Amelia, is a woman who does speak and who does feel passion. Truly virtuous passion, although people disapproved of her. The other thing the contemporary public disapproved of was Baron Wildenheim finally being persuaded by his son not only to take his illegitimate son into the house as his child, equal to his legitimate daughter, but to marry the woman he has seduced and betrayed, which is what Henry Crawford conspicuously doesn't do with Maria at the end. The little parallels run. Nevertheless, it must be clear to anybody that Baron Wildenheim's conduct is virtuous. If you have seduced and betrayed a woman, it is better to marry her even if her son is by now grown up. And at first the Baron proposes to make her a little separate establishment where she can live quietly and be visited, which is exactly what happens to Maria. And Frederick says, 'No, no, you can't do that, she is my mother, you must marry her in public.' And this was German Romantic morality. But you wonder how much it actually differs from Jane Austen's morality, because it sees the emotions and situations truthfully, and it says there are certain things that it's obviously right to do. It produces all sorts of curious reverberations, doesn't it?

SODRE: Yes, and ambiguities as well. Amelia is not supposed to be so bold as to declare herself to Anhalt, and yet, as you say, it must be right that she does. Mary, who is much bolder than Fanny, and badly brought up, half does that by accepting to play Amelia, but in fact she never actually tells Edmund that she loves him.

BYATT: No, she goes through an agony of waiting to see if he will declare himself to her. Just as much agony as Fanny goes through knowing that he wants to declare himself to Mary and that she doesn't come in anywhere.

SODRE: The only woman who shows her emotions openly is Maria, who is adulterous – the woman who does speak is this woman who wants to get out and doesn't know how to in a way that is morally acceptable. Maria doesn't have any other choice: either she is claustrophobically imprisoned with Mr Rushworth, or she's having an adulterous affair which leads to her ruin – there isn't any possible good moral outcome.

BYATT: There is, of course – that's the glory of Jane Austen; there is a moment at which she makes it perfectly clear that what Maria should have done is tell her father that a mistake has been made. And he would have got her out of it. She walked herself into being engaged and Mrs Norris pushed her. And you don't even quite know which of them to blame, although at that point the narrator blames Sir Thomas.

SODRE: But this doesn't even occur to Maria – of course there is a choice, but not in her mind. She doesn't conceive of the possibility of not marrying Mr Rushworth, and not marrying Henry Crawford either. In the chapel scene at Sotherton, Henry whispers to her 'I do not like to see

Miss Bertram so near the altar'. In other words, 'I don't want you to marry Mr Rushworth.'

BYATT: He does do that, and then he just goes away.

SODRE: Then he goes away, without saying anything to her, so he is tremendously cruel, and she is totally at a loss to understand what is going on. I think she expects Henry to propose to her, and then she can go to her father and tell him – she does not know how to act in this intermediate position in which she might not have one or the other.

BYATT: Again, the reader has to do so much moral work, because at the moment when Henry goes away without saying anything to Maria, Jane Austen doesn't give you a lot to go on in which to imagine Maria's state of mind. And yet if you choose to do so, you wholly can.

SODRE: But going back to the ambiguity implied by the use of *Lovers' Vows*, it is clear in the play that if Frederick and Amelia *hadn't* behaved unconventionally, horrors would have ensued: if Amelia hadn't told Anhalt that she wanted to marry him, she would have married Count Cassel, which would be like Maria's marriage to Mr Rushworth, conventionally right but morally wrong. This acceptance of the unconventional is implied (but kept encapsulated in the play – made safe by being a 'fiction' inside the 'true' story), whilst simultaneously traditional values are praised and recompensed, which makes it all more complex and more ambiguous.

BYATT: That's why it's so important to have read it. Because Marilyn Butler rightly points out that there was a whole tradition of Romantic art which said that the important thing was to liberate the passions and that people should act on their impulses, and that if you were in a confining situation it was bad for you, you must throw it over. She sees Jane Austen's art as a conservative art which sets itself against Romantic freedom and Romantic passion, which for Jane Austen, and for people like her, culminated in the French Revolution and in blood and terror. It used also to be fashionable to say that Jane Austen lived during the Napoleonic Wars and recorded nothing and knew nothing. But in fact her cousin Eliza's first husband's head was cut off by the guillotine, and her brothers fought in big naval engagements. Jane Austen knew perfectly well what world she was living in. And it produced a kind of caution; it made a decorous and well-ordered society seem important. I think Marilyn Butler is very wise. But I think what you have just said and what I feel, after reading *Lovers' Vows*, is that the kind of emotional truths that are in *Lovers' Vows*, even if they are truths about openness and making an escape from bad convention, do operate at some level in

Mansfield Park. It's not simply silly and bad, *Lovers' Vows*, because the truth of the feelings does matter. Maria is acting out a conventional plot constructed by Mrs Norris, which says that you have to marry a large fortune and the important thing is to get married quickly. And she's doing it because she doesn't want to be restrained by Mansfield Park. And this is worse than what Amelia does in *Lovers' Vows*. Amelia sees right through Count Cassel and says, 'I can't marry anybody so silly who goes about seducing people.' In many ways of course Count Cassel is a wonderful combination of Henry and Mr Rushworth: he's an idiot like one of them and a seducer on principle like the other, in his pink cloak.

I think the play is one paradigm of how to tell a story about seduction, and love and truthfulness and families, and in *Mansfield Park* it's rejected, and yet it's also accepted. The Cinderella story and various other fairy-story structures of brothers and sisters and mothers and fathers and renewal and balls and princes, are another paradigm. Fanny is Cinderella, even down to sitting next to a fire that doesn't exist, she's the daughter of the ashes, and when she finally gets a fire it's like being the real daughter instead of the stepdaughter. There are a number of fairy stories in Grimm and Perrault where the resourceful princess, having won her prince, then loses him again and has to go off on a quest, or some witch magics him into forgetting her. The prince then agrees to marry someone else, the witch, or the witch's daughter, and when the whole wedding with the second bride is set up the first one then comes in and reveals: 'I am your true love, you can't marry this person.' She casts off her servant's disguise, or the dirty donkey-skin. She throws away the ashes and comes out in her beautiful dress with stars and moons on it, rather like Fanny's beautiful dress with the silvery spots on it, and claims her lover.

SODRE: Yes, and it is interesting that these particular fairy stories are very much to do with sibling rivalry which, as we've said, is an important theme in *Mansfield Park*. Like the stories in which the third is always the one who gets the prize, never the first. A bit sad for you and me! The first and second are either bad or silly, and the third one gets the prize; probably a reaction to the privileges granted to the first-born. This is also interesting in connection to the third Miss Ward, the first Fanny Price. Fanny Ward is the only one who marries for love, like Amelia, and she's certainly not recompensed for that, it's a complete disaster. The other two sisters do better from marrying completely for interest. So there is also another interesting version built into the first paragraph of the book, in which the person who did the right thing, who married for love, has a terrible fate. The third sister in the Ward story doesn't get the prince, she gets horrible Mr Price.

BYATT: She gets horrible Mr Price and very large numbers of children, which is what is likely to happen to you if you marry for love. A very dry comment on marrying for sex, in a way, that. It's completely anti-romantic. It starts out with a fairytale structure – 'There were once three sisters' – and then it says something completely unexpected about all of them.

SODRE: The first one, Mrs Norris, was a wicked witch, the second one was almost as bad and married for money, the third one was good and married for love – and look what happened to her!

There are several contrasting structures and themes at work here, but the dominant one is that you have to be constant to your original family, and that in an ideal world you would never leave your home. Fanny and Edmund in the end move happily back into Mansfield; Jane Austen herself refused a marriage of convenience and stayed firmly rooted at home.

BYATT: I do feel that a lot of the insistence on home and constancy is to do with Jane Austen's own realisation that she had reached an age where she has ceased to be a princess. As you have pointed out, she wrote a letter at this time saying 'from now on I shall sit on the sofa'. ('By the by, as I must leave off being young, I find many douceurs in being a sort of chaperone for I am put on the sofa near the fire and can drink as much wine as I like.') She has in a sense identified herself with Fanny and Lady Bertram, who watch from the sofa. And there is a sense in which Fanny is the novelist who doesn't miss anything, but doesn't act except by noticing. There's a sense in which Jane Austen has ceased to think of herself in terms of all these myths, all of which end with a prince, and has instead decided to put family affections at the centre, and the men to whom she was most attached really from then on were her brothers, her sailor brothers, her good sailor brothers. She loved her sister, with whom she shared a bedroom. Like Fanny's, her space was small and cramped. She seemed to cease to look outside it. Again, if you read *Persuasion*, that looks different.

SODRE: Yes, it does. *Persuasion* is much more hopeful on the subject of marriage; we believe that Anne and Captain Wentworth will have a good marriage, because they have shown they could maturely recover from old wounds and disappointments; it is fundamentally a story about repairing the seemingly irreparable damage done in the past. The successful marriage is seen as the consequence of a painful, but healthy, process of growing up. Whereas in *Mansfield Park* Jane Austen is clearly writing about the impossibility of good marriages. The only possible good marriage in the whole novel is that of Fanny and Edmund, but their future happiness is presented rather hypothetically. At the point in her life when Jane Austen was writing *Mansfield Park*, she had refused a marriage of convenience, and presumably had made a conscious choice of spinsterhood. I think she probably did feel it was the right choice. She'd rather be a novelist, a woman 'lying on the sofa', but mentally the opposite of Lady Bertram, somebody with an active, creative mind. It would have been very difficult to be a novelist if she had lots of children. Like Fanny left sitting on her own in the wilderness in Sotherton, the rooted, immobile character may be lonely, but behind the apparent passivity there is an active, observant mind taking everything in: in this rather theatrical scene, while all the other characters rush in and out in a mindless way – all 'rush-worths', as it were – Fanny is the only person who knows what is going on in the minds of all the other characters. I think the position of the unmarried novelist is being examined through the apparently passive heroine.

BYATT: Because Jane Austen became engaged for one night, didn't she: she accepted an offer of marriage and was brought home in considerable disarray the next day because she'd come down to breakfast and announced that she couldn't go through with it. I find this intensely moving. She may of course, come to think of it, have felt rather like Fanny refusing Henry Crawford. 'Everybody thinks I ought to do this, but when I really think about it I see I can't.' So she went home. And then she started thinking about the values of home and independence. But she doesn't have an independent woman in this novel. It's amazing how, throughout the whole history of novels by women, it is held against the author who is the independent woman that she hasn't created a heroine who is an independent woman. Which seems to me quite wrong. What you do is create an image of dangers and possibilities that other women run through. George Eliot is accused of having betrayed Dorothea by not making Dorothea into George Eliot. And you could accuse Jane Austen of having betrayed Fanny by not making her into Jane Austen. But it would be wrong. It's just that Jane Austen is herself Jane Austen, and *observes* Fanny.

BYATT: I did feel as a child, as a young woman, as a critic, as a teacher, that whereas her not telling you about the final dialogue between Darcy and Elizabeth is fine, and her not telling you about exactly what Mr Knightley and Emma said to each other is fine, there is something very depressing about her not giving us the scene in which Edmund realises how long Fanny has loved him, and understands exactly what the real relationships between all the people were during all that time. I feel this partly because it causes you to dislike Edmund quite a lot, the way she narrates the final meeting between prince and princess.

SODRE: I think that's right. There is an irony in the narrator's voice that makes you feel there's no reason why you should believe that this marriage will be all right.

BYATT: I agree with you.

SODRE: The satirical way in which she talks about Edmund's 'unconquerable passions' doesn't allow us to take his love for Fanny seriously: 'Scarcely had he done regretting Mary Crawford . . . before it began to strike him whether a different kind of woman might not do just as well'. This goes beyond the witty author poking gentle fun at her character: 'might do just as well' shows an Edmund functioning in 'Crawfordian' mode. She continues by inviting the reader to speculate:

> I purposely abstain from dates on this occasion, that every one may be at liberty to fix their own, aware that the cure of unconquerable passions, and the transfer of unchanging attachments, must vary much as to time in different people. – I only intreat every body to believe that exactly at the time when it was quite natural that it should be so, and not a week earlier, Edmund did cease to care about Miss Crawford, and became as anxious to marry Fanny, as Fanny herself could desire. (Ch. 48)

I thought that her not allowing Fanny to tell Edmund how long she had loved him for, even after he had told her that he loved her, was rather mean! Because once Edmund has told her, the whole question of silence should end. After all, Edmund had much appreciated her 'constant little heart' before. She doesn't give us enough to convince us that there is such a thing as a good marriage.

BYATT: She tells us about this marriage after dismissing Maria and Henry Crawford and saying 'Let other pens dwell on guilt and misery.' But she then does not dwell on happiness or recognition or warmth. The actual sentence has a very curious grammatical structure here for what is in a sense the romantic denouement: 'His happiness in knowing himself to have been so long the beloved of such a heart, must have been great enough to warrant any strength of language in which he could cloathe it to her or to himself; it must have been a delightful happiness!' (Ch. 48). Now here is an author who puts it as a hypothesis; she doesn't say 'it was', she says 'it must have been', and he 'could' possibly find some language in which to clothe his delight. And I agree with you, it feels as though Austen is holding back; she says 'You imagine it if you like.' It's like 'Let other pens dwell on guilt and misery'. 'Let somebody else imagine the language in which Edmund may be supposed to have declared his gratitude or love to Fanny.' In that sense of course – I've only just thought of this – it's not unlike the end of *Villette* where the narrator draws back and says 'If you want to imagine that Paul Emanuel and Lucy were happy together you may.' Why is there this reluctance to imagine happiness?

SODRE: Austen is usually rather good at imagining happiness; I think the specific problem here is linked to what we were saying before: she is exploring the negative side of marriage, at the point in her life when she was working through her disappointment at not marrying and coming to the conclusion that being a single, intellectually productive woman *was* the best position for her. And yes, it is a bit like the end of *Villette*, teasing in a similar way; it frustrates our wish to have a good marriage at least at *some* point, after the series of horrible marriages. The central thesis is that ideally one should remain 'not out', as close to one's original love objects as it is possible to be, without either being incestuous (Maria and Henry acting mother and son) or entirely narcissistic (Lady Bertram who is forever 'constant' to herself).

BYATT: Yes, this brings us back to Mary Crawford's question about Fanny Price – is Miss Price 'out' or is she 'not out'? It brings us back also to Mansfield, which is an enormously enclosed world. It has a far more enclosed landscape than any of Jane Austen's other novels, where people are always going on walks across the countryside – they go on a lot of walks in *Persuasion*. Elizabeth Bennett does all this very rapid walking to see Jane. Fanny gets exhausted if she walks anywhere, and likes the feeling of being enclosed by the shrubbery near the house; you get the feeling that the woods enclose the castle, moving back to the fairytale image. You get the feeling that autumnal weather, and slightly bad weather which keep you in one place, are actually very agreeable. Which may be interesting. And Sotherton, in itself, contains in and out, because the outside is what Henry Crawford is going to improve; they're going to make all these vistas and views and rides where you can move away from the house, and everybody goes and sits in the little wilderness with the wicket gate, which is an ancient literary image of the way into the Wild Wood, or the Wood of Error. But they go out. And as has been endlessly pointed out, everybody squeezes out through the fence and doesn't even go out through the gate (therefore taking themselves away for ever from Bunyan's Christian Pilgrim who was prohibited from succeeding in his quest if he didn't go through the wicket gate). But the centre of Sotherton is the chapel, which is *in*. And which Fanny deeply feels ought never to be changed, ought not to be improved, to be left as it is because countless generations of people have worshipped there. It's Mary who criticises the family structure, of the family with servants who are worshipping there very reluctantly and not wishing to be servants and not wishing to worship. Fanny and Edmund reprove Mary for this frivolity. Both Mansfield and Sotherton are in some sense connected with Christianity. The centre of them both is the Anglican Church and the truths of the human spirit, which matters a great deal to Jane Austen, a kind of piety. And the imagery of Mansfield as the enclosed place invaded, which we have compared to paradise invaded by the serpent and subsequently by sin and death, goes with the sense that the chapel is enclosed and should be preserved inside Sotherton. And perhaps there's a fear that some sort of religious, accepted structure is threatened in all the places in *Mansfield Park*.

SODRE: The question of place is a central one. Mansfield and Portsmouth, and also London and Sotherton, have particular meanings and the characters, especially Fanny, have particular relationships with the places themselves; place is more than a mere location for this or that family, or this or that character. Mansfield stands in total contrast to Portsmouth: their qualities are entirely opposed. Fanny loves Mansfield as a place independently from her love for Edmund; its order and tranquillity make it possible for her to feel calm and integrated herself. Portsmouth – her original home – is a place where she feels desperate. I think what's invested in *place* is a relationship, not with the people who live there, but with a 'model' of a person in the mind – so all the characteristics of Mansfield that make it good are also the characteristics of the relationship Fanny would like to have with an ideal partner.

I think it's as if, unconsciously, the place represents a parent; Fanny's relationship with Mansfield symbolises a very early relationship, with a parent who, in her mind, is much better than the parents she has to contend with in reality: the horrible mothers and the neglectful father. Portsmouth represents a chaotic relationship with a *bad* parent; it's not just the place where she meets Mr and Mrs Price, it represents, in itself, the psychological relationship that she gets immersed in by virtue of *being* in that actual place. So that the cure for that is being inside a different place; symbolically a place in the mind of a more ideal parent, a parent who could hold her securely in a tranquil, quiet way.

BYATT: Yes, one of the things that interests me in terms of what you've just said is the long speech about the nature of memory that Fanny makes to Mary, just after Fanny has grown up, when they are beginning to speak to each other. I think she only comes to love Mansfield as a place when she has a memory of it as a place where she thought, where she read, where she grew up, where she had her own room even without a fire in it. I'll read you a bit of this:

> 'Every time I come into this shrubbery,' says Fanny, 'I am more struck with its growth and beauty. Three years ago this was nothing but a rough hedgerow along the upper side of the field, never thought of as any thing, or capable of becoming any thing; and now it is converted into a walk, and it would be difficult to say whether most valuable as a convenience or an ornament; and perhaps in another three years we may be forgetting – almost forgetting what it was before. How wonderful, how very wonderful the operations of time, and the changes of the human mind!'
>
> And following the latter train of thought, she soon afterwards added:
>
> 'If any one faculty of our nature may be called *more* wonderful than the rest, I do think it is memory. There seems something more speakingly incomprehensible in the powers, the failures, the inequalities of memory than in any other of our intelligences. The memory is sometimes so retentive, so serviceable, so obedient – at others, so bewildered and so weak – and at others again, so tyrannic, so beyond control! We are to be sure a miracle every way – but our powers of recollecting and of forgetting, do seem peculiarly past finding out.'

This is about the longest speech Fanny has ever made, it's the first time she's made a public speech, I think, almost to anybody but Edmund. And it's very sad that the next sentence is: 'Miss Crawford, untouched and inattentive, had nothing to say' (Ch. 22). Because at this point Miss Crawford is not listening to Fanny. But it seems to me that the image of the shrubbery growing and the hedgerow growing and the place changing, clearly represents Fanny – it began as something rather small or almost nothing, and it only means something to her when it's contained in her memory of its growth. She herself at the point when people begin to see her, because she's now visible and a pretty woman, has also got a past which is deeply valuable to her. And then she is cast off into her original past which is Portsmouth, which becomes a kind of horrible, demonic place of terror. It's a beautiful piece of construction by Jane Austen, and it's a beautiful moment in Romantic observation.

SODRE: Yes, I think it's very beautiful, and so interesting that this scene in the shrubbery precedes her visit to Portsmouth, her contact with the real past which, presumably, is different from her construction of the past in memory; her reference to eventually 'forgetting, almost forgetting what was before' – the rough hedgerow – is connected to the wish to forget her bad experiences. What she says about the wonderfulness of memory is also linked with the central theme of constancy: remaining attached to one's good experiences, and being faithful, and grateful, to the past. Discovering Mansfield as her true home, when she only has the *memory* of it, means she has established it firmly in her internal world as the container for her past good experiences.

BYATT: I was thinking when you were speaking about constancy of Anne Elliott's remarks to Captain Wentworth about 'All the privilege I claim for my own sex is that of loving longest, when existence or when hope is gone' (*Persuasion*, Ch. 23). A sense of long attachment was deeply valuable to Jane Austen.

And about reflection, I think the other thing that happens in all novels is that because you read a novel by yourself in a room, inner space in your own mind and outer space in novels become somehow equivalent, images of each other. And Fanny is very much a reading person, she reads by herself in her room, in the east room without the fire, this is what she does there. And we said earlier that Fanny becomes the image of Jane Austen the novelist sitting on the sofa and observing the life and making sense of it. There's a way in which the whole landscape is *inside* in a novel, even if it's said to be outside, which I find peculiarly exciting. I think to myself about the world in the head. And Mansfield at some level that I can't even quite explain is a very powerful image of that experience of having a whole world in your head, which grows there like the shrubbery in Fanny's remarks about memory. And which can't happen in the noise in Portsmouth, either. That kind of meditation can't happen.

SODRE: Yes, Jane Austen makes the whole of Mansfield into that sort of space; it becomes the world 'inside', in which everything can take place.

The idea is that if you have 'Mansfield' you can have a meaningful internal world, which means you don't need to 'go to London', in practice or metaphorically, you don't need external excitement, innovations.

BYATT: There's a wonderful scene which fits exactly on to this, and epitomises many things, which is the scene when Henry Crawford reads *Henry VIII*. When Sir Thomas brings Henry to see Lady Bertram and Fanny, it says they're sitting in deep tranquillity – it uses both those words, 'deep' and 'tranquillity' – and they've just been reading *Henry VIII*, which is slightly comic, because that play is anything but deeply tranquil, it's full of endless beheadings and abandoned wives and guilt and misery. And Henry then moves into this reading and animates it, and he reads all the parts with his wonderful voice and brings alive this whole inner world of Shakespeare, which of course is ambivalent in this case because it's a book and an inner space, and he makes it into a one-man drama. Rather like Satan who *informs* the serpent by going into it and speaking with its voice in paradise. So Henry speaks the text of *Henry VIII* in Mansfield Park. And then he talks about Shakespeare and says he's part of an Englishman's constitution. It's as though the nature of Mansfield, the nature of being English and the nature of Shakespeare and the nature of deep tranquillity, and even the fact of Lady Bertram, who has apparently been enjoying Shakespeare, are all part of one thing which is all right. And you believe it is. And for that moment Henry is subsumed in Mansfield and you can almost love him.

What he is really giving her is Shakespeare, which is the richest possible experience.

SODRE: I have just noticed something funny, a joke from Jane Austen; after Henry finishes reading *Henry VIII*, he makes a whole speech about the value of constancy: 'Constancy, I am not afraid of the word. I would spell it, read it, write it with any body. I see nothing alarming in the word. Did you think I ought?' when we are supposed to have noticed that he is just like his extremely inconstant namesake. The other funny thing is that Lady Bertram says that Fanny 'was in the middle of a very fine speech of that man', who turns out to be the malevolent Cardinal Wolsey, who is in the same position in court as Mrs Norris is in Mansfield! Again Lady Bertram shows that she has no idea at all of what is going on. What I find most striking about Lady Bertram is that in her the much praised quality of tranquillity becomes a horrible caricature; you could say she is more constant than everybody else, because she only has one love object: herself. The picture of narcissism is quite extraordinary. She so loves herself that she isn't even aware other people exist: she is the mad extreme of tranquillity and of constancy.

BYATT: One could move out from that observation of the complete passivity of Lady Bertram into thinking about energy. I used to think that most great novels by women were about what to do with energy that might be stopped off. And that's certainly true, for instance, of *Emma*, it's true of *Persuasion*, it's true of every novel by George Eliot, there is a woman in it possessed by a power which is thwarted. This is not true in *Mansfield Park* because anybody – apart from William – who has any energy is bad. It says at the beginning Mrs Norris had a spirit of activity, and all her activities are dangerous. And Maria praises Mary Crawford for having an energy of character. And it's Mary who produces a sort of absoluely wonderful paradox: 'resting fatigues me', she has to be on the move. Now when you get to the end everybody starts settling down, Mr Rushworth decides that acting is a bad thing, and says it's much better to be 'sitting comfortably here among ourselves doing nothing'. It is better always to do nothing. And right at the end when Mr Yates has been married to Julia, the narrator says 'there's some hope of his becoming less trifling, of his being at least tolerably domestic and quiet'. He is praised for being quiet. I think it's unlike any other book, except possibly *The Vicar of Wakefield*, for caring about people not bustling, not moving, not acting, not doing things. And in that sense you have to think twice about Lady Bertram, because there is a sense in which she is the spirit of Mansfield Park. The scene you've left out of your account of her is the moment at which she is stirred to real feeling, and she sends all these stupid letters when Tom is ill and hurt to Fanny, just saying the conventional thing, 'we must all do our best, we must be as helpful as we can'. And then when she sees Tom she actually really does get distressed and she says to Fanny 'he's so changed' and begs her to come home. And Fanny goes home and Lady Bertram falls on her neck. And actually at that moment as a mother, when Tom is hurt, Lady Bertram is roused to real maternal feeling, briefly. Which proves that at the centre of Mansfield, however buried in fat and conventional doing nothing and looking exactly like a pug, is something living: she does have a maternal heart, she really is surprised by how upset she is about Tom being ill. And Fanny is moved by her being moved. Fanny does love Lady Bertram, she doesn't love Mrs Norris. And she doesn't love her own mother. But I think she rushes home to Lady Bertram out of slightly more than duty; I think she rushes home to answer this cry from somebody who didn't even know she was a mother until she thought her child might die. And that is a moment of high drama, although it's slipped over in all the other things that are going on.

SODRE: Yes, I think that's true, but this is the only moment in the novel where she becomes properly connected; Fanny responds to that and is loved. But on the whole I think she loves Lady Bertram because Lady Bertram is quiet. There are positive reasons for liking quietness; but it is also Fanny's fragility that makes her prefer Lady Bertram's unresponsiveness to other people's intrusiveness, because she is often desperately in need of somebody who will engage with her. When she is comparing Portsmouth to Mansfield, she says that at Mansfield 'every body's feelings were consulted', which is patently not true: her feelings were not consulted for most of her life in Mansfield. But there is a quality of tranquillity that answers a very profound need to be protected from anything that impinges on her, like Mrs Norris's intrusive bustling.

BYATT: There's that wonderful moment when Sir Thomas returns from Antigua and the house is got ready to welcome him, and the fire is laid by the butler. That is as it were the house doing things itself. And then as we've said, Mrs Norris comes along and spoils the fire the butler has made, who otherwise doesn't exist, though he does have a name. There is a sense that the house carries on its life because it knows its own order. As the garden does, which is an extension of the house. There isn't anything wild beyond the garden.

I think one of the critics who has really understood this paradoxical lifelessness at the centre of what Fanny values, is Lionel Trilling, whose essay on *Mansfield Park* refers to Fanny as one of the poor in spirit out of the Bible. Trilling points out that the Christian heroine in the seventeenth, eighteenth and nineteenth centuries tended to be sickly, ill, passive, to make a good death, to be self-denying, to be very good at giving things up, and that Fanny has all these virtues, along with the human virtues of observing other people's feelings and hearing things. He says rather beautifully,

> This strange, this almost perverse rejection of Mary Crawford's vitality in favour of Fanny's debility lies at the very heart of the novel's intention. 'The divine,' said T. E. Hulme in *Speculations*, 'is not life at its intensest. It contains in a way an almost anti-vital element.' Perhaps it cannot quite be said that 'the divine' is the object of Fanny's soul, yet she is a Christian heroine. Hulme expresses with an air of discovery what was once taken for granted

> in Christian feeling. Fanny is one of the poor in spirit. It is not a condition of soul to which we are nowadays sympathetic.

More recent readings of *Mansfield Park* have been readings which regard it as a criticism of the patriarchy and wish to see Fanny as a feminist heroine opposing the mistakes of Sir Thomas and actually dying to burst out. Or they try and read Mary as the real heroine and Fanny as the secret villain. Or there have been more widespread political interpretations which say that Fanny and Sir Thomas represent Tory political stability and country houses and not changing the gentry, and owning slave plantations on the side in Antigua but not saying that your source of money is corrupt. I can see no authorial intention on the part of Jane Austen to emphasise these points; she knew they were part of her complex world. But I do think that we have forgotten what Christian belief about how to behave meant to people who had it. Ignes, you grew up in a Brazilian Catholic tradition. I am talking about the English Anglican tradition – the *via media*, full of good sense, but constantly on the watch for excess, a constantly self-denying Christian tradition. If you read the prayers that Jane Austen wrote as a young woman, they're very beautifully written; they're prayers asking (a) to be able to deny oneself, and (b) to be able always to be on the watch so that you never hurt anybody else, so that you always notice other people's feelings. Here is one of her prayers:

> Teach us to understand the sinfulness of our own hearts, and bring to our knowledge every fault of temper and every evil habit in which we have indulged to the discomfort of our fellow-creatures and the danger of our own souls. May we now, and on each return of night, consider how the past day has been spent by us, what have been our prevailing thoughts, words and actions during it, and how far we can acquit ourselves of evil. Have we thought irreverently of thee, have we disobeyed thy commandments, have we neglected any known duty, or willingly given pain to any known human being?

I found these little prayers very moving and they are part of what Trilling says.

SODRE: A response to the Christian theme: I take the point about Jane Austen and thinking about other people's feelings. This informs the whole book, people are defined by being or not being able to empathise and sympathise with others. But from a psychoanalytic point of view, the poor in spirit, this Christian person who is so good and modest, is somebody who always has a relationship with God, and is therefore like a child who has a very good parent. The poor in spirit don't exist in an empty world, they exist as dependent modest children of a very ideal parent. You could say about the idealisation of Mansfield as a place, that it has a similar psychological meaning, that Fanny can develop like the shrubbery and grow in this quiet, modest way if she has in her mind a relationship with God or an ideal parent or with this paradisical home, the recipient for herself as a child in a dependent relationship, on a symbolic level. For Fanny, becoming Sir Thomas's beloved child is as important as becoming Edmund's wife.

BYATT: And one would say 'Our Father which art in Heaven, hallowed be thy name,' and one would go on to say 'Forgive us our trespasses as we forgive those that trespass against us'. You can hear Fanny saying this every night. In a sense what we are partly saying is that you can give a psychoanalytic explanation of why religious certainty makes people better, which is nothing to do with whether the religion is true or not. It just makes them better because there is Our Father which art in Heaven. But you can also say that the form of the European novel is related to the form of the biblical narrative. There are rules of conduct and laws of human feeling which have been assumed by the whole of the society in which we live to be derived from a good parent in heaven, even if one has no good parent on earth, or even if one loses one's good parent on earth. I think the form of the novel went on having a relation to the form of the Bible, long into the time when most of the people writing it had completely lost faith in the biblical narrative as history. These ideas will come back in terms of all the other books we're talking about up to and including *Beloved*, which is an extremely Christian novel, and completely haunted by biblical rhythms, as is *Villette*. So it's rather nice that we have raised this very large point at the end of this discussion.

Chapter 2

Charlotte Brontë: *Villette*

Villette (1853), Charlotte Brontë's last, strongly autobiographical, novel is narrated in the first person by Lucy Snowe. She opens by remembering a visit to her godmother, Mrs Bretton, and the attachment her son, Graham John Bretton, forms with a little girl, Paulina Mary Home, who has also come to stay. Lucy then loses touch with the Brettons, and, after eight difficult years, becomes companion to elderly Miss Marchmont, after whose death she crosses the Channel in search of a new life. On board the *Vivid*, she meets a spoilt young lady, Ginevra Fanshawe, on her way to a *pensionnat* in a town called Villette. In the absence of any other plan, Lucy turns up at the same *pensionnat*, is scrutinised by the formidable headmistress, Madame Beck, and her cousin, a despotic little man, teacher of literature, Paul Emanuel, and taken in as governess. Before long she is forced by circumstance to take an English class, and, despite initial fears, flourishes as a teacher.

Lucy works hard, but is lonely, and becomes attached to the amiable local doctor, Dr John. She is disappointed, however, to realise that he is infatuated with the pretty but mindless Ginevra Fanshawe (and during a play directed by Paul Emanuel in which she agonisingly has to act and play a man, she parodies his position, which she considers absurd) especially as Ginevra prefers the foppish Monsieur de Hamal, with whom she eventually elopes.

Left alone except for the company of the 'cretin' during the long summer vacation, Lucy wanders out into the streets of Villette in a kind of delirium. Despite being Protestant, she 'confesses' to a Catholic priest, Père Silas, after which she faints. She wakes up to oddly familiar surroundings: Mrs Bretton, now in Villette, has taken her in. Unexpectedly, Lucy now admits to having always known that Dr John was her godmother's son. They become firm friends, and Dr John's attentions and letters become a lifeline. On one occasion, having been frightened by what she thinks is the ghost of a nun, she mislays one of his letters and is deeply distressed. He reassures her that the nun is the product of a fevered brain, and indeed, towards the end of the novel it emerges that the nun, a famous 'Gothic' element in Villette, was none other than de Hamal, in disguise. Several weeks later, they go to the theatre, to see a famous actress, Vashti. However, a fire breaks out mid-performance, and Dr John is reunited with Paulina Mary. Lucy watches as their courtship leads inevitably to betrothal, much to the initial horror of Paulina's possessive father, now an aristocrat by inheritance, Monsieur de Bassompierre.

The perverse attentions of Paul Emanuel, which have been in the background, take on a new importance: Lucy finds that she is prepared to commit herself to becoming his 'friend', and makes him a beautiful watchguard. Envious, Madame Beck sends Lucy on an errand to witch-like Madame Walravens. From her, and Père Silas, she learns of the tragic story of Paul's love for a young girl called Justine Marie who died in a nunnery after their marriage was forbidden. The true quality of Paul's nature becomes clear: despite their disapprobation, he has continued to support Justine Marie's grandmother, Madame Walravens. This story, intended to keep Lucy away from Paul Emanuel – ostensibly because Lucy is a Protestant, but really because those who benefit from his generosity want to keep M. Paul for themselves – only serves to deepen her feelings of love. However, she then learns with shock that Paul is to go to the West Indies (to manage an estate owned by Mrs Walravens).

She is devastated, thinking he has left without explanation. Under the influence of a sedative given by Madame Beck, she again wanders the streets, and is amazed to see Paul himself. He at last turns up to explain, and, in a violent scene, lashes out at Madame Beck who tries to separate them. It turns out that he has been busy securing for Lucy a home and a schoolroom for herself – and for him to return to her in Faubourg Clotilde. After three years of waiting, however, it is strongly suggested, in an ending which is famously ambiguous, that he is drowned at sea on his way home from the West Indies.

BYATT: Let's start with Lucy Snowe the character. The thing that interests me is, I think, of all the narrators in novels which are very carefully placed socially, Lucy Snowe is the one with the least previous history. She speaks to us and tells us nothing of her parentage, her family history, of any relation in the world. She appears for the first time completely isolated, as somebody's god-daughter on a visit. All she says is, 'When I was a girl I went to Bretton about twice a year, and well I liked the visit' (Ch. I). We never find where she's come from and very little about where she goes to. What do you think about this shearing off of any normal parentage?

SODRE: I think this is part of Lucy's determination to re-create herself as the 'Snowe' character, as if she is saying: I will tell you, reader, only as much as I choose to; and I don't choose to reveal my past to you – and she repeats this show of mastery over the reader when she doesn't tell us anything factual about the eight years between the first visit to Bretton and her starting to live at Miss Marchmont's. (She says just enough to tantalise the reader!) Charlotte Brontë has created a heroine who reinvents herself as a character.

BYATT: As a child and as an adult reader, I always thought of the name Snowe in terms of coldness. But as you spoke I saw it in terms of an image of a great white blank plain with no footprints on it. If anyone is going to walk on it, it shall be she. It has this printless quality.

The other thing she doesn't do for quite a long time in those early chapters is tell you how old she is. I am interested in the moment when Paulina the child is brought in for the first time. Here is a figure arriving with a bundle of blankets, and this is an almost archetypal image, it suddenly struck me, being an eldest child, of what is seen by the eldest child when the new usurping child arrives in the house. There is a bundle of blankets, and then you find your bedroom has been changed and a new little bed has appeared, and everything that was yours (though in Lucy's case only on loan) suddenly becomes shared with somebody. It is customary in criticism to say that Paulina is an *alter ego* of Lucy, that these two female children, in a house where they are both isolated, represent different attitudes to Graham Bretton and the world. But there's also a sense in which Paulina appears as Lucy's younger sister who is not acknowledged and partly not wanted. Lucy refuses to respond to Paulina, as she refuses by instinct and nature to respond to the world. Though, as an elder sister, I remember that it is one of the ways you feel, with the great threat of a new young child arriving, you freeze up. This led me on to think, that during the whole of Charlotte Brontë's time in Brussels in the *pension* of Monsieur Héger there were actually *two* girls there. There was Charlotte Brontë and the next sister down, Emily Brontë. There wasn't just one isolated woman. There was one woman and a very difficult sister, to whom she wrote a lot of letters when she did later become isolated there.

SODRE: I think your point is interesting. I hadn't visualised the birth of the new baby in that scene at all, until you said it, and then it seemed clear to me that it must be so. Of course one of the possible reactions of the older child to the younger one is to become ultra-grown-up. This must be one of the reasons why Lucy doesn't tell us how old she is – she leads us to believe she was much older than she was. In fact, we don't know in the beginning of the novel that at the time of the Bretton visit she was still a child.

BYATT: There is one very strange point early on where she actually says 'As I write now my hair is white'. It's an eerie moment, slipped into a parenthesis – she says 'Fifty miles were then a day's journey, (for I speak of a time gone by: my hair which till a late period withstood the frosts of time, lies now, at last white, under a white cap, like snow beneath snow)' (Ch. 5). There she gives you a sort of look into the gulf of the future, and allows the reader to know that the person now writing is an old woman with white hair under a white cap, which of course goes with the white snow. It intensifies somehow this agelessness. She tells you once and once only that this book is being written by a very old woman. That too, I think, once you realise it, casts you back to seeing that the figure who is narrating this to us is doubtful in age as in face as in character.

SODRE: This connects to the end of the novel as well, when she is being mysterious about what happened to M. Paul, whilst at the same time making it clear that he dies by saying: 'they were the three happiest years of my life' (Ch. 42). But in relation to the period between Bretton and Miss Marchmont, something extremely interesting happens in the text: she refers to going through some horrible experience using shipwreck metaphors:

> Picture me then idle, basking, plump, and happy, streched on a cushioned deck, warmed with constant sunshine, rocked by breezes indolently soft. However, it cannot be concealed that, in that case, I must somehow have fallen over-board, or that there must have been a wreck at last. I too well remember a time – a long time, of cold, of danger, of contention. To this hour, when I have the nightmare, it repeats the rush and saltness of briny waves in my throat, and their icy pressure on my lungs. I even know there was a storm, and that not of one hour nor one day. For many days and

> nights neither sun nor stars appeared; we cast with our own hands the tackling out of the ship; a heavy tempest lay on us; all hope that we should be saved was taken away. In fine, the ship was lost, the crew perished. (Ch. 4)

So the old Lucy is describing her traumatic experiences between the ages of fourteen and twenty-two through the use of metaphors created from her adult traumatic experiences, of reliving through identification her lover's death by drowning. The imagery that belongs to the more recent past is cast backwards to convey symbolically an emotional childhood experience. The reader can only understand that on rereading the novel; but again, we have an instance of having to reflect on Lucy's, rather than Charlotte's, use of language.

I wanted to go back to the question of Lucy and Paulina, because I think Paulina's agelessness – her being perpetually small – confirms your idea of her as the younger child: in the older child's mind, the younger one is the baby for ever. Paulina is always small in size, she is described as a changeling, she's got a pygmy head and pygmy hands. But I don't think that this necessarily excludes thinking about Paulina as the container for Lucy's temporarily discarded infantile feelings. In effect, Lucy says, I, Lucy Snowe, plead guiltless of that curse, an overheated and discursive imagination, and you know she is lying.

BYATT: I read that as a child myself, and I knew she was lying, then. Even as a child I felt her suppressing something. I felt her making a decision to say this, and even possibly a decision to say it inadequately so that you sense she knew perfectly well about passion if she felt it appropriate, but she wasn't allowed to. Another thing that strikes me about Lucy and Paulina, and sisters and women and children, is that Lucy at first refuses to help Paulina dress, and Paulina is always very anxious to dress herself.

SODRE: Paulina wants to be a grown-up lady, a little wife for her father. She needs, presumably, to protect herself from the pain of being a motherless little child (Charlotte Brontë's mother died when she was five. Her relationship with her father was very far from the adoring one between Paulina and her father). Lucy is cold to Paulina, or she wants us to believe she is, when she is describing to us her own invented 'Snowe' character. She is not motherly except at the moment when Paulina is in distress about having to leave Graham, when she invites Paulina into her bed and warms her up. She claims to be too wise to have that sort of passion, but we know she can understand Paulina precisely because she can identify with her.

BYATT: Yes, constantly at every turn; as she later explains, she has to renounce that kind of passion because it's inappropriate to somebody of her kind and situation. I don't know if this is a real connection, but I found it moving later on in the story when Lucy is taken out by Dr John unexpectedly to see Vashti in the theatre. He gives her half an hour to get dressed, and she can't get her dress on. She picks out her dun-coloured crêpe, she doesn't pick out the pink dress which she's been given by the Brettons when she went to the concert, and she has to have Rosine to help arrange her clothes. For a moment she is Paulina, she is somebody who is allowed to have somebody to help her to look beautiful. Then she goes out with Dr John and in a way that's the beginning and the end of her real relationship with him. It's the moment when he invites her for herself, but equally it's also the moment when he rediscovers Paulina at the theatrical performance to which he has taken Lucy. I always feel, when Lucy's putting on this garment and arranging the lace round her neck, it's as though she has been allowed to be the little princess, the little countess almost for this moment, with a maid, and then it's taken from her. You had some interesting ideas about Paulina as the princess, the fairy princess, and the names of the homes and –

SODRE: Paulina is both a bereaved little child struggling to survive and an uncanny little being, not quite human: she is called a changeling, an elf, a little ghost. I think the fairytale aspect of Paulina is used by Charlotte Brontë to work out the question of childhood imagination and the creation of fantasy worlds, like the Angria world that the Brontë children imaginatively inhabited. Mature creative imagination is rooted in infantile desires and conflicts, but also has to be distanced from these to produce something less wish-fulfilling, more realistic and more connected with adult functioning. Using the example of Lucy being helped to dress by Rosine: Lucy is, for a moment, allowing herself to be a princess; but only partially, since by putting on her dun-coloured dress she is *not* putting on the pink dress, she is also saying, this is my reality.

When Paulina explains her new surname – 'We are Home and de Bassompierre' – I thought Brontë was making the differentiation between homely ordinary life and life in the underworld (i.e. in an Angrian world, as it were) as her new aristocratic name suggests 'under the stone' ('debas' and 'pierre'); such was the reality of Angria to the Brontë children that they could have said they lived at Home and in Angria simultaneously. Paulina belongs both to fairytale and realistic novel. Lucy now has to give up her fairytale-ish passion for Graham

Bretton, who will be absorbed into his prince role in the de Bassompierre world; this will eventually free her to fall in love with M. Paul, an adult passion that includes both sexuality and intellectual communion. In her biography, *Charlotte Brontë: A Passionate Life*, Lyndall Gordon shows very clearly how difficult it was for Charlotte to give up finding refuge in the Angria world even after she was quite grown up, how difficult to make the step from wish-fulfilling fantasy world of counts and countesses into creating an imaginary world rooted in her real experiences. In *Villette*, exploring the world of real personal experience includes exploring the very real need for the fairytale world. Paulina is given a happy end; Lucy isn't.

BYATT: The novel does start in the 'real world', the Bretton home.

> The house and its inmates specially suited me. The large peaceful rooms, the well-arranged furniture, the clear wide windows, the balcony outside, looking down on a fine antique street, where Sundays and holidays seemed always to abide – so quiet was its atmosphere, so clean its pavement – these things pleased me well. (Ch. 1)

This is the essence of the prosaic and comfortable home. Except it isn't her home. Then her godmother's house reappears in a completely hallucinatory way in Villette. Even the furniture has been moved from England to Belgium. She wakes out of madness after she's collapsed in the street, out of loneliness and despair – she wakes to see exactly the same furniture, a reality experienced as hallucination. And this has an effect on the reader; there are dreams in which one sees one's own childhood furniture – you struggle out and think 'But I'm not there any more.' But Lucy does find herself in the little sea-green room of her childhood – although it wasn't her childhood because we haven't any idea what that was like, she hasn't told us and never will. She has her little sea-green room, so she was the little mermaid.

> My calm little room seemed somehow like a cave in the sea. There was no colour about it, except that white and pale green, suggestive of foam and deep water; the blanched cornice was adorned with shell-shaped ornaments, and there were white mouldings like dolphins in the ceiling-angles. Even that one touch of colour visible in the red satin pincushion bore affinity to coral; even that dark, shining glass might have mirrored a mermaid. (Ch. 17)

SODRE: Her waking up in the sea-green room is reassuring but also alarming, she doesn't know if it is real or not. On the other hand, what you said reminded me, she also says to the *bonne* who is looking after her that she wants to get dressed and go downstairs because she's feeling dull here. She makes it clear that although there is a part of her that would like to go back to the sea-green world in which she could be Mrs Bretton's adopted daughter, she also needs her own space and her own mind; later in the novel this will link up with Graham's lack of space for her in his mind.

BYATT: A wonderful thing, how the metaphors and images will be called up even when you're discussing the plot. There was the sea-green room, and you said she found it too dull. Then one thinks of her setting off, this prosaic solitary woman, to cross the Channel, which is the sea, green, blue, in a ship called the *Vivid*. She chooses the ship called the *Vivid* to travel in. Poor Lucy, although her name is Snowe, she terribly wants something big and bright and glowing and shining like Angria. And what's more, we always know it, even when she's assuring us she doesn't.

I've seen it said that Lucy Snowe confines herself typically in households where the head is a solitary woman, which is interesting considering that the Brontës grew up in a household where the head was a widowed father trying to look after a large family. Lucy Snowe is always an isolated being. She moves from Mrs Bretton's house to Miss Marchmont's house where a disappointed spinster is grieving for a dead lover. And from there to Madame Beck's seminary. I remember as a child being completely baffled by the portrayal of Madame Beck. When I first met Madame Beck I thought, this is going to be a bad character, a frightening character. Then she turned out to be terribly good at her housework and kind, and not to have those characteristics that terrified me in my own mother, of extreme bad temper and hysteria. She was always good-tempered. I (again as a child) began to think that Madame Beck was a model and wonderful mother figure. Then you realise that Lucy hates her, partly because she's a rival for the affections of M. Paul – which comes out in the very last scene where Madame Beck actually gets slapped, a moment of real violence as opposed to emotional violence. I have thought that perhaps Madame Beck's mystery is partly a mystery of Charlotte Brontë not knowing what to say about Madame Héger. But I don't think it's that, I think she's actually an extremely complex and beautifully realised character.

SODRE: I don't get the impression from reading the biographies that Madame Beck is very much like Madame Héger. Lucy, of course, eventually becomes the spinster headmistress herself.

When Lucy describes Madame Beck, she says she won't tolerate any display of emotion because this will make her aware that she doesn't have a heart; but she has to have enough of a heart to feel pained by its absence.

BYATT: She is a very enabling person. She sees that Lucy can do better and will be able to teach better, and makes a space for Lucy to fulfil an ambition that Lucy didn't even know she had. When Lucy arrives there is no idea in Lucy's head that she can be a teacher. That is put there by Paul Emanuel and Madame Beck, and Madame Beck starts the process by using her to take the place of a missing teacher. It is as though she brings her up and says, 'Look, there isn't much to you, but there is this. This is something you can do with your life and energy.' And Lucy accepts it from her, and (without thinking at all that Madame Beck is an *alter ego* for Lucy, as I think Paulina is), I think it is legitimate for the reader to say to herself, 'Perhaps Madame Beck, like Lucy, is not saying all she feels, not saying all she knows, all she desires, all she is.' It is Lucy who thinks Madame Beck is complacent and happy at being a widowed lady running a school efficiently. How do we know? Madame Beck doesn't know about Lucy; how do we know that Lucy knows about Madame Beck? I think Charlotte Brontë allows you to ask this question legitimately.

SODRE: Yes; one doesn't believe that Madame Beck's jealousy of Paul and Lucy is only to do with practical school matters. That she needs to be slapped to be got rid of shows that her intrusiveness is not solely motivated by machinations to control Paul: she is a jealous woman who cannot bear to see that Lucy is Paul's beloved. But Lucy benefits from Madame Beck's perceptiveness: when she encourages Lucy to teach, she has obviously sensed her strength underneath the timid exterior; and when Lucy finds herself on the stage in the classroom, she becomes this terribly powerful teacher who is capable of locking up one of the bullies.

BYATT: And when she takes this very large, rude, angry girl – which is every teacher's dream and every oppressed girl's dream – and shuts her in a cupboard and immediately changes the loyalties of the whole class, this is real power. It's the unleashing of energy: 'In an instant, and with sharpness, I had turned on her. In another instant she occupied the closet, the door was shut, and the key in my pocket.' Very satisfying.

You mentioned the word 'stage'. We were saying when talking

about *Mansfield Park*, that theatrical presentations in many of these novels give us a kind of image of possible power or self-expression or possible emotional space, which are not offered to the characters in their daily lives. It's interesting how differently Lucy Snowe finally takes the requirement that she act a part in a play from the way in which Fanny Price did in *Mansfield Park*. I remember – it's funny how reading this book all my childhood feelings come back in my own body – the acting frightened me as a little girl, and I remember worrying about why Lucy wouldn't wear men's clothes, what was it that Lucy didn't want to be, that she wouldn't put on trousers? All she says is 'To be dressed like a man did not please, and would not suit me. I had consented to take a man's name and part; as to his dress – *halte là!* No. I would keep my own dress; come what might' (Ch. 14). She simply adds 'a little vest, a collar, and cravat, and a pâletot of small dimensions'.

I remember thinking how ridiculous she must have looked with a man's jacket over a skirt; she had made a complete doll of herself, what kind of object was she that she wore these symbolic tokens of being a man? I remember as a girl myself in a girls' boarding school working my way through Shakespeare, and being good at acting you were required to take all the male roles. And I was afraid I was losing my sex. I didn't want to be Prospero, I wanted to be Miranda, because I wanted to be quite sure I was a woman. I think this is a normal emotion in a building full of women, and no men. There's M. Paul in this particular case, the one male teacher, but on the whole you can see that Lucy felt 'I am a woman, nobody sees I am a woman, now they're getting me to dress as a man.' Yet when she got on the stage, she was completely liberated. But liberated because she was acting at Dr John, whom she had perceived to be in love with Ginevra who was the coquette, whom the foppish character which Lucy was acting was meant to run off with. Thus paralleling on the stage what was happening in real life, where M. de Hamal was much more attractive to Ginevra than the good and upright and much more sexually beautiful Dr John. I suppose the two scenes, where she shuts the girl in the cupboard, and then the scene where she takes over the play, moved me as an ambitious child terribly, as well, because give such a child an inch where it can show what it can do, and it will do it. It's just that it's afraid of never being given an inch. And Lucy is so used to saying 'I can't do anything, I won't expect to be asked to do anything, given anything' – then when she gets on the stage she blossoms and flourishes.

'By-and-by, feeling the right power come – the spring demanded gush and rise inwardly – I became sufficiently composed to notice my fellow-actors.' Then as she thinks of Paul Emanuel and Dr John, she grows into and *changes* her role:

> Ginevra was tender; how could I be otherwise than chivalric? Retaining the letter, I recklessly altered the spirit of the *rôle*. Without heart, without interest, I could not play it at all. It must be played – in went the yearned-for seasoning – thus flavoured, I played it with relish. (Ch. 14)

How much do you think that's to do with personal ambition, and how much to do with the relationship with Ginevra and Dr John and M. Paul?

SODRE: I think it's probably both, but much more importantly to do with self-expression and strength. The first time I read it I thought she was too embarrassed to impersonate a man, too anxious about her sexuality. But as I read it later it seemed much more clear that keeping her skirt is a powerful affirmation of her personality and of her womanhood. When discussing her clothes, M. Paul says, 'certain modifications I might sanction, yet something you must have to announce you as of the nobler sex' (Ch. 14), and one senses she might say to herself, 'Right! I must keep my skirt, then.'

BYATT: It comes back to the idea of helping people to get dressed – they all try to help her to get dressed, and on this occasion she goes away and shuts herself up and puts her own bits of men's clothes on, and comes out and says, 'This is what I am.' I suppose what she's giving is an exhibition to Dr John of just what a silly sort of man can win a girl like Ginevra, and he's too stupid to read it.

SODRE: That's right. And she's also taking revenge on Ginevra by making her fall for the stage fop as well, which is interesting, because Ginevra always thinks of Lucy as a man. She calls her Diogenes and Timon.

BYATT: And she's always taking her arm, and always pressing up to Lucy. It never goes the other way. I don't agree with the reading that says that Lucy actually is a powerful lesbian who doesn't know it and is attracted to Ginevra. This seems to me to be nonsense. Lucy is a heterosexual woman who terribly wants to be noticed to be one. As often happens in all-female communities, she's afraid of an attraction to and for other women – and Brontë obviously knew all about the rushes and shifts of intense feeling between women in such communities.

Ginevra I think likes power over everybody, and is actually attracted to Lucy. This is the only explanation for the way in which Ginevra cannot bear it if Lucy doesn't respond to her little advances.

SODRE: Ginevra is excited by, and attracted to, Lucy's capacity to see right through her; she despises Graham because he thinks she is so pure.

BYATT: It is done with such beautiful realism by both Lucy Snowe and Charlotte Brontë. The degree to which Lucy likes Ginevra is most beautifully done: she doesn't like her an inch further than she morally ought to, but you never have the feeling of embarrassment with Ginevra that you do with Mary Crawford in *Mansfield Park* where you feel that both Fanny and Edmund are getting over-hysterical in reaction to Mary's silliness and naughtiness and vulgarity and flirtatiousness. Lucy has got Ginevra exactly placed, she knows just how silly she is, and she is prepared to like what little is good in her. In a very measured way, really, considering Lucy's such a deeply hysterical character at one level.

Speaking of knowing people – one of the sentences that most baffles me in the whole of *Villette* is where Lucy remarks 'If anyone knew me it was little Paulina Mary.' You really don't feel that this can possibly be true. It's when they're discussing their childhood memories, and at that moment of discussion, the memories of Lucy and Paulina seem to become amalgamated, of Paulina reading to John, or Graham as he then was. Or of John reading to Paulina.

> The light in which M. de Bassompierre evidently regarded 'Miss Snowe', used to occasion me much inward edification. What contradictory attributes of character we sometimes find ascribed to us, according to the eye with which we are viewed! Madame Beck esteemed me learned and blue; Miss Fanshawe, caustic, ironic and cynical; Mr Home, a model teacher, the essence of the sedate and discreet: whilst another person, Professor Paul Emanuel, to wit, never lost an opportunity of intimating his opinion that mine was rather a fiery and rash nature – adventurous, indocile and audacious. I smiled at them all. If anyone knew me, it was little Paulina Mary. (Ch. 26)

That's a very bizarre end to that paragraph, because I think both you and I feel that one of the glories of this novel is the sense that it's M. Paul who really knows Lucy's nature, when he says she's fiery.

SODRE: Yes, and this is what is most exciting about him. In relation to Paulina, we are often told that she doesn't know; and specially that she does not know Lucy. So is Lucy being sarcastic?

I want to go back to Lucy's feeling of power on the stage: she becomes somebody full of energy who can actually impersonate this fop, who is so entirely different from her; she says:

> That first speech was the difficulty; it revealed to me the fact, that it was not the crowd I feared, so much as my own voice. Foreigners and strangers, the crowd were nothing to me. When my tongue once got free, and my voice took its true pitch, and found its natural tone, I thought of nothing but the personage I represented – and of M. Paul, who was listening, watching, prompting in the side-scenes. (Ch. 14)

This is fascinating as a description of the novelist at work: she finds her true pitch when she can fully imagine – mentally inhabit, as it were – her characters.

BYATT: I think what Charlotte Brontë is saying there is something analogous. 'I am a successful novelist, I actually do have a way of saying something nothing to do with my immediate grief, which changes my whole world.' I think it is about that, you're right, it's about what art can do, even that art, even acting a fop. And if you're going to be a good novelist, if you can't get a good fop in your novel, or a good somebody who is not a high-minded young woman trying to write a novel, you can't write a novel. I think it's partly that. It's being able to see the other and take pleasure in it.

SODRE: Even de Hamal, a relatively minor character, cannot be just 'a fop' – she has to imaginatively wear his jacket to make him real.

BYATT: And this is both the way to take on your own power and release yourself from yourself. Which in terms of *Villette* is absolutely wonderful. If ever there was a book about the impossibility of releasing yourself from yourself and the pain of being yourself and the pain of being alone with yourself and having no power of self-expression and no right to self-expression, it's *Villette*. And yet within it there are these moments of pure glee. Partly Lucy's extremely good caustic comic voice, which is what attracted Ginevra to her, of course.

Lucy is in a position where no man will want her, both because she's ugly or not beautiful and because she's penniless. Which was the case of her creator. Or how we imagine her creator saw herself in her own days in Belgium.

SODRE: And she really doesn't want that pathetic role. On the other hand the disguises (like the dun-coloured dress) are there so that she 'looks the part' which is really her part. She dresses like a governess and behaves like one, but feels this is her disguise. It hides her vulnerability. It reminds me again how Charlotte Brontë, like Lucy, thought that one of her only defences from the horror of being a governess was that in her silence and her invisibility she would be taken to be somebody who didn't have a mind, and she could then triumph over everybody. Because she obviously had a much greater mind than everybody else. Brontë put on pretend shyness to disguise her real shyness. And because she felt she was disguised as a shy governess, she created more space in her mind for her secret passionate self.

BYATT: Lucy trips herself when she starts explaining how absolutely terrified she was of going into the class and standing on the estrade, the teacher's platform. Because the moment she gets there, you see that she isn't terrified, she isn't the person in a pathological state of fear she's been telling the reader she was.

I don't know what feeling you get about Lucy Snowe's sexuality? I feel she is somebody who would like to be in love, would like to know passion, although she despises the other teachers who so openly save pathetic dowries, or dream of catching M. Paul. She does an enormous amount of rationalisation when Dr John starts writing to her. She explains precisely that she knows not to read too much into these letters which she so badly needs. And she describes how she always wrote two letters back, one of them saying what she really felt and one saying what she knew she ought to say. Then in the attic, after seeing the nun, she is completely abased, when she's scrabbling away like a mad thing in the dust on the floor, looking for the dropped letter, and Dr John comes up behind her and says 'Is it my letter?' In a way that's a complete humiliation because he has seen how desperately she cares about his letter.

SODRE: She feels intensely sexual, she's very interested in the way Dr John looks, and above all she desperately wants to be loved. She is not particularly interested in his mind. The gradual change of sexual interest from the more prince-like Graham to M. Paul who isn't at all beautiful is brilliantly done. But Brontë makes it clear that Lucy is attracted to *both* of them, in the same period of time – which is extremely brave for a nineteenth-century novelist! In fact, even right at the end, when Lucy is very much in love with Paul, she sees Graham in the festival scene, and imagines him to have a little closet in his mind called 'Lucy's room', and then she says 'I kept a place for him, too . . . All my life long I carried it folded in the hollow of my hand – yet, released from that hold and constriction, I know not but its innate capacity for expanse might have magnified it into a tabernacle for a host' (Ch. 38).

There is a part of her that she feels will forever long for what Graham represents, for the perfect world of ideal happiness and beauty. That Lucy chooses the religious terms 'tabernacle' and 'host' to convey this implies her awareness that this is infantile idealisation. On the other hand, the relationship with M. Paul is exciting from the beginning, even when she doesn't like him: his intelligence and his passionate nature powerfully attract her.

BYATT: Yes, he's presented as a person of huge and prickling physical energy and you feel him come into a room. She makes it quite clear that everybody felt him come into the room, that he had a kind of magnetism. Whereas Bretton is more the image of the English gentleman with red whiskers who could turn into George Eliot's Grandcourt, who *was* an English gentleman, with red whiskers. Lucy shows her awareness of limitations in John Bretton, or Graham Bretton, as with Madame Beck.

I think Charlotte Brontë's heroines always respond to kindness. In novels by men about the relations between men and women, on the whole women are somehow expected to respond to masterfulness. In novels by women, on the whole, what they respond to is people observing their feelings, people treating them as people, people being kind. And what is both unexpected and dramatically satisfying about those two men is that Graham Bretton *is* very kind, and *almost* sees Lucy as a human being who has a right to his attention as a human being, but not quite. Whereas M. Paul reveals that he knows her when he hisses at her, 'sibillating' like a 'sudden boa-constrictor'. 'Petite chatte, doucerette, coquette! Vous avez l'air bien triste, soumise, rêveuse, mais vous ne l'êtes pas; c'est moi qui vous le dis: Sauvage! la flamme à l'âme, l'éclair aux yeux!' (Ch. 27). She uses satanic imagery about him, but he is totally kind. There's a wonderful moment when he shares his brioche with her and then she pleads to be allowed to get him a baked apple. She tempts him because she knows he likes sweet things, describing the wonderful spiced apples in the kitchen. She brings him the apple, Eve offering the fruit, but intending to run away immediately. And is tempted to share the fruit herself, by male gentleness and masterfulness mixed.

> That intolerably keen instinct of his seemed to have anticipated my scheme; he met me at the threshold, hurried me into the room, and fixed me in a minute in my former seat. Taking the plate of fruit from my hand, he divided the portion intended only for

> himself, and ordered me to eat my share. I complied with no good grace. (Ch. 30)

She's teasing and tormenting him in this scene. You've said there's an element of playful sado-masochism in the relationship between them, which is part of the pleasure of falling in love. They tease each other to see how far the other one will go, they insult each other. Whereas with Dr John, the conventions of British politeness have to be absolutely observed.

SODRE: Life with Dr John would be exceedingly boring for her, however kind and handsome he may be, because he is so entirely out of touch with who she is, and because of how different they are. Lucy – like Jane Eyre before her – wants to be profoundly known; sexual passion, for both Jane and Lucy, is at its highest when the man can look inside them and see their passion. This mental penetration isn't meant to be just a metaphor for physical contact: there is tremendous excitement in the coming together of minds.

In the extraordinary scene where Paul hisses 'Sauvage! La flamme à l'âme, l'éclair aux yeux' she is sitting next to Graham Bretton, who, in contrast, is entirely blind to her. In his eagerness to be helped in his conquest of Paulina he treats Lucy like a spinster who needs no sex.

BYATT: This echoes *Mansfield Park* where Edmund and Mary Crawford constantly come to Fanny and expect her to be nobody and to further their relationship with each other. But whereas Fanny rather gloomily suppresses all her feelings and does what they ask, Lucy gets very angry and calls up an embodiment of her own anger who hisses 'You have fire in your soul and flames in your eyes', like a serpent.

SODRE: So you feel that part of his attractiveness to Lucy at that moment is that M. Paul is so much like her, he can voice her emotions; this makes a lot of sense, psychologically. The violence of his jealousy is therefore gratifying to Lucy, both because this is her first experience of being sexually desirable and because she can see her own intense jealousy in him. She can both project it – this tormenting thing is now inside him – and be closer to him through identification.

BYATT: Jealousy is usually such a negative force, but as you describe it there it's a kind of wonderful empowering. This is partly because M. Paul is a very intelligent, humane man, so when he's absolutely assured that there's no cause for jealousy he stops showing it. Whereas a pathologically jealous person wouldn't. It's perfectly natural, territorial, male jealousy. Which is very pleasing.

SODRE: Lucy loves discovering he is a 'sauvage' himself, he's got flames in his soul. And of course he is behaving like an absolute savage, going around hissing 'You are coquettish!' in the middle of this grand party!
BYATT: Yes, it's as full of passion as Angria, though as you've said, it's the de Bassompierres who are the presence of Angria in this text. M. Paul is an entirely real, rather ugly, bespectacled, small teacher with a funny little hat, and his sexual jealousy is perfectly realistic, ordinary sexual jealousy, nothing to do with Byronic heroes. Nevertheless it takes you out into a world where things are full of power and reality and really matter; space is created. And all the diamonds and the glittering somehow bear no relation to all that.
SODRE: No, because there is real glittering, in his eyes and her eyes.

BYATT: I knew nothing about Roman Catholicism when I first read *Villette*, and I was baffled by how wicked Catholicism was felt to be. I could feel that Charlotte Brontë was making an effort at generosity towards M. Paul's Jesuit upbringing and towards the saints of the Church. As a child I found it completely impossible to imagine what the scene of confession meant because I didn't know what it was. It does add a dimension, the way in which Lucy's low point, the long empty period where she's left alone in the school, ends in her confessing, trying to communicate with somebody, confessing her sins, to a Catholic priest in a Catholic church, knowing that that is a structure within which there would have been room for her to speak. Whereas her Protestantism is a completely suppressed religious structure in which all she can do is keep silent and be respectable. But in this novel Catholicism is identified with an atmosphere of creeping and spying in ways I don't quite understand.
SODRE: I only read *Villette* as an adult – as a Catholic child, I would have found the hatred of Catholicism quite disturbing. I read Mrs Gaskell's *Life of Charlotte Brontë* before I read *Villette*, and therefore knew the background, and kept anxiously hoping that *Villette* would never be published in Belgium! The reader believes that Père Silas is going to be helpful to her, to start with; and indeed Lucy says 'He was kind when I needed kindness; he did me good. May Heaven bless him!' (Ch. 15). I felt quite shocked when the Catholic conspiracy was revealed – that Père Silas and Madame Beck want to own Paul's soul, and to keep Paul and Lucy apart. The reader identifies with Lucy's need for somebody who will listen (it is not really a 'confession'), the need not to be alone with her madness.
BYATT: Someone who will listen. Like the analyst?

SODRE: Yes; Lucy describes her experience as follows: '– the mere pouring out of some portion of long accumulating, long pent-up pain into a vessel whence it could not be again diffused – had done me good' (Ch. 15). This is exactly what Bion describes as one of the analyst's most essential functions, to be a container for the other's disturbing internal states; Lucy's phrase, 'whence it could not be again diffused' describes the need for the containing object not to re-project these states again into the person who is communicating them. In *Daniel Deronda* Daniel, who doesn't really ever completely understand Gwendolen, is very much put in the position of listening to what is unbearable when he receives her 'confession'.

BYATT: George Eliot uses the conversion experience in intense scenes where one character confesses to another, and the lives of both are changed – most strikingly between Rosamond and Dorothea in *Middlemarch*. In a way one could look back, to thinkers before Freud, and see that the whole structure was in place long before his discovery that telling your life history, what he called the talking cure, could change you. And you can see Charlotte Brontë reaching out for that. I suppose you could argue that writing a novel is another way of giving form to that confession or that desire to tell the story of your life and understand it.

SODRE: In this particular novel, Brontë is so consciously aware of the existence of the reader – she was an established author by then.

BYATT: There is a difference between a first novel by someone young, who's simply writing for a kind of *abstract* reader, and the work of an established writer who knows she has people who have understood what she has already said. That knowledge makes you both more evasive and more direct, in curious ways.

SODRE: I suppose this must work both on the level of external reality – there is a readership out there – and also, symbolically, on the level of internal reality – not feeling alone when you have a listener in your mind, capable of receiving even your most difficult thoughts and emotions. You, the writer, have the blank page, and things in your mind, and you hope there will be a reader. But the moment you start writing, the page becomes symbolically the other, as well as a part of yourself: providing a container for the things in your mind, and providing the possibility of distancing.

BYATT: Can you say why the figure of Madame Walravens, who appears all of a sudden and then vanishes again, except for the last line of the book, has such power? Why is that scene so peculiarly gripping, where

Lucy is sent by Madame Beck on this curious errand, to take Madame Walravens the 'pretty basket of fruit' like Red Riding Hood out into the forest?

SODRE: Lucy has been living in a realistic world, and one could say that her child self, who is now in Paulina, is living in a fairytale one. When Lucy is sent by Madame Beck to Madame Walravens she re-enters the fairytale world, but in its negative aspect, the world of the witches who own Paul Emanuel's soul.

BYATT: There is Justine Marie, Madame Walravens's granddaughter, who is the dead princess, the dead beloved – the girl Paul loved until she died in the convent.

SODRE: As the dead beloved, she is idealised, a princess to whom the prince Paul Emanuel has to be faithful for ever. The realistic version of this is the Catholic conspiracy to have power over him; the illusion of Justine Marie is used by Père Silas and Madame Beck to enslave Paul Emanuel.

BYATT: Yes, and the Catholicism is somehow a religion which puts a premium on not getting married, which is how you have priests and nuns. And it puts a premium on Paul Emanuel's duty not to get married. It is amazing how their account of him turns him into a slightly soppy, glib, slightly too saintly figure. All his actions have been virtuous, but it needs Lucy to know that they are the actions of a waspish little man who keeps losing his temper and behaves badly. The witches tell a highly hagiographical story about this very good man, which is true but not the whole truth, and somehow makes him inaccessible to Lucy, which is what they intend. They are very cunning. One thing their cunning does, tangentially, is to release Madame Beck from imprisoning the hero, release her into being a woman in a curious way. She too has tried to rescue the hero from the tower and failed. She's now not going to let Lucy rescue him.

I love the size of Madame Walravens – I don't know how Charlotte Brontë thought of making her only three feet tall, but –

SODRE: Perhaps the idea is to make her symmetrical with Paulina, who is also a dwarf. Paulina is so small that her size feeds her father's illusion that she is still a child. These very little people belong to the same world, light, fairylike Paulina with her rich beautiful clothes, and crippled Madame Walravens with her rich grotesque clothes.

BYATT: And her ivory stick and the jewels in her hair which she has to have. They both have to have jewels, they have to be looked after. Paulina is always being carried as if she couldn't walk, although she insists that she can walk. But she comes in being carried. Then again she's rescued and carried by Dr John out of the fire. Then again she appears as a child, a snow child, crowned with ivy leaves, behind Lucy in Lucy's mirror, a kind of childish version of Lucy.

> It wore white, sprinkled slightly with drops of scarlet; its girdle was red; it had something in its hair leafy, yet shining – a little wreath with an evergreen gloss. Spectral or not, here truly was nothing frightful, and I advanced. (Ch. 24)

And of course the other old woman with white hair in the story, apart from the witch Madame Walravens, is Lucy herself, when she's telling the story, and she says 'My hair is now white as I write.' It's Lucy as the Fairy Godmother, or Mother Goose, who tells stories by the fire.

Madame Walravens is a sort of stumplike pygmy, as though she's rooted into the ground. With her ivory stick – because it's ivory it's like a third bone, skeletal. I know what I always saw Madame Walravens as: she's Coleridge's figure of death-in-life, life-in-death, from the *Ancient Mariner*: 'the Night-mare Life-in-Death is she, who thicks man's blood with cold'. She's a ghoul, isn't she? You can feel she's going to suck their blood and throw their skulls out. And what she does is turn their life-blood into jewels. This is one of the most ancient and terrifying images, the jewelled skeleton, a thing that has sucked the life out of real fruit but you've still got jewels shining among the dead hairs and bones. Terribly powerful, all the more because of its rather stolid realism at the same time. It doesn't get too fanciful; you can actually see that this person might have existed. And the last sentence of the book is about her, about how very long she lived, about how the destroyers prosper. 'Madame Beck prospered all the days of her life; so did Père Silas; Madame Walravens fulfilled her ninetieth year before she died. Farewell' (Ch. 42).

The ending of the love story is very ambivalent. Brontë allows the reader to imagine a happy ending – her father wanted one – but it is clear that she felt Paul Emanuel must die. She wrote a rather flirtatious, sidestepping, facetious letter to her publisher, George Smith, after various anxious ladies had asked for clarification.

> With regard to that momentous point M. Paul's fate, in case any one in future should request to be enlightened thereon, he may be told that it was designed that every reader should settle the catastrophe for himself, according to the quality of his disposition,

> the tender or remorseless impulse of his nature: Drowning and Matrimony are the fearful alternatives. The merciful – like Miss Mulock, Mr Williams, Lady Harriet St Clair, and Mr Alexander Frazer – will of course choose the milder doom – drown him to put him out of pain. The cruel-hearted will, on the contrary, pitilessly impale him on the second horn of the dilemma, marrying him without ruth or compunction to that – person – that – that – individual – 'Lucy Snowe'.

She manages to suggest in these letters that both were equally horrible for Paul Emanuel so he may as well be drowned. She leaves fairytale happiness and stark tragic 'realism' (which is Romanticism, of course, with its storm) side by side at the end. It makes an interesting comparison with *Mansfield Park* and its evasions both of 'dwelling on guilt and misery,' and of telling Fanny's happiness. And nevertheless Brontë ends *Villette* as though it was a novel by Sir Walter Scott, with an informative last sentence about what happened to these minor characters.

SODRE: This is what is fascinating about the way the fairytale elements and the more realistic elements intertwine: they are both convincing in their different metaphors and levels of experience.

BYATT: *Villette* is full of varied personifications of female energy. We could start with the passage where Lucy personifies Reason, which is the force that is stopping her from behaving extravagantly. She speaks to Reason and says:

> 'But if I feel, may I *never* express?'
>
> '*Never!*' declared Reason.
>
> I groaned under her bitter sternness. Never – never – oh, hard word! This hag, this Reason, would not let me look up, or smile, or hope: she could not rest unless I were altogether crushed, cowed, broken-in and broken-down . . . Reason is vindictive as a devil: for me, she was always envenomed as a step-mother. If I have obeyed her it has chiefly been with the obedience of fear, not of love. Long ago I should have died of her ill-usage: her stint, her chill, her barren board, her icy bed, her savage, ceaseless blows; but for that kinder Power [Imagination] who holds my secret and sworn allegiance. Often has Reason turned me out by night, in mid-winter, on cold snow, flinging for sustenance the gnawed

> bone dogs had forsaken . . . Then, looking up, have I seen in the sky a head amidst circling stars. (Ch. 21)

It's full of fairytale language, the hag envenomed as the stepmother, the crusts and the bones. But it also brings a slightly repetitive, pressing, hysterical note which has made many readers frightened of *Villette*.

SODRE: I think it's the fear of madness – Lucy goes mad so realistically! Here is this extremely controlled heroine, who finds herself utterly alone in the school holidays except for the 'cretin' (who is described both as a victim and as evil, but who is happy because mindless), and through having no voice and no one to listen to her gradually starts going mad, getting overwhelmed by the violence of her inner world. She uses images of terrible violence – like the story of Jael and Sisera, the nail going through the temples; Lucy may look cut off and withdrawn, but she is being tortured by a kind of energy gone wild. (And yet she exclaims: 'How I pity those whose mental pain stuns instead of rousing!' (Ch. 21) – she is being sarcastic, but also truthful.) When she's mad, she's mad in a terribly excited way – an excess of life, rather than a cold withdrawal into a deathlike state. Later on, when Madame Beck gives her opium – when she thinks Paul has left without seeing her – instead of going to sleep she goes wild and runs out into the town, in a semi-hallucinated state. Lucy's madness will never be of the 'reasonable' kind, so that she could be put away somewhere with the cretin.

BYATT: Brilliant, yes.

SODRE: In her image of the nail, she doesn't die when it goes through her brain, the brain gets convulsed and moves around, it gets much more active instead of inactive. I think this links to the question of what happens to the energy, so suppressed and controlled by this witch Reason that it causes madness. Reason is the 'baddie' here.

BYATT: Wonderful, because usually it's unreason and the imaginative that are portrayed as being witches and demons, and here imagination is a soothing and calming force, and it's also a power to which she's constructed this temple which has no walls and no dome. In the temple of Imagination you have all the space you need. She is almost screwing herself down into a bottle like a genie. In the world of imagination the thing had room to come out.

SODRE: Lucy and Freud would certainly have agreed as to excessive repression causing mental illness! She had to screw Graham's letters into a bottle, and she goes through the most elaborate ritual to hide them.

BYATT: The cork is sealed into the bottle and she buys oiled silk to put round the letters, which means she intends to preserve them. In parenthesis – I was very amused when I reread this passage which I had forgotten, to realise I had used it in *Possession* when the character went out and bought a glass bottle with a stopper and then bought oiled silk, and I knew I had some immensely sensuous memory of wrapping things in oiled silk, and I didn't know where it came from – but of course it came from burying the letters in the bottle. And from the pain of that, and burying the bottle in the cleft tree. And making a little shrine to it. You can see that this is a perfect powerful image for life-in-death again. I think Coleridge's images of life-in-death run all the way through. There are also references to Desdemona and Othello, as though she's trying to kill herself. And the genie from the *Arabian Nights*, always representing space and power and possibility which isn't actually ever there.

SODRE: There is a great loss when she realises she can't have Graham Bretton, but the essential thing about the oiled silk is that her passion is not allowed to die; it is kept secretly alive. It couldn't be a more sensuous image, of elaborately wrapping and burying something in this grave to keep it alive.

BYATT: What it's describing of course is the pleasure of the writer in making that image, the pleasure Charlotte Brontë must have had. A normal depressive woman who decided to get rid of the letters would have just torn them up and put them in the fire. Or lost them. You can lose letters quite easily. To invent this complicated rite and make so sure that they were buried and not dead because they couldn't be rotted, is an artistic or creative act.

SODRE: The past resurrected into the present, both in its idealised and in its persecuting, ghostly aspects, will come up in different ways in all our novels.

BYATT: There are three creations of art or the imagination, three huge female figures in which Charlotte Brontë allows all her imagery of Lucy's state of mind to play. There are the paintings in the art gallery, the picture of Cleopatra, and the rather dull little pictures of a woman's life. Then the whole problem of the spectral nun. And finally Vashti, the actress. The art gallery is very funny. There is Lucy in front of the painting of Cleopatra, which is I think the most purely comic moment in the whole book, the description of the enormous areas of flesh of this completely sexless woman, sitting on this immense seat, who manages *not* to cover herself with yards and yards of drapery. (We have been thinking in terms of people being dressed and undressed – Lucy being made ready to go out with Dr John, or Paulina being made ready to see her father.) The comedy works by obtruding precise reasonable measurements.

> It represented a woman, considerably larger, I thought, than the life. I calculated that this lady, put into a scale of magnitude suitable for the reception of a commodity of bulk, would infallibly turn from fourteen to sixteen stone. She was, indeed, extremely well fed: very much butcher's meat – to say nothing of bread, vegetables, and liquids – must she have consumed to attain that breadth and height . . . Pots and pans – perhaps I ought to say vases and goblets – were rolled here and there on the foreground; a perfect rubbish of flowers was mixed amongst them, and an absurd and disorderly mass of curtain upholstery smothered the couch and cumbered the floor. (Ch. 19)

It's not a tone Lucy uses exactly anywhere else. It's an imitation housewife, of a Yorkshire kind in my view, solidly refusing to be impressed. And that's not the only picture – there are the four images of 'La vie d'une femme', which are flat, dead, pale and formal. There's a *jeune fille* coming out of church, a bride with a long white veil 'holding her hands plastered together, finger to finger', and a young mother hanging disconsolate over 'a clayey and puffy baby with a face like an unwholesome full moon' – there's Lucy's attitude to maternity! Then there's the widow, 'a black woman holding by the hand a black little girl'. 'Angels', that is 'women grim and gray as burglars, and cold and vapid as ghosts' (Ch. 19).

SODRE: I love the way Lucy pretends not to understand the Cleopatra: she would say pots and pans rather than goblets and cups. She calls it 'an enormous piece of claptrap' (Ch. 19). Through her humour she conveys, 'I despise this kind of art, I despise this kind of woman.'

BYATT: Both.

SODRE: But as soon as Paul Emanuel appears on the scene, she pretends to be interested, just to provoke him, declaring, 'It is a very ugly picture, but I cannot at all see why I should not look at it' (ibid.).

BYATT: And he decides to protect her from it, and says she shouldn't look at it because she's an unattached lady.

SODRE: He thinks the picture will have some power over her; but we know it doesn't. She can mock it (and him!) as much as she feels like. But the Cleopatra must be there to say something about a horrible kind of sexuality, a gigantic grotesque version of completely mindless female sexuality, which she is repelled by.

BYATT: As if the expanse of flesh represents the absence of mind, and she responds to it in a mindless way by simply weighing it up and analysing it into its constituent parts. Though I think it's important that the idea of cups and goblets and offering people life-giving drinks, with the connotation of the chalice of the Communion, runs all the way through this book. People give each other real cups, and there are a lot of metaphorical cups. The image of Christ in the garden asking that the bitter cup should be taken from him crops up in all sorts of places. And there is Paulina drinking Graham's 'Old October', which he says is 'perilously sweet' (like something from a fairytale). She sips from the cup in his hands, and then is dismissive: 'I find it anything but sweet; it is bitter and hot, and takes away my breath. Your old October was only desirable while forbidden' (Ch. 25). Cleopatra isn't drinking anything, although she's well fattened up by having drunk quantities of liquid.

SODRE: If you have in mind the chalice, then it is a desecrated one, used as a repository for mindless stuff.

BYATT: Yes, she makes repulsive everything that matters to Lucy in ordering her life neatly – cups, clothes, the flesh underneath the clothes. These all come together beautifully of course when M. Paul builds the beautiful kitchen with the lovely cups for Lucy at the end, and in the wonderful scene where they actually have their one meal together on the little balcony looking out, the cups are perfectly described – 'he said I should offer him chocolate in my pretty gold and white china service' – and they eat delicious fruit and bread. As they do at M. Paul's picnic earlier, which is a simple pastoral feast: 'Our meal was simple: the chocolate, the rolls, the plate of fresh summer fruit, cherries and strawberries bedded in green leaves, formed the whole' (Ch. 41).

SODRE: In this chapter, 'Faubourg Clotilde', sexuality is hinted at rather beautifully, as in 'cherries and strawberries bedded in green leaves', and earlier, when he says to her that when she thought he had abandoned her, he had her constantly in mind: 'Lucy and Lucy's cot' (ibid.).

BYATT: I found that very moving.

I think that Vashti, the actress, is meant to be set up as the opposite of Cleopatra. They are both large, oriental women, who represent some real violent powerful female force. I was interested to discover who Vashti was, because I had always supposed that she was some kind of oriental harlot or Queen of Sheba figure, but in fact she was the first wife of King Ahasuerus who later married Esther. She was very beautiful, and was called forth at the feast of the king to display her beauty to all his guests – at a feast indeed where goblets and cups and wine are emphasised. 'And they gave them drink in vessels of gold, (the vessels being diverse one from another) and royal wine in abundance, according to the state of the king. And the drinking was according to the law; none did compel . . .' (Esther 1: 7–8). And she wouldn't come out – she said no, she wouldn't be looked at. And everybody said she had betrayed the king and the needs of the Persians, the guests, and therefore she should be put away as a wife. She refused to be a spectacle, a performer. Then an innocent young virgin was advertised for and found who was Esther, the Jewish lady.

It's interesting that the name of the woman who wouldn't act is chosen by Lucy/Charlotte as a name for the great Jewish actress Rachel, in the scene in which the sweet young virgin is found by Dr John to replace Lucy Snowe. He goes with Lucy and goes home with Paulina. Lucy has decided to display herself – she worries about the propriety of dressing up to go out with a man alone, but decides it's all right because he's the son of her godmother. And the actress incarnates all her paradoxical fears of displaying passion and of not feeling.

Brontë creates an extraordinary sustained imagery of fire and ice, of red and white, volcanoes. It feels as though she wrote it at great speed, and with great concentration.

> Suffering had struck that stage empress; and she stood before her audience neither yielding to, nor enduring, nor in finite measure, resenting it: she stood locked in struggle, rigid in resistance. She stood, not dressed, but draped in pale antique folds, long and regular like sculpture. A background and entourage and flooring of deepest crimson threw her out, white like alabaster – like silver: rather be it said, like Death (Ch. 23).

It doesn't say, white as snow. But Lucy is snow, is white. And the background is red, and the actress has already been compared to a dying sun or a volcano, 'a chaos – hollow, half-consumed: an orb perished or perishing – half lava, half glow'. Lucy/Brontë compares Vashti to the Cleopatra, the 'mighty brawn, the muscle, the abounding blood, the full-fed flesh . . .' (Ch. 23). Vashti is a woman who isn't flesh, she's Death. And so connects to Madame Walravens and her white bony staff. She is also a fallen angel, which connects her to the Romantic Satan, and the Angrian image of the underworld (De Bas-en-Pierre, as you said). The Cleopatra is materialism and the flesh, like the solid, stolid girls of Labassecour.

'Place now the Cleopatra, or any other slug, before her as an obstacle, and see her cut through the pulpy mass as the scimitar of Saladin clove the down cushion.' That's a reference to the wonderful scene in *The Talisman*, where Walter Scott's delicate Oriental, Saladin, cleaves the cushion in front of the great heavy English crusader knight, who is Richard the Lionheart in disguise. Rachel, the Jewish actress, is a type of oriental subtlety and grace.

SODRE: This links with Saladin and Richard the Lionheart in *The Professor's House*. Godfrey St Peter ought to prefer reliable Scott/ Richard but he feels gradually more drawn to the intelligent and passionate Louie/Saladin.

BYATT: Yes, and here the Richard the Lionheart is Dr John, who is sitting there as stolid as anything with his red beard. Lucy says her heart is a sunflower turning from the south to 'a fierce light, not solar – a rushing, red, cometary light – hot on vision and to sensation'. This is a disclosure of female power – acting which is entirely satisfying, which 'instead of merely irritating imagination with the thought of what *might* be done, at the same time fevering the nerves because it was *not* done, disclosed power like a deep, swollen, winter river'. The fiery comet is the opposite of the plain of snow. It's in motion and it's red. Then she goes on to say that Dr John didn't respond to this. 'His natural attitude was not the meditative, nor his natural mood the sentimental; *impressionable* he was as dimpling water, but, almost as water, *unimpressible:* the breeze, the sun, moved him – metal could not grave, nor fire brand.' And then Lucy says his sympathies were callous, and that he disapproves of Vashti as a woman and therefore can't see that she's a great artist. This is Charlotte Brontë getting a whole theme into a very small space and moving on. But it is to do partly with the reception of *Jane Eyre* –

SODRE: Being accused of coarseness.

BYATT: Yes, and extravagant passion for a maiden lady. She wonderfully comes back to the red and white and says 'That night was already marked in my book of life, not with white, but with a deep red cross' (Ch. 23). She's got the crusader cross branded on her. She can be branded, as Graham cannot. And just at the moment where you feel that you are being moved by Charlotte Brontë into a world of almost religious, simple, symbolic, powerful metaphor – the comet, the flood, the fire, the ice, the dead marble, the bones – she suddenly does something I find quite extraordinary, because a real fire starts up, and everybody starts shouting 'Fire!' And you the reader are still in an unreal world because it's an imaginary world, an imaginary theatre. You have to respond to real fire – which is partly a kind of tremendous come-down from this cosmic battle. But it is also as though the world of Lucy's imagination, as opposed to the world in which she was sitting quietly next to Dr John, has invaded the real world. So real fire has come. What real fire does, which is terrible for Lucy, is reunite Dr John with Paulina. He carries his princess triumphantly through a wall of flesh, as it were, through the Red Sea.

SODRE: I think it's marvellous too. She says of the performance: 'It was a marvellous sight: a mighty revelation. It was a spectacle low, horrible, immoral' (Ch. 23). So she places you right inside her conflict, her ambivalence towards a powerful experience which simultaneously attracts her and repels her. The imagery is so intense that the text has almost the same impact on the reader as Vashti has on Lucy.

BYATT: Brontë curiously never tells you what part the actress was playing. I've always assumed it was Phèdre.

SODRE: I never thought of it. If that was true, one could have a clearer picture of what Lucy could have felt was immoral in the play itself. Is there any reason to believe that?

BYATT: One of the reasons I think so is because you get this amazing description of her playing Phèdre in Proust. I tend to associate the two scenes. It's amazing how many times Rachel's acting appears in novels as a kind of touchstone for female power and for art controlling passion – just. Another passionate Jewish actress is Daniel Deronda's mother, the opera singer.

Coming back to the fire – the other thing is that it turns out that this was a rather small fire in some 'drapery', which might be clothes, costumes or possibly curtains.

> Next morning's papers explained that it was but some loose drapery on which a spark had fallen, and which had blazed up and been quenched in a moment. (Ch. 23)

SODRE: But Lucy is being consumed by the very real fire of her desires! When Paulina makes her reappearance Lucy feels she loses her love; but even before this happens, in the passage you quoted, whilst she is looking at Vashti with tremendous intensity of feeling she suddenly becomes aware that the actress has no impact on Graham. So however much she may desire him, there is a level on which she realises he could never entirely fulfil her most profound needs. He has no real passion.

BYATT: In that context his hair is interesting. Everybody is always avoiding calling his hair red. They say it's chestnut or titian. And Paulina once rescued becomes extremely white and icy and snowy, and dances about like a snow fairy with ivy leaves in her hair. It's as though his 'not quite red' is all right for Paulina's whiteness, but it won't do for Lucy's real passion. As a child I think I instinctively knew that the real flamboyant energy was in the very beautifully embroidered watchguard with all the wonderful colours and jewels that seemed to be somehow alive, that Lucy made for M. Paul. That's my own metaphor, flamboyant. It *has* got flames in it. There is something flaming about M. Paul's brightness of costume as opposed to Dr John. As though he could respond to the heat of passion.

SODRE: But that's also the scene in which Lucy doesn't give Paul the watchguard; she is in the grip of her perversity, and causes him to become completely distraught and furious. She enjoys her power to inflict pain – and this scene is followed by the one in which he ransacks her desk, a powerfully sexual interchange. This fiery man won't accept her coolness to him, and this gives her intense pleasure.

BYATT: Yes, and then he asks inch by inch about the watchguard, whether any inch of it was made with any other person in mind.

> 'Then it is not necessary that I should cut out any portion – saying, this part is not mine; it was plaited under the idea and for the adornment of another?'
>
> 'By no means. It is neither necessary, nor would it be just.'
>
> 'This object is *all* mine?'
>
> 'That object is yours entirely.' (Ch. 29)

SODRE: He is both the passionate man full of desire, and the small child being jealous. There is something very touching about his need for reassurance, his pleasure in seeing all his initials embroidered. Her tantalising of him is in part her flirtation, but also in part her cruelty, which she is aware of.

BYATT: And wonderfully contrasted with the sense that Dr John, who is taking de Bassompierre's child from him, is a man taking a child. De Bassompierre says to Lucy: 'It is strange; I had lost the just reckoning of her age. I thought of her as twelve – fourteen – an indefinite date; but she seemed a child.' (Ch. 37) You feel all of them are children compared to Lucy and Paul who are playing at being children and bringing out childish emotions, which are actually grown up.

SODRE: Paulina never grows up, and she manages to organise this infantile *ménage à trois* in which she remains 'married' to her father and Graham just comes to live with them. But what you said reminded me that one of the last times we see the three of them together, they are sitting in the park, and she is plaiting together bits of her hair with their hair. So she's making this object which is in complete contrast to the flamboyant watchguard; the watchguard is something totally new as a creation (as opposed to the sentimental commonplace use of a locket) and made specially for Paul Emanuel.

BYATT: It is actually a work of art. I *knew* it fitted on to Vashti and Cleopatra. In fact it is the work of art made by Lucy Snowe. And the way it's described, it's a wonderful work of art.

> All my materials – my whole stock of beads and silk – were used up before the chain assumed the length and richness I wished; I had wrought it double, as I knew, by the rule of contraries, that to suit the particular taste whose gratification was in view, an effective appearance was quite indispensable. As a finish to the ornament, a little gold clasp was needed; fortunately I possessed it in the fastening of my sole necklace; I duly detached and re-attached it, then coiled compactly the completed guard, and enclosed it in a small box I had bought for its brilliancy, made of some tropic shell of the colour called 'nacarat,' and decked with a little coronal of sparkling blue stones. Within the lid of the box, I carefully graved with my scissors' point certain initials. (Ch. 29)

One of the things I enjoy in feminist criticism is the amount of work that's been done on how important works of embroidery and needlework are in women's images of making things. There's a wonderful moment where Lucy actually compares the head of Paulina's needle to the head of a little golden snake moving along – 'the golden head of some darting little yellow serpent' – as though her sewing was somehow subversive or serpentine. There's a scene where Lucy breaks her sewing-scissors, out of rage with M. Paul. But she finally makes him this wonderful thing, which he then wears out in the open, right across his breast like the knight with the red cross. It's a series of positive powerful images. Very good.

The third personification of female power, besides Cleopatra and Vashti is the spectral nun. The nun is ambivalent in the sense that it's partly a motif out of a gothic novel in which people see ghostly figures representing guilt or fear rushing through the corridors of castles, and partly realistic. It's realistic in two ways – psychologically and banally. Dr John is quite convinced that the nun is a kind of boiling of Lucy's brain, Lucy's anxiety impressing itself on the air so that she can actually see it, a hallucinatory creature. Then there is the final almost farcical complete explanation of the nun, which was actually a man, de Hamal, dressed up as a woman, who has come in to make love to Ginevra Fanshawe. It was in fact illicit sex being facilitated by the legend, the myth, the fear of the nun. But the nun is also a link between Paul Emanuel, Madame Beck and Lucy, because M. Paul believes when he sees her that it's Justine Marie come to tell him not to be in love with Lucy. And Lucy believes that it's a buried nun who did wrong, a spectre produced by her burial of the letters, by her own buried life and buried sexuality. How do you think one responds to it?

SODRE: Lucy effectively says at one point 'So much for this sort of romanticism, of people who really believe in ghosts and nuns.' In the end, when she sees the nun on her bed, she doesn't run away, she pounces on it and tears it apart – and it's just a costume with a note. It's wonderful. But that is also when she has gone through experiences of being haunted by ghosts and nuns from her internal world, which are much more real than Gothic invented ghosts. So that her own brand of Gothic is much more to do with internal reality than with made-up fantasies and stories. The Lucy who has gone through horrible experiences of madness, who is haunted by the conspiracy against her involvement with Paul Emanuel, who is so tormented by this horrible catastrophe of the loss of her love, is not frightened by that sort of ghost any more. I think it's a wonderful passage about the contrast between real imagination in contact with internal reality, and made-up stories about nuns.

BYATT: It does bother you as a reader, when you find out that the nun was only M. de Hamal dressed up. You feel that Charlotte Brontë has slightly betrayed you, she has made you share all Lucy's emotions, which turn out to be about nothing. It's interesting how the nun becomes more and more human. When Lucy first sees it it doesn't really have eyes, but later she actually meets its eyes, that glitter. So in some curious way it's beginning to get more real. More real in a concrete sense, as it gets more into the story. It can finally become completely real and only a set of clothes which have been abandoned.

SODRE: The treatment of the nun does touch the whole question of what's 'real' in fiction.

BYATT: Lucy sees herself as an unwilling nun.

SODRE: Lucy takes the veil in the beginning of the novel, because snow is a veil. She isn't really snow, she's fire. But she wraps herself in 'Snowe' . . .

SODRE: There is something important in relation to creative writing, as opposed to daydream, wish-fulfilling writing, which I think Charlotte Brontë refers to at various points, which comes through in the narrative. She illustrates this through her use of fairytale: she examines the question of imagination being used to create gratifying false worlds. This is what George Eliot calls 'mists of feelings instead of substantial realities'. In *Villette,* in her use of fairytale, Angria-like characters, Brontë is truthfully exploring the mind's capacity to create lies – exploring, ultimately, the infantile need to invent fictions that console, rather than fictions that struggle with the working through of painful conflicts.

BYATT: Or capacity to create images with which to interrogate reality. I think you can use fairytales to understand reality – just as much as you can use religion. They come together as being rather the same thing in this book. Charlotte Brontë has set up the whole structure of Protestant Christianity, and the whole structure of Catholic Christianity, and the structure of witches, stepmothers, princesses, princes, fire, ice, the kind of archetypal world of enchanted castles, dungeons, ghastly nuns. All these are images with which you present your reality to yourself and see what it is that matters to you in it. You can understand a lot about yourself by working out which fairytale you use to present your world to yourself in. For that matter I suspect you could do that with Christianity too, whether it's the Virgin and Son or the figure on the Cross you choose to devote yourself to. *Villette* is a novel by somebody who was terribly conscious of the temptation to escape into the worlds of myth, or to invent places where desire could be satisfied, rather than living in reality. And in a sense both Charlotte Brontë and Lucy Snowe are fighting an almost desperate and almost unnecessary battle to stay only in reality and not to rush off into imagination, because they think that might lead into madness and they think it might kill them. Whereas in fact it is their lifeline. That's how I see it. The book is uneasy, it isn't a book in which the mythic world, or the world of cosmic struggle, wholly reinforces the search for reality. First the search for reality knocks the cosmic world on the head, and then the cosmic world rushes in and makes reality into hallucination, and the balance is very hard to find. I think in the end it works, I think it is a very great novel, because in the end, at least for the reader, it's possible to hold both these worlds together in one place and see that they are both part of the whole world of writer, narrator and reader.

SODRE: I think it is a very wonderful novel, in spite of its occasional unevenness, moments when one feels things are not entirely worked out. It is in complete contrast with the perfect symmetry of *Mansfield Park*. *Mansfield Park* is not impoverished by the symmetry and sharpness of focus, but it is a completely different way of thinking about the world. *Villette* is much more a novel about the life of the mind, about imagination. Creative imagination, which transforms Charlotte's raw experience into the wonderful story of Lucy and Paul; uncontrolled imagination, which Brontë sees as the mind violently rebelling against excessive repression, and being overwhelmed by the horrors of internal reality, which is madness; and over-controlled imagination, which is used defensively against knowledge of internal and external reality.

BYATT: There is a point I have been wanting to discuss – this is the only first-person novel among those we have chosen to talk about. The only one where the novelist has put on a narrative voice. And that of a character who is quite close to her, if not very close, who can be recognised as having many of the same emotions. One of the theories I have about the George Eliot third-person narrator is that actually you can get much closer to a character if you don't write in the first person, than if you do. It seems to me that Lucy is much the most tricky central character of all the ones we are discussing. I was reading through *Daniel Deronda* and looking at what George Eliot feels she can with authority tell you about that very difficult, complicated person Grandcourt. And she just says: 'he felt this, he felt that'. And you know this is what he felt. And you know she has a right to say so, and you know that your own imagination can take over from there, and imagine the things she doesn't tell you. But with Charlotte using the first person as she does here, it is actually a barrier, an interesting barrier between the writer and the reader, Lucy's own narrating of her own fate.

SODRE: Yes. Lucy makes you curious and angry when she is particularly teasing and tantalising; specially when you are not sure if this is the writer's controlled construction of her character's personality, or if this is Charlotte simply being nasty to you.

BYATT: Do you feel that somebody is being aggressive to the reader? Somebody is not in alliance with the reader, somebody wants the reader to have a bumpy ride and to think one thing is happening and then another will. In a way the novelist is hiding behind the narrator, the character.

SODRE: Yes, I have the feeling that it is very convenient for Charlotte to have Lucy doing to the reader what *she* wants to do. I felt most betrayed by Lucy not telling me that she had discovered Dr John's identity. Critics have said that maybe Brontë wanted to increase the suspense, but I found it most disconcerting, I felt teased in a disagreeable way. I don't think it works, in the novel.

BYATT: I have wondered if it was a sort of exhaustion or incompetence. All through *Villette* there is a feeling of somebody, the writer, not only the character but the writer, being at the end of her tether. And when you read the biographies, you can see that she must have been at the end of her tether. Branwell was dead, Emily was dead, Anne was dead. Was she married? It was before she married.

SODRE: Before she married, around the time she was involved with her publisher, George Smith (her Graham Bretton).

BYATT: So she was afraid. She was both very famous, and afraid of having no life as a woman. The book is full of strain and effort of will. Every now and then, I think in the Vashti chapter, or in the Cleopatra chapter, you know she's got it absolutely right and she says 'Aha, I can do what I like with the language', as Lucy felt when she was acting: 'I can do it, I can do it.' Every now and then you feel her thinking, 'I have got to push this on, I have got to make it work.' And sometimes you get the very high-flown passages at that point, which strike one as false because you feel she's working herself up. As Dr Leavis once famously said about Othello, 'working himself up' to being in a passion. You feel sometimes Charlotte is working herself up, or Lucy is, to being in a passion.

SODRE: She was feeling completely haunted at that time, she couldn't sleep at night thinking of the deaths of Emily and Anne, so there must have been moments when she was writing in states of mind not dissimilar to Lucy's in her breakdown. Lucy is haunted by nightmarish images of death, but also at one point says something that conveys very movingly one of the most profoundly painful experiences of mourning:

> I rose on my knees in bed. Some fearful hours went over me: indescribably was I torn, racked and oppressed in mind. Amidst the horrors of that dream I think the worst lay here. Methought the well-loved dead, who had loved *me* well in life, met me

> elsewhere, alienated: galled was my inmost spirit with an unutterable sense of despair about the future. (Ch. 15)

Despair becomes absolute when you feel that even your internal loving objects have turned against you, the beloved dead have forsaken you. Lucy's extreme suffering must be close to Charlotte's experience of bereavement at the time of writing *Villette*.

BYATT: Exactly. She must have been quite near that. I think that comes through, and you sense her trembling on the edge of things. In many ways of course, you could argue that she needed Lucy Snowe to be so cold and repressed and tiresome, in order to write a book at all, given the state she was in. She must have felt Lucy was quite a useful tool.

SODRE: On the other hand, there is something that I find extraordinary in *Villette*, which is the fact that there isn't a separate character who is the 'mad woman in the attic': the madness is not split off from the central character, like in *Jane Eyre*, in which there is an actual mad woman who is sexually voracious and violent and crazy, whilst Jane is passionate but sane. Part of the greatness of *Villette* comes from the integration of madness and sanity in the same character. This links to what you explored in detail in the text, the richness and complexities of the different uses of the 'fire' metaphor, compared to which the fire in *Jane Eyre*, however powerful, seems one-dimensional.

BYATT: It is an immensely complex and courageous book.

Chapter 3
George Eliot: *Daniel Deronda*

Daniel Deronda, published in 1876, is the last of George Eliot's novels. It has a double plot, which follows the interconnecting lives of Gwendolen Harleth, a spirited, beautiful, much-courted heroine with high self-esteem, and Daniel Deronda, of uncertain parentage, who has been attentively brought up by an English aristocrat, Sir Hugo Mallinger. The two first come across one another in a striking opening scene, set in a gambling house.

Gwendolen's mother, a widow, and three younger sisters, are struggling. Helped by a brother-in-law, Mr Gascoigne, they move into a pleasant country house, Offendene. Gwendolen rejects an offer of marriage from eligible Rex, and shortly after is threatened with the necessity of taking more humble accommodation. The thought of further hardship horrifies Gwendolen, and she is determined to protect her mother, to whom she is very close, and herself from destitution. Her first thought is to make a living as a singer, but she is brutally put off by Herr Klesmer, the musician, who tells her she will never be a true artist. As a result, with no other avenue open, she agrees to marry an English gentleman, Grandcourt, despite having been warned against it by Lydia Glasher, a woman who was previously his mistress, and by whom he has children. Almost immediately Gwendolen suffers, from guilt, and more directly from the realisation that her husband himself is a cold, sadistic man whose desire to have power over her is absolute. In one powerful scene, she receives diamonds with a terrifying note from Lydia Glasher, which sets the unhappy tone of her marriage to come. Her buoyancy and self-esteem are eroded, and at every opportunity she turns for guidance to Daniel Deronda, whom she has invested from the first with a mysterious authority.

Daniel Deronda himself is peculiarly sensitive, sympathetic and idealistic. At first sight he was struck by Gwendolen, but it is with a young Jewish woman, Mirah, whom he saves from drowning herself, that he falls in love. Daniel entrusts her to the care of the family of a close university friend, artist Hans Meyrick, who warms quickly to her, and there she flourishes. Herr Klesmer, who is by now married against her parents' wishes to an ex-music-pupil, Englishwoman Miss Arrowpoint, is called in to train her lovely singing voice, which she begins to use professionally. Mirah craves reunion with a missing brother: her mother is dead, and her father abusive and alcoholic. In the attempt to find the brother, Daniel ventures into the Jewish quarter of London. There he comes across an ardent, intellectual Jewish nationalist called Mordecai, to whom he is curiously drawn. Mordecai proves to be Mirah's brother, and, after a while, Daniel reunites them, to their mutual joy. Mordecai sees in Daniel a future leader of the Jewish people; at first this bewilders, but does not repel him.

The denouement occurs in Genoa, where Daniel and Gwendolen meet again and where revelation and trauma await them respectively. Daniel is there to meet his mother, who has written to him at last. In her, he finds an extraordinary, powerful woman: an actress and singer known as the Alcharisi. She reveals that she renounced her son in order to pursue her career, and also in order to disguise his true identity, which is Jewish. His mother will remain remote, but the discovery of his Jewish identity has a profound effect on Daniel, and makes sense of his love for Mirah and the role cast upon him by Mordecai.

Gwendolen and Grandcourt are there on a tormenting yachting holiday, ironically instigated partly to keep Deronda and Gwendolen apart. After a brief, surprise meeting between Daniel and Gwendolen, Grandcourt falls from his yacht and drowns at sea. Gwendolen, persecuted by guilt because she neglected to try to save him, 'confesses' to Daniel, who finds the burden of it hard to bear.

Gwendolen's despair is at first deepened when she learns that Daniel is to marry Mirah and to devote his life to the founding of a Jewish National home, as Mordecai had predicted he would. However, it is suggested that, although suffering appallingly, she will recover, and that she will, in time, learn how to live with more honesty, humility and happiness.

SODRE: Shall we start, like all readers, with the opening scene?

> Was she beautiful or not beautiful? and what was the secret of form or expression which gave the dynamic quality to her glance? Was the good or the evil genius dominant in those beams? Probably the evil; else why was the effect that of unrest rather than of undisturbed charm? Why was the wish to look again felt as coercion and not as a longing in which the whole being consents?
>
> She who raised these questions in Daniel Deronda's mind was occupied in gambling: not in the open air under a southern sky, tossing coppers on a ruined wall, with rags about her limbs; but in one of those splendid resorts which the enlightenment of ages has prepared for the same species of pleasure at a heavy cost of gilt mouldings, dark-toned colour and chubby nudities, all correspondingly heavy . . .' (Ch. I)

BYATT: It's one of the greatest openings of any novel. Partly because it starts with a series of questions, rather than descriptions. So whilst appearing to set a scene, it hesitates to do so for quite a long time. The series of questions begins with 'Was she beautiful or not beautiful?' This is the fairytale question, except that in tales there never is a question: all princesses are beautiful. I admire the courage of an author who can then go on 'Was the good or the evil genius dominant in those beams?' She's starting on a very high note. She's put good and evil in, and then she answers her own question: probably the evil. Except in the next paragraph you realise that your point of view is not that of an impersonal author but of somebody called Daniel Deronda, about whom you're told nothing except that he's watching. So he becomes a kind of second author, and it puts the object of the questions at a distance from reader, author and Deronda.

SODRE: What is fascinating for a psychoanalyst is that the questions immediately link external reality to internal reality – as if the reader is drawn into a position of psychological curiosity, almost of scientific enquiry in relation to the inner world of a character. And then we discover this is Daniel Deronda's point of view, so the author is focusing on the mind of another character, who is defining someone whom he does not understand in moral terms: 'Probably the evil'. The reader is now wondering about the secret of this mysterious woman, whilst very subtly being informed about the man who asks the questions.

BYATT: And then: 'Why was the wish to look again felt as coercion and not as a longing in which the whole being consents?' That's an immensely loaded question. It has to contain sexual desire, and yet it's desire which is coerced rather than consented to. It's somebody feeling fascination against his will, though we don't know he's a he until the first sentence of the next paragraph. Then Eliot immediately goes into the story: 'She who raised these questions in Daniel Deronda's mind was occupied in gambling'. Which somehow you simply don't expect. I remember the first time I read that, thinking, what an extraordinary shock.

SODRE: I think this shock is meant to pull the reader even more closely into Daniel's state of mind: this heroine who gambles also immediately attracts and repels the reader, who becomes powerfully engaged with this beautiful woman involved in something which is by nature fascinating and addictive. The novel is partly going to be about relationships that are disruptive and destructive, because based on the wish for total power.

BYATT: I suppose that it means the narrator has immediately set up the whole novel to make you feel there's something evil about Gwendolen, which lingers even when Eliot later takes you very close and makes you sympathise with her and feel all her feelings. In this opening scene she is seen from outside, as an attractive and dangerous being. What Eliot then does is create a whole European atmosphere of a gambling house, with wonderful narrative authority. She claims that this is a European novel, sets it in an enormous racial mix, all these people who are present:

> Those who were taking their pleasures at a higher strength, and were absorbed in play, showed very distant varieties of European type: Livonian and Spanish, Graeco-Italian and miscellaneous German, English aristocratic and English plebeian. Here certainly was a striking admission of human equality. (Ch. 1)

Everybody's equal before the force of gambling and the force of money in a way. But it's not, apparently, going to be an *English* novel. Gwendolen is seen not in an English setting, and looking rather exotic. And for a long time you don't see her at all, all you see is the thing which isn't, which is the Spanish child gambling on the wall, whom Deronda compares her to, a ragged Spanish child whom he would rather see. Interesting.

SODRE: A child who is in fact closer to him and his Mediterranean origin (although it is of central importance in the novel that this is not known at this point). But there's another child as well, a melancholy little boy in fancy dress, apparently in complete contrast with the imaginary Spanish child and with the excited Gwendolen, but in fact bringing into the picture what you will eventually discover and sympathise with in Gwendolen, a melancholy child who creates for herself a life which is a masquerade.

BYATT: The whole scene is full of artifice. There is the old woman, 'prematurely old, withered after short bloom like her artificial flowers', and the child is in fancy dress. You get the first mention of the jewels. We discussed the importance of jewels in *Villette* and the theme connects to Miss Havisham in *Great Expectations* and the witch in the fairy story. 'The white bejewelled fingers of an English countess were very near touching a bony, yellow, crab-like hand stretching a bared wrist to clutch a heap of coin'. Beautiful.

SODRE: And it goes on, the description: 'a hand easy to sort with a square, gaunt face, deep-set eyes, grizzled eyebrows, and ill-combed scanty hair which seemed a slight metamorphosis of the vulture.'

BYATT: Both very witty and – it has exactly the same quality, a total precision and total mystery. And then Eliot moves on into describing the money, and we still haven't seen Gwendolen at all. We've seen all these other people. And there is this wonderful observation that runs all the way through the scene, that the air is bad: 'the atmosphere was well-brewed to a visible haze' it says at the beginning of the third paragraph. And Eliot keeps coming back to that and making the air worse and worse. Two pages later: 'Deronda's first thought when his eyes fell on this scene of dull, gas-poisoned absorption was that the gambling of Spanish shepherd-boys had seemed to him more enviable'.

Eliot's first description of Gwendolen starts with a description of her effect on Deronda: 'The inward debate which she raised in Deronda gave to his eyes a growing expression of scrutiny, tending farther and farther away from the glow of mingled undefined sensibilities forming admiration' (Ch. 1). We see his eyes following her movements, which is very beautiful. One moment his eyes 'followed the movements of the figure, of the arms and hands, as this problematic sylph bent forward to deposit her stake with an air of firm choice'. We still can't see her really, can we? The word sylph obscures rather than depicts . . .

SODRE: Up to this point we don't see her from inside, we see her from Daniel's external point of view; as 'probably evil', which here is associated with power, arrogance and maybe ruthlessness. The paragraph you're quoting says, 'she looked round her with a survey too markedly cold and neutral not to have in it a little of that nature which we call art concealing an inward exultation' (Ch. 1). Deronda's psychological perception of her is of a witch disguised as a princess.

BYATT: It's quite interesting that throughout the novel nobody likes her. Some people fall in love with her; Rex falls in love with her, Daniel Deronda doesn't fall in love with her. In fact Rex is the only person throughout the novel who really likes her. Everybody else reacts with immediate suspicion and says that she's pushing it too far, she's acting. In any conventional novel, a person introduced in this way would be the villain, the person you were really going to dislike, who was going to damage everybody. In fact what we're meeting is the victim, on the whole. She hurts nobody directly except Rex, and is deeply hurt by many people. Although she is extremely selfish and unpleasant, also.
SODRE: But she's also completely lacking in insight, and that's basically what George Eliot says she suffers from; that her hurtfulness to others is based on her incapacity to see rather than a more active wish to hurt. George Eliot does not see her as 'evil', she sees her as psychologically immature and disturbed. When Gwendolen angrily says to her mother, 'Why did you marry again, mamma? It would have been nicer if you had not' (Ch. 3), a question that comes from her intensely possessive self, her mother answers, 'with a violence quite unusual in her – "You have no feeling, child!" ' And she is right, she is psychologically an insensitive child; she has no idea she is being cruel. And yet she loves her mother, but only as an extension of herself.
BYATT: It's a kind of driven cruelty. Rather like some of the cruelties in Toni Morrison's *Beloved*.
SODRE: Going back to the first scene, this is Gwendolen's point of view:

> But in the course of that survey her eyes met Deronda's, and instead of averting them as she would have desired to do, she was unpleasantly conscious that they were arrested – how long? The darting sense that he was measuring her and looking down on her as an inferior . . .' (Ch. 1)

You have the feeling she must be used to being looked at with admiration, but at this point you discover that her awareness of being scrutinised by this particular man makes her feel uncomfortable, almost desperate: her 'inward exultation' is shattered by his scrutiny.
BYATT: I do love Eliot's use of different vocabularies: 'he was of different quality from the human dross around her, that he felt himself in a region outside and above her, and was examining her as a specimen of a lower order'. The examining her as a specimen comes out of the vocabulary of science, and the epigraph to this chapter talks about both art and science. But the idea of Deronda coming from a region outside and above is

actually much more a religious idea, as though he's an angel or a demon, looking down on her from some other world. Which she has also said. And then you get 'Deronda's gaze seemed to have acted as an evil eye'. Up till then he's been goodness and she's been evil. The word evil is applied to what he now does to her. And he stops her from winning. He stops off her energies, the theme which for me recurs most powerfully in all the novels we are looking at. In many ways Gwendolen, of all our heroines, is possessed of the most energy and gets the most stopped. Here she appears to be winning. And then this good man, or this man who feels he can judge her, looks at her and is read by her as the evil eye. He stops her. And that is when she starts exerting all sorts of muscular control on herself. 'Since she was not winning strikingly, the next best thing was to lose strikingly. She controlled her muscles, and showed no tremor of mouth or hands. Each time her stake was swept off she doubled it.' Now this is how Gwendolen will be seen reacting to everything: she controls her muscles. This control is the stopping off of energy, an extreme form of pain; all she does is stand there looking beautiful, whereas before she's been swooping about the table with all these elegant movements: ' "Le jeu ne va plus", said destiny.'

SODRE: But you feel that for Gwendolen 'destiny' is really Deronda, who is this angel and demon at the same time?

BYATT: Destiny is your sex, a thought which it is also possible to read into this moment.

SODRE: But I think Deronda is felt by Gwendolen as the powerful person who can stop her winning because she feels he can see her soul; 'le jeu ne va plus' because he knows her, what she is playing at, as it were . . . Gwendolen, in contrast to Brontë's Lucy Snowe, does not want to be understood, since all her mental energies are used to maintain the belief – in herself as much as in others – that her disguise is her true self. Lucy's power comes from self-knowledge; Gwendolen's from self-deceit. But the 'flames in the eyes' are, in a negative way, as important here as in *Villette*: 'Yet when her next stake was swept away, she felt the orbits of her eyes getting hot' – this is such a fantastic description – 'and the certainty she had (without looking) of that man still watching her was something like a pressure which begins to be torturing' (Ch. I). She feels mentally absolutely invaded by him.

BYATT: And this is treated with the metaphors that then begin to appear, as a cosmic drama as well as a simple human drama. Continuing with the science image, Eliot says that 'it was at least better he should have kept his attention fixed on her than that he should have disregarded her as one of an insect swarm who had no individual physiognomy.' One of the main interests of the naturalists in the nineteenth century was the similarities and differences between the social insects and human beings. I remember reading Michelet's book *L'Insecte*; he spent a long time torturing an ant by putting it under a glass and taking away its oxygen, and it began to rub its head with its feelers and felt great pain. And Michelet then has an immense page on how an ant has no face, you cannot meet its eye, you can't understand what it is. Here Gwendolen has been reduced to having no individual physiognomy, just being one of a swarm, by Deronda's look. Yet on the next page she's compared to a serpent, and the serpent comes totally out of German mythology, Greek mythology and biblical mythology, in the sense that Gwendolen is a Lamia, she is a water nixie, which is a spirit of the outer air looking for a soul.

> The Nereid in sea-green robes and silver ornaments, with a pale sea-green feather fastened in silver falling backward over her green hat and light-brown hair, was Gwendolen Harleth . . .
>
> 'A striking girl – that Miss Harleth – unlike others.'
>
> 'Yes; she has got herself up as a sort of serpent now, all green and silver, and winds her neck about a little more than usual.'
>
> 'Oh, she must always be doing something extraordinary. She is that kind of girl, I fancy. Do you think her pretty, Mr Vandernoodt?'
>
> 'Very. A man might risk hanging for her – I mean, a fool might.'
>
> 'You like a *nez retroussé* then, and long narrow eyes?'
>
> 'When they go with such an *ensemble*.'
>
> 'The *ensemble du serpent*?'
>
> 'If you will. Woman was tempted by a serpent: why not man?' (Ch.1)

I love the way it's done in a comic, English, Jane Austen kind of speech. 'Yes, she has got herself up as a sort of serpent now, all green and silver, and winds her neck about a little more than usual.' This makes you see entirely what kind of woman she was, and yet it makes you see her not as a woman but as a creature or a demon. And then you get the doubleness again, when Mr Vandernoodt says that her long narrow eyes 'go with such an *ensemble*', the *ensemble du serpent*, 'If you will. Woman was tempted by a serpent: why not man?' But it's Deronda who's just cast an evil eye on Gwendolen. So you do feel that a cosmic drama is being enacted at this table of chance or destiny by these two figures, with this kind of Walpurgisnacht crew of minor demons or death's heads looking on. Wonderful scene.

SODRE: In George Eliot the line of serpent women starts with Berthe in 'The Lifted Veil' – a woman whose terrible power over her husband comes from her absolute psychological opacity. And in *Middlemarch*, although Lydgate can understand Rosamond, she is psychologically impenetrable, which is what gives her power to defeat him. Poor Gwendolen thinks she can be a serpent, but it only takes this man to look into her for a second and her psychological masquerading is dismantled. The choice of gambling as a metaphor for Gwendolen's life is brilliant: she feels triumphant in her conviction of being a winner; and never was a loser portrayed with more psychological insight than this! Gwendolen's destiny is to be married to a serpent rather than to be a serpent.

BYATT: Indeed. Wonderful image later on of Grandcourt curled like a particularly ornamental serpent in the corner of the cabin when they are flying about in the boat. The Lamia, the Undine, the water nixie, all of them are creatures of the middle air, who needed to marry a human being in order to get a soul. And I'm quite sure George Eliot is thinking also of Lilith, the first wife of Adam in the Garden, and other daemons. These were serpent beings, serpent angels, in Hebrew mythology. Whereas Daniel Deronda, in the way in which you have just described the metaphor, is as it were St Michael striking down the original dragon.

BYATT: One of the places I keep coming back to is the place where Gwendolen sees that her home wasn't her home.

> Pity that Offendene was not the home of Miss Harleth's childhood, or endeared to her by family memories! A human life, I think, should be well rooted in some spot of a native land, where it may get the love of tender kinship for the face of earth, for the labours men go forth to, for the sounds and accents that haunt it, for whatever will give that early home a familiar unmistakable difference amidst the future widening of knowledge: a spot where the definiteness of early memories may be inwrought with affection, and kindly acquaintance with all neighbours, even to the dogs and donkeys, may spread not by sentimental effort and reflection, but as a sweet habit of the blood. At five years old, mortals are not prepared to be citizens of the world, to be stimulated by abstract nouns, to soar above preference into

> impartiality; and that prejudice in favour of milk with which we blindly begin, is a type of the way body and soul must get nourished at least for a time. The best introduction to astronomy is to think of the nightly heavens as a little lot of stars belonging to one's own homestead. (Ch. 3)

That again looks so simple and is one of the most complicated bits of prose in the English language, I think. The way it moves from the local image to its immense implications and out to the abstract. I think she is taking the idea of 'memory inwrought with affection' back to Wordsworth's idea of things and thoughts being felt along the blood.

SODRE: Yes, George Eliot makes it quite clear that Gwendolen isn't sufficiently rooted, which is interesting because Gwendolen is in fact excessively close to her mother, psychologically still a baby at the breast. Something is not internally established firmly enough for her to be able to separate. Wordsworth's 'infant babe' in the *Prelude* grows from having established his mother's breast firmly in his inner world, and, as the psychoanalyst Ron Britton has shown, Klein's theory of the building up of internal reality is very close to Wordsworth's view of the development of his infant self. The passage you quoted also reminds me of Maggie's decision to be loyal to her earliest bonds in *The Mill on the Floss*. One feels this is one of George Eliot's deepest convictions. But Gwendolen doesn't have a father, and presumably had a very depressed widowed mother when she was very little; she sells the Etruscan necklace, which was made of turquoises from her father's chain, to pay for her gambling, and tells herself it doesn't matter because she has no memory of her father. I think the death of her father – in external reality but also in internal reality since she has no memory of him – followed by the death of a hated stepfather, are the basis for the rootlessness that informs all her relationships with men. I suspect the death of the stepfather (who she must have wished dead) is the cause of her terror of the 'dead face' when the panel flies open.

BYATT: There is also – I remember having a real thrill of horror when I read it – there is the fact that she strangled the canary. So Gwendolen as a child was capable both of strangling her canary because it annoyed her, and of wishing her stepfather dead, if you are right. She committed an actual very small murder, and wished for a very large murder. And in the paragraph about Offendene, George Eliot does tell us that you should feel 'kindly acquaintance with all neighbours, even to the dogs and donkeys'. Gwendolen is a small pet-bird murderer. The whole structure of the canary murder has changed in my mind every time I have read this book, because the first time I was so shocked that I was being required to sympathise with somebody who had murdered a canary at all. It is, in a way, exactly the same feeling you get from Chapter 1, the feeling that the author is insisting on the evil of the presence of Gwendolen. But when you look at the way George Eliot describes it, she does it with such precision.

> Though never even as a child thoughtlessly cruel, nay, delighting to rescue drowning insects and watch their recovery, there was a disagreeable silent remembrance of her having strangled her sister's canary-bird in a final fit of exasperation at its shrill singing which had again and again jarringly interrupted her own. She had taken pains to buy a white mouse for her sister in retribution, and though inwardly excusing herself on the ground of a peculiar sensitiveness which was a mark of her general superiority, the thought of that infelonious murder had always made her wince. Gwendolen's nature was not remorseless, but she liked to make her penances easy, and now that she was twenty and more, some of her native force had turned into a self-control by which she guarded herself from penitential humiliation. There was more show of fire and will in her than ever, but there was more calculation underneath it. (Ch. 3)

Now, that is George Eliot at her very best. Everything is qualified, your emotional response to it cannot be simple. The word murder is used, but the section begins with her delight in rescuing drowning insects. So she isn't a pathological animal killer. Nevertheless at the centre of it are this extraordinary egotism and narcissism, both of which are her nature; the canary jarringly interrupted her own singing, as indeed her sisters do, she doesn't like them, she doesn't really want them to exist.

SODRE: Pathological narcissism, which Eliot is exploring throughout the book, is a kind of psychological murder, the mental annihilation of the other person. When she tells us the cause for the murder, Gwendolen's extreme rivalry, we feel this is linked with the fact that she didn't think her mother ought to have had all those babies, whom she despises *en masse*. So we also wince at the awareness that such extreme possessiveness of the mother, the wish for no rivals, implies unconscious violence.

BYATT: This does seem to lead naturally to the scene in which she enacts Hermione from *The Winter's Tale* in front of the strange little panel which flies open. It seems important – in terms of narcissism being a wish to murder everybody but yourself and possibly your mother – that on both occasions when the panel flies open her sister Isabel is the agent who causes it to fly open.

> The opened panel had disclosed the picture of an upturned dead face, from which an obscure figure seemed to be fleeing with outstretched arms. 'How horrible!' said Mrs Davilow, with a look of mere disgust; but Gwendolen shuddered silently, and Isabel, a plain and altogether inconvenient child with an alarming memory, said –
>
> 'You will never stay in this room by yourself, Gwendolen.' (Ch. 3)

And it's Isabel who has opened it.

SODRE: Isabel, who is so curious, has stolen the key and left the cabinet unlocked. I am interested in that description of Isabel, 'a plain and altogether inconvenient child with an alarming memory'. It occurs to me that Gwendolen's terror of the dead face is connected to her own 'alarming memory', her not being able to entirely forget her stepfather who haunts her as this dead face. What is so horrifying about this panel, which after all is only a painting, must be that it reawakens some terrifying memory. What is being enacted in this scene is the negative of the Hermione situation, in which the past is revived and healed: here it is the dread of the past being resurrected.

BYATT: It's a story exactly about the way in which what you don't know about the past, or what you try not to remember about the past, is the thing that is actually driving all your actions. You feel that without benefit of Freud George Eliot knew all this. Knew it consciously, perfectly well, and was able to construct it. I think that Isabel has an alarming memory because she remembers that Gwendolen was frightened of some death, and chooses to play with this.

SODRE: I completely agree with you, that George Eliot had profound understanding of how the past powerfully influences, in an unconscious way, all our life. There's one more thing I wanted to say about the panel scene: Gwendolen has this terror of death, and it is such a beautiful idea to make her be acting Hermione when she's confronted by the dead face suddenly appearing. The first time Gwendolen sees the panel, at their arrival in Offendene, she is terribly upset, and she and Mrs Davilow go upstairs and enter for the first time what will always be referred to as their black and yellow bedroom, 'where a pretty little white couch was prepared by the side of the black and yellow catafalque, known as "the best bed" ' (Ch. 3). This is just amazing: the parental bed is immediatly associated with death. There isn't an alive father in this bedroom, there are two dead fathers. Gwendolen's first impulse is to look at herself in the mirror, and Mrs Davilow says 'That is a becoming glass, Gwendolen; or is it the black and gold colour that sets you off?' Gwendolen is 'set off' by the colours of death; she can have her little white couch, be always with her mother, because of the death of the fathers; but also, she can't be alone, separate from mother, because of her dread of the dead. Later on George Eliot quotes Shelley, in her epigraph to Chapter 54. It is curiously appropriate:

> The unwilling brain
> Feigns often what it would not; and we trust
> Imagination with such phantasies
> As the tongue dares not fashion into words;
> Which have no words, their horror makes them dim
> To the mind's eye.

This yellow and black bedroom always makes me imagine that she had Shelley's 'Ode to the West Wind', which is all about death and resurrection, in mind:

> . . . like ghosts from an enchanter fleeing,
>
> Yellow, and black, and pale, and hectic red,
> Pestilence-stricken multitudes: O thou,
> Who chariotest to their dark wintry bed
>
> The wingèd seeds, where they lie cold and low,
> Each like a corpse within its grave, until
> Thine azure sister of the spring shall blow . . .

I was wondering if one could actually think about bits of poetry, that may be somewhere in the writer's mind, even if not explicitly, consciously there, having an evocative function – like the way you said you had used the bottle and waxed silk image from *Villette* in *Possession*?
BYATT: I'm sure that's right. I think one gets haunted by rhythms and phrases and images and patterns of colour. I felt that the yellow and black was loaded with meaning that I couldn't quite place, and was trying uneasily to fit it on to Edgar Allan Poe's 'Masque of the Red Death'. And the colours take us back to the gambling den in which there's the gold of the money. What they are not is pleasant colours, are they, not warm or friendly, for a bedroom. In a sense, if we take the

bedroom forward to the scene with Hermione, and the seeds of the things growing – if you take the imagery of the 'Ode to the West Wind' which ends with the buried seed coming up again, and then you think of Hermione and Perdita as Demeter and Persephone, which I always do, you have the image of a dead and resurrected goddess.

SODRE: But also Demeter and Persephone represent the closest possible relationship between a mother and daughter. I hadn't thought of that, but it does seem relevant, when you think that Gwendolen would have preferred to stay for ever with her mother who protects her from terror, and that she is kidnapped into the underworld by Grandcourt.

BYATT: This also anticipates *Beloved* in a strange way. In a way a tableau is a form of life in death, it's people representing a moment and then holding it. Thus in a sense introducing a kind of death to it. It is interesting that Gwendolen's mother is enacting Paulina, who orchestrates the awakening of the statue: ' "Music, awake her, strike!" said Paulina (Mrs Davilow, who by special entreaty had consented to take the part in a white burnous and hood)' (Ch. 5). Now, later on we have Gwendolen in a white burnous, don't we, which is being put round her shoulders by Grandcourt at thc ball.

SODRE: Which she's very reluctant to accept, but excited by as well, 'submitting very gracefully'.

BYATT: Yes. And this cloaked and veiled figure calls up the Gothic atmosphere of nuns, as in *Villette*. In the tableau Herr Klesmer strikes a thunderous chord and 'the movable panel . . . flew open on the right opposite the stage and disclosed the picture of the dead face and the fleeing figure, brought out in pale definiteness by the position of the wax-lights' (Ch. 5). 'Pale' and 'wax' and 'light' take you back to the image of death. What happens is that the mixture of the very loud music and the image freezes Gwendolen. I've only just thought of this – this is wonderful –

> Gwendolen, who stood without change of attitude, but with a change of expression that was terrifying in its terror. She looked like a statue into which a soul of Fear had entered: her pallid lips were parted; her eyes, usually narrowed under their long lashes, were dilated and fixed. (Ch. 5)

I'd like to stress two things there. One, that again her energy has been suppressed, as in the first scene where she's moving her wonderful arms gracefully like a sylph, but when Daniel Deronda looks at her she suddenly controls her muscles and becomes rigid. This is Gwendolen's normal response to fear. But in terms of the image of Gwendolen as a nixie, and looking for a soul, it says she looked like a statue into which a soul of Fear had entered. And fear here has a capital letter. When we've talked earlier about this book, we have always immediately said the most interesting thing in it is Gwendolen's fear. What is the fear fear of?

SODRE: Again I think it is fear of somebody dead who comes back, it's essentially the ghost of the father or the stepfather, or both merged. From the point of view of psychoanalytic thought, I think it's a marvellous description of the relationship with ghosts, who, as Freud said, populate the unconscious seeking revenge for having been murdered by death wishes. Gwendolen, who is somebody who lives in dread of a ghost, chooses, possibly unconsciously as a way of triumphing over her own fear, to play Hermione, who is supposedly a completely benign ghost who becomes alive again. And at the moment she is actually enacting that, something terrifying happens, the malevolent dead reappears, and immediately reverses the end of *The Winter's Tale*: we are supposed to see a statue turning into a woman, and we see a woman turning into a statue. I think that is so marvellous!

BYATT: I feel there is more in it there as well, because she has chosen to be a statue of somebody whose whole nature is that of a mother, a wronged wife and a mother. I've always had a sort of horror of Hermione as a figure of death. I find her deeply alarming. Possibly because Shakespeare invented her, and literary criticism seems quite happy to accept her, as a benign figure of resurrection. She's in fact somebody who has had all her adult life and the growing up of her children taken from her by being closed in the tomb, and is only allowed to come to life when she's too old to live her life. And so she is in a sense a real figure of life-in-death, which was Coleridge's great terror, and which George Eliot understood. A fear of having a life that isn't a life. Why did Gwendolen not choose to play Perdita?

Why did Mrs Davilow not play Hermione, and Gwendolen play Perdita, watching her mother come to life? Why did Gwendolen play the mother and Mrs Davilow play the magician or witch who kept the woman in the tomb? And the other thing I thought, is that, seeing this scene in terms of arrested energies and released energies, Gwendolen is useless as an artist, she is standing on that pedestal in order to show off a pretty instep. George Eliot tells us this. Nevertheless she's surrounded by the terrible forces of real art. We have the real artist in the book who is Klesmer, doing a great thunder roll on the piano, we have the greatest English artist, Shakespeare, who is evoked here, there and everywhere

throughout this novel as a kind of comparison for what you might be able to do if you do art properly, i.e. produce your energies properly. And here is Gwendolen trying to reduce Shakespeare to her size. But Klesmer says no, I will show you what this truly means, I will make a great banging noise. And this causes the panel to fly open and between the painting, the music and Shakespeare's deep knowledge of what it meant to be dead and come to life, Gwendolen becomes a statue into which the soul of Fear has entered. In a sense she's *responding* to art, without being able to *make* it. Because she can't, so she becomes paralysed. Which is what she does when asked to respond to anything. And yet I return to the original idea: she appears to be a figure of enormous energy, she rides around on horseback, she can control a bow and arrow so that she can shoot to the bull's eye every time. She even manages conversations with her little whip. Whenever she is seen as attracting people her body is seen in perpetual motion, she's always snaking her hands around. And so you get a double image of her, because men see her as wonderfully mobile, and yet her real self is something very stiff and paralysed.
SODRE: But also I think there is another difference between what Gwendolen is doing and Art. The point you are making about this kind of fantasy, as opposed to being a real artist, is that it corresponds to a state of mind in which the life energy has to be used psychologically in a defensive way all the time. So that Gwendolen is always using her power, not to do something constructive but to control men and to control her fear. What I don't like about the resurrection of Hermione is that it is what psychoanalysts would call a 'manic reparation'. Leontes has done terrible things to his wife in the first act, and then he is very, very sorry but he doesn't really do anything good, and then she's magically resurrected. Gwendolen, by wanting to be Hermione, is just magically trying to repair the past, or to make it disappear by locking it away (she is terrified by the unlocking of the panel). She's not repairing the past by trying to understand what happened to her (which she begins to be able to do at the end). She tries to believe in her power to create a life from the outside, by marrying the right kind of husband, or becoming the most admired woman.

BYATT: I think this takes us on to what she feels about men. I was thinking about Lucy Snowe as you were speaking, and thinking that Lucy Snowe too has fantasy ways of dealing with her own powerlessness, though she's a much more intelligent person. But they both have the same problem – the one we find in all these novels by women – of marriage being the only fate for a woman, and also the only career for a woman. And unlike Lucy Snowe and Fanny, Gwendolen is both beautiful and marriageable. You were saying that *Mansfield Park* is a novel against marriage, and *Villette* is a novel in which marriage, though intensely desired, is not permitted to its heroine. One of the striking things about *Daniel Deronda* is that Eliot has depicted a terribly marriageable girl with no idea in her head of any other thing she wants to do, who nevertheless is terrified of being married and doesn't want that way out.

SODRE: Well, she hates men. She doesn't just hate horrible men, like Grandcourt; she hates male sexuality. Throughout the book, Gwendolen is depicted as dreading male sexuality: not just because Grandcourt is a monster, a perverse sadistic man, she also hates it in Rex: 'The perception that poor Rex wanted to be tender made her curl up and harden like a sea-anemone at the touch of a finger' (Ch. 7). It's not just that she isn't interested or frigid; she feels a terrible repulsion towards men which is very striking. After the scene with Rex she is very distressed, because she realises she will never be able to love anybody. And again I suppose in terms of her biography it must come from having hated her stepfather and not having had a father she could love. But I think it's interesting if we compare her with Lucy Snowe, because Lucy claims to be cold and frigid and snowy and yet she is so passionate and sexual. Whereas Gwendolen is certainly not unaware of sexuality, but she is afraid of it, and feels repelled by men.

BYATT: When she's waiting for Klesmer, when she's asked Klesmer to come and see her in order to ask if she can be an actress to repair the family fortune, Eliot follows a striking image, as she often does, with an abstract narrator's comment. The image is of Gwendolen being diverted to the contemplation of the image of herself which she sees in a glass panel. She's dressed in black without a single ornament 'and with the warm whiteness of her skin set off between her light brown coronet of hair and her square-cut bodice'. The narrator comments, 'she might have tempted an artist to try again the Roman trick of a statue in black, white and tawny marble.' It's a *trompe-l'oeil* statue she's saying she might represent. 'Seeing her image slowly advancing she thought, I am beautiful. Not exaltingly, but with grave decision.' Because she feels her beauty is going to free her.

Being beautiful was after all the condition on which she most

> needed external testimony. If anyone objected to the turn of her nose or the form of her neck and chin, she had not the sense that she could presently show her power of attainment in these branches of feminine perfection. (Ch. 23)

And then she waits for Klesmer. She 'dreaded Klesmer' – here's the word dread which always goes with Gwendolen – 'as part of that unmanageable world which was independent of her wishes – something vitriolic that would not cease to burn because you smiled or frowned at it'. It is arresting and shocking, that vitriol is an image for her fear of Klesmer coming. Vitriol is what spoils beauty, vitriol is what jealous women threw at beauty.

> Poor thing! she was at a higher crisis of her woman's fate than in her past experience with Grandcourt. The questioning then, was whether she would take a particular man as a husband. The inmost fold of her questioning now, was whether she needed a husband at all – whether she could not achieve substantiality for herself and know gratified ambition without bondage. (Ch. 23)

Now, ambition is interesting there, because it suggests some drive in her beyond the mere fear which you've been suggesting is the main centre of her being. I love the fact that, the moment after she's produced this image, of 'something vitriolic that would not cease to burn', George Eliot can say 'Poor thing!' I think that 'poor thing' asks the reader to identify with the narrator in looking at Gwendolen with warmth and terror from a long distance.

SODRE: 'Poor thing!' asks the reader to sympathise with her horror of feeling forced to marry. But she is also a 'poor thing' because not only can she not be a true artist, but she actually has not the faintest idea what a true artist is. When she's thinking about her ideal destiny – 'gratified ambition without bondage' – this has nothing to do with art, but all to do with a purely narcissistic endeavour – she will be entirely dependent on a thing that is external, her beauty. Entirely dependent on other people's eyes – in total bondage, in fact – in a way that a real artist isn't; a real artist is primarily involved with the internal creation of art, and only secondarily with it being something to be seen from the outside. And Gwendolen just doesn't know this; what is so mortifying for her in this scene with Klesmer, apart from the narcissistic wound, is that for the first time she gets an inkling that she is entirely blind as to what art is.

BYATT: One of the things Bradley says about Shakespeare is that after writing *Hamlet* he decided that never again would he create an intelligent tragic hero, and that all the tragic heroes after Hamlet are actually rather stupid people. Macbeth, Lear, Antony, Othello – people with very little self-understanding. I think the glory of Gwendolen's stupidity, because she *is* very silly and stupid, is that George Eliot has understood that point, that there is something more tragic about the crushing of a human being who isn't thinking right, even than the agony of a human being whose intelligence you share and communicate with. There's something terrible about Gwendolen, because of the limitations of her understanding. Right up to the very end of the book, she doesn't really see most of what's going on. It's incredibly moving when she doesn't begin to imagine that Daniel might have had a life of his own in which something different is going on.

SODRE: Which is so painful. But I think the other thing about that – and George Eliot was writing before Freud conceptualised this – is that Gwendolen's psychological stupidity – the fact that she doesn't think or understand – is not to do with her being 'empty'; she is full of psychological drama and complications, only she doesn't know it. But we know it. So that in fact, a superficial young woman with no insight is somebody whose mind, whose internal world, is infinitely complex and fascinating.

BYATT: Somebody who is being pulled around by demons and forces.

SODRE: Gwendolen tells herself she is in control, she can dominate this man Grandcourt, this world – and this is all so fragile. We can see how she thinks she can invent her life, like she invents *tableaux vivants*. Throughout the novel George Eliot brilliantly conveys the interplay between Gwendolen's conscious perception of herself, her motives, her capacities, and the forces that are unconsciously driving her.

BYATT: How successful do you think she was with Daniel, who grew up not knowing who he was and then supposing himself to be Sir Hugo's illegitimate son? Do you feel that he is a created human being in the way Gwendolen is?

SODRE: No, not at all. She hasn't succeeded in making him real enough. I think that's why so many people really feel that the Gwendolen part of the novel is infinitely better than the Daniel part, the Jewish part. There is something about Daniel which isn't properly developed. Although there is a quest for a mother, for Jewishness, for his origins, a longing for something unknown which makes sense at different levels, his anguish about his past remains a bit theoretical, one doesn't believe in his anguish about being an orphan. I like the scene when he's talking to his tutor about nepotism, and it suddenly occurs to him that maybe he is Sir Hugo's son; the reader believes this almost until the end, when Sir Hugo tells him he isn't. But often I don't entirely believe in Daniel, he is a bit too good. I like him most when he is afraid of Gwendolen, at the time when she most needs him to understand her, and he can't, or does not want to – after Grandcourt's death. The way that his angelic goodness fails him and that he psychologically recoils from her – in his mind he forsakes her – is beautifully analysed. Gwendolen asks him if he thinks she could be a murderer:

> 'Great God!' said Deronda, in a deep, shaken voice, 'don't torture me needlessly. You have not murdered him. You threw yourself into the water with the impulse to save him. Tell me the rest afterwards. This death was an accident that you could not have hindered.' (Ch. 56)

Daniel's very human selfishness – 'don't torture *me*' – absolutely redeems him; whilst he listened to her with an averted face 'he felt as if he were putting his name to a blank paper which might be filled up terribly'. Throughout the scene this movement continues, with Gwendolen desperately needing to tell everything, Deronda in desperate conflict with his wish not to know; I think this is one of the greatest scenes in literature. But the more idealised Deronda, in his wonderful quests, I don't like so much.

BYATT: There is a question to be raised there. Different critics have seen him differently. I think different readers see him differently. When I first read the novel I thought oh yes, he is being built up as the opposite of Gwendolen: he has a very secure childhood, although he has no parents; she has a very insecure childhood although she has too many parents. He is an English gentleman who has grown up as part of the rooted life in a particular place which George Eliot so values and feels that Gwendolen hasn't managed to have. And of course all this is a kind of fiction. I don't know how far she explores the effect on him of this being a fiction? How far his upbringing as an English gentleman modifies, as it would have to, his final discovery of his identity as a Jewish messiah. Because whether he likes it or not, all those childhood years which were so formative have been passed with a very strong but not very clever and affectionate father figure, and a rather silly but agreeable mother figure who is eventually depressed because all she can produce is daughters. Everybody in this book has a great many daughters, not so many sons. In a way Daniel's sexuality seems to come from nowhere, there isn't an adequate description of his good nature and he's on the whole at ease with himself as a human being. And again, he must be predicated, right from the beginning, as an example of the debate between nature and nurture, and George Eliot didn't know about genes, but she obviously did believe that his racial and blood identity as a Jew were more powerful than that upbringing in English countryside which she said brought itself into your very blood if you were an English person. She's far too intelligent not to have been aware that she was creating a kind of conflict there. What perhaps she just about *does* succeed with, is that when you meet his parents you feel you understand him better than when you've only known Sir Hugo who has been his stepfather. You feel, yes of course, that explains him better, when you see that his father was very delicate and womanly and subordinate and quiet and full of Jewish idealism, and that his mother was not motherly and didn't want to love him, and was able to give him away without trouble. And you think, yes these facts which he never knew have nevertheless formed his identity.

I think the whole book is about determinism and chance, it opens with gambling and dice and chance, and asks whether Daniel was formed by determinism or chance. So in a sense Eliot has asked all the right questions about his nature. I suppose it's at the moment when he represents himself as a saviour to Mirah, or even worse when Mordecai makes a messiah of him and he takes the mantle on, that you feel that Daniel's just a stick. Then you ask yourself, and I have never answered this question adequately, whether George Eliot knew this. And there's a further thing: there seem to be a very large number of Jewish readers who find Daniel completely satisfactory as a Jewish leader and character, in a way an English reader of the English novel doesn't. So there's all sorts of questions about him. Which raises the further question: can you write a great novel in which one of the characters is somehow insubstantial even at the end – the eponymous character, moreover, and in many ways the central character? And the curious answer is yes, you can, this is one of the greatest novels ever written, even if on a first reading one felt that one half of it would have been better excised and forgotten.

SODRE: I agree, of course, this is one of the greatest novels ever written, even with its problematic aspects. But just going back to the question of parentage, it occurs to me that one could think that Daniel's terror of Gwendolen's inner world might be truthfully linked with his terror of woman, like Gwendolen's terror of man. Mirah is most definitely not like a mother to him, and their relationship is rather idealised. But one shouldn't think about Daniel as not having known a mother: he does not remember, but he did know a terrible (quasi-murderous) mother, the Alcharisi, who didn't want him.

BYATT: Yes, you don't get any sense of this woven into the depiction of his character, which is where the failing comes.

SODRE: When he isn't drawn with depth, then we don't believe in him and it gets dull, which links to why the Jewish part is boring (although you say it's not boring to some Jewish people). There is something distasteful about it, which bothers me, about the way she portrays the Jewish question. I think the Messiah image does link to the idea of people who have to be extra good, as a defence against the fact of having been a baby who wasn't wanted. The Messiah is the most wanted baby in the world, the opposite of Daniel.

BYATT: Yes, and the form that Daniel's messianic qualities take is this extraordinary maternal caring for people: he cares for the Meyricks, he has to rescue Mirah, and having rescued her he has to make her a life. He has to respond to Mordecai's terrible need for him to be something, although he dreads responding to Mordecai in some ways as much as he dreads responding to Gwendolen. But he feels he has to respond, he has to be good, to give people things; he has to make the world good for people. And in many ways that is a perfectly plausible character cast for somebody who has had a good childhood but still doesn't know who he is. It does work as a construct, though you don't feel it in your blood as you feel Gwendolen's terror.

SODRE: That's the point, that's so interesting. I would like to hear more about it from your point of view as a writer. Theoretically it makes sense; somebody who doesn't know who his mother is, but who has in his unconscious mind a mother who hates him, embarks on a quest for something that could symbolise ideal motherhood: religion, faith, that reconstitutes an ideal family, of the whole humanity of Jews. You could say it makes psychological sense. And yet, as you say, it's not worked enough into your blood. George Eliot falls for the idealisation, I think, because of her own wish to do something heroic, of her wanting to save the Jewish people.

BYATT: It's just occurred to me that of course Daniel Deronda does in this sense very precisely represent George Eliot. This is her last novel, and as we say of some of the other novels, these are all novels written by women who knew themselves to be major professional novelists, who were treated seriously as major artists. George Eliot particularly had had it laid upon her that she was a great teacher, very much as Christ was, and she kept talking in very interesting semi-Christian imagery about what she was doing. She stated that the only way she could teach was by making her ideas 'thoroughly incarnate', in particular human beings. And I think also, if you read her biography, it's clear that by the time she wrote *Deronda* she had acquired a crowd of largely female disciples who sat at her feet and begged her to understand and change their lives. And she was partly repelled by them. This is clear if we look at her attempts to mitigate Edith Simcox's attachment to her. I think she's transposed herself, and her sense that she's been asked to do almost more than a novelist can do, into Daniel Deronda. There's a certain wry humour, I think, in her presentation of his inadequacy to what's being demanded of him. A rather different point is that Elinor Shaffer compares Daniel to Renan's portrait of Christ in *La Vie de Jésus* as an oriental man of immense emotional susceptibility, very sentimental, very gentle, who naturally attracted people to him and made disciples of them, and then was somehow trapped by their discipleship. Elinor Shaffer makes the very brave and terrifying assertion that what George Eliot was trying to do was write in modern realistic fiction an image of what it had felt like when Christianity, a religion proclaiming the coming of an incarnate Messiah, grew out of the forms of Judaism. Another thing that Elinor Shaffer suggests is that in this context the local English life of this novel is the Old Testament, out of which Daniel Deronda's new Jewish testament which speaks to the whole world will spring, thus reversing the idea of universal Christianity springing out of locally rooted Judaism.

What I've always felt about Deronda's mother, and this is a personal remark – is that of all the characters in fiction she was the one who I felt I was, as opposed to feeling I ought to be or wanted to be, or might have been. In that sense there must be some great power in her as a woman artist; she says that terrible sentence about 'you can never imagine what it is to have a man's force of genius in you.' Daniel has just tried to translate the stopping off of this princess's energy into his own terms, saying, in his slightly patronising way,

> 'I gather that my grandfather opposed your bent to be an artist. Though my own experience has been quite different, I enter into the painfulness of your struggle. I can imagine the hardship of an enforced renunciation.'

> 'No,' said the Princess, shaking her head, and folding her arms with an air of decision. 'You are not a woman. You may try – but you can never imagine what it is to have a man's force of genius in you, and yet to suffer the slavery of being a girl. To have a pattern cut out – "this is the Jewish woman; this is what you must be; this is what you are wanted for; a woman's heart must be of such a size and no larger, else it must be pressed small, like Chinese feet; her happiness is to be made as cakes are, by a fixed receipt." ' (Ch. 51)

And when I read that, I thought that's it. This is a truth. Although I've had a good education and I've had chances and I might do it, nevertheless, there is this sense of what to be a woman is, that is imposed upon you, that doesn't include being a great artist. And that must have been George Eliot speaking, although she makes this woman rather repellent and harsh, and deliberately makes her unmotherly and the opposite of Daniel who has all George Eliot's own madonna-like qualities – George Eliot was by then known as Madonna to all sorts of people. Here is this harsh, tough, Jewish woman who will not be a Jewish woman, and she cuts right across George Eliot's and Mordecai's and Daniel's sentimentality about being Jewish, and says, I won't be it. I was moved. There is no other claim of a woman to be an artist, in art, that is that fierce.

SODRE: She's a terribly brave woman, which is what makes her attractive even though there's something about her that is so hard. What I find striking in this scene is that Daniel, who is partly attracted and partly repelled by her, wants to be good to her in the way he's learned how to be good to people. But she won't permit that – which is precisely right for the character. There is a sentimental scene of reconciliation waiting in the wings, as it were, begging to be allowed in, which George Eliot brilliantly keeps out. And this paradoxically leaves the space for the reader to imagine, for instance, that the Alcharisi might have an unconscious wish to see her child before she dies.

BYATT: As you speak, it brings me back to Hermione again. Because of course this is another variant on that. This is not the sentimental reconciliation scene at the end of *The Winter's Tale* which so offended you and me, where at the last moment everybody puts aside the offence they have caused – Leontes has caused terrible offence to Hermione by putting her from him, he has thrown away his daughter and killed his son by neglect, or heartbreak, and now he's allowed to have everything absolutely back. One of the things George Eliot wrote against in her youth was what she called 'compensation'. She said, if you renounce something for virtuous reasons, you are not compensated for that renunciation. If you give something up, you give it up. And you become the person who has given that up. If you are virtuous, virtue doesn't bring rewards other than being virtuous. She was terribly straight. And the Alcharisi is George Eliot in that sense too, in her knowledge that what you have done you cannot undo, you have made your own fate. And she has undone it exactly as far as she can, which is to take a look at Daniel. She could have sent him the papers, without seeing him.

SODRE: She takes a serious look at Daniel. She doesn't take a wish-fulfilling look at Daniel.

BYATT: No, it is entirely he who tries to do the wish-fulfilling. And when you said earlier that he feels repelled and attracted, of course this is exactly what he feels towards Gwendolen. Jenny Uglow has pointed out that he *feels* the same about his mother and Gwendolen; when he sees his mother he thinks 'Her worn beauty had a strangeness in it as if she were not quite a human mother, but a Melusina, who had ties with some world which is independent of ours.' (Ch. 51) She is a serpent woman, a spirit without a soul, as Gwendolen is a nereid or a water nixie. In that sense his coiling back from women, apart from Mirah, is an equivalent of Gwendolen's coiling back, as though they are both afraid of something in parents of the opposite sex who have let them down by either dying or vanishing.

SODRE: Taking up the point about Daniel and Christ, in connection with the scene where he is terrified of being told about Gwendolen's murderousness: he psychologically forsakes her in her despair, when she feels she will be crucified, because he feels he is the one who is being crucified by having to accept her sins. Gwendolen has invested Daniel with qualities belonging to an ideal parent, who can offer unconditional forgiveness; something Freud described as an aspect of the transference.

BYATT: It's interesting, because when we were discussing *Villette*, Lucy Snowe went off and confessed to Père Silas, because she had all this burden inside her that had to be given to somebody. That wasn't exactly a transference because –

SODRE: . . . Lucy didn't know him; so, she invested him with a particular quality of containment only for a very brief moment.

BYATT: Yes, and what's more she didn't like him or what he represented. But it was the same compulsion. And Daniel here is saying he's rejecting that function, he's not a priest, which makes him closer to the analyst. It's one of the very few treatments I know in fiction of what must be a very common situation, people trying to give you a lot of emotions that you simply don't want. It's terrible to be loved if you don't love. In a way analysis must provide a kind of medium figure who can take all this and not die under it.

SODRE: When Daniel thinks that 'he was not a priest. He dreaded the weight of this woman's soul flung upon his own with imploring dependence' (Ch. 56) he could as well be saying 'I'm not a psychoanalyst!' We'll soon also move to the question of being loved and not loving when we do *The Professor's House*, where St Peter says 'The saddest thing in the world is to fall out of love.' It's a greater burden not to love, than it is not to be loved. Which is what Lydgate says in *Middlemarch*, about falling out of love with Rosamond: to be expected to love when you don't is the greatest pain, greater than not being loved.

BYATT: Yes, it's something which Charlotte Brontë knew nothing about at all.

SODRE: Such a craving for being loved.

BYATT: And loving.

SODRE: If you think of Gwendolen as absolutely dominated by Fear, with a capital F, it's fascinating that she actually marries Grandcourt, who has a dead heart; his internal face, as it were, is dead. When she meets him she describes him negatively as not having any of the characteristics that she doesn't like in men: 'He isn't ridiculous.' But very soon you can see going through her mind a horror of him, that she keeps pushing out again. She is of course repelled by him, not just because she's repelled by men in general, which she is, but because she knows there is something horrible about him. She tries to deal with it by making herself hold on to the illusion that it doesn't matter that he's powerful, because she is going to be infinitely more powerful. But she really dreads him, and not only because of his mistress Mrs Glasher, although she also wished to have never known about her. 'Something, anything she wished for that would have saved her from the dread to let Grandcourt come' (Ch. 26). She believes this marriage represents salvation in that it will deal with the practical realities – it will save her mother from poverty; but Grandcourt coming has the same meaning to her as the panel door opening. Grandcourt too has a dead face and she has some awareness that he needs to control her and murder her soul.

BYATT: Yes, there's a wonderful mixture of language before that line about dread.

> A few minutes before she was looking along an inescapable path of repulsive monotony, with hopeless inward rebellion against the imperious lot which left her no choice: and lo, now, a moment of choice was come. Yet – was it triumph she felt most or terror? Impossible for Gwendolen not to feel some triumph in a tribute to her power at a time when she was first tasting the bitterness of insignificance: again she seemed to be getting a sort of empire over her own life. But how to use it? Here came the terror. Quick, quick, like pictures in a book beaten open with a sense of hurry, came back vividly, yet in fragments, all that she had gone through in relation to Grandcourt – the allurements, the vacillations, the resolve to accede, the final repulsion; the incisive face of that dark-eyed lady with the lovely boy; her own pledge (was it a pledge not to marry him?) – the new disbelief in the worth of men and things for which that scene of disclosure had become a symbol. (Ch. 26)

Pictures in a little book, beaten open, is like the panel flying open, but she hasn't yet got to the last picture of course. There is an element of the uncanny here, of the marvellous, the magical, because the last picture is the dead face and the fleeing figure. And then you get the image of her freezing. 'That unalterable experience [talking to the dark-eyed lady] made a vision at which in the first agitated moment, before tempering reflections could suggest themselves, her native terror shrank.' And yet Grandcourt presents himself as an outlet for energy. At the bottom of the same page,

> The young activity within her made a warm current through her terror and stirred towards something that would be an event – towards an opportunity in which she could look and speak with the former effectiveness. The interest of the morrow was no longer at a deadlock. (ibid.)

The poor woman does think that he offers a chance to her energy, whereas in fact he's a complete energy devourer, soaker-upper, energy stopper. He's so much more an accomplished sadist than she is.

SODRE: Like a vampire.

BYATT: Yes, and it is she who appears to be a vampire at the beginning.

SODRE: But she isn't really, it's just make-believe, a masquerade, whereas he is the real thing, the devil who takes over her soul. Another image of death comes in Lydia Glasher's letter when she sends the diamonds: 'The man you have married has a withered heart. His best young love was mine; you could not take that from me when you took the rest. It is dead; but I am the grave' (Ch. 31). Gwendolen does not just feel guilty towards this woman who ought to have married him; something ghostly and deadly accompanies the message – Mrs Glasher, the vengeful ghost condemning her to live with a corpse.

BYATT: One of the amazing things about Grandcourt is that he is not simply, as he could have been, a function of Gwendolen's imagination. It isn't her fear that makes him a killer. She doesn't call up a killer, he's a fully accomplished destructive force when he walks across her life. He's actually just as stupid as she is. He knows vaguely what he wants to do, but he's stupid about what she's thinking or feeling. And also he doesn't even care. He says so quite often to himself. He doesn't love her. There is one wonderful moment when George Eliot tells you he came near to loving her – the moment before he goes in to take her down to dinner when she starts screaming at him like a banshee. With all the diamonds falling over the floor. Which again is a wonderful Gothic scene. I love the way in which George Eliot very slowly lets you into his life. You see him at first in relation to Gwendolen. I think, in terms of conventional fictional expectations, the fact that he has a bald head with only a little fringe of hair is terribly upsetting to the novel-reader. It makes him sort of banal and slightly ridiculous at exactly the moment when Gwendolen is saying there's nothing ridiculous about him. Then of course – when you get to Chapter 12 and see him with the dogs, you realise – when you're alone with him you see him as totally sadistic and destructive. There's this terrible scene at the breakfast table:

> Everything around them was agreeable: the summer air through the open windows, at which the dogs could walk in from the old green turf on the lawn; the soft, purplish colouring of the park beyond, stretching towards a mass of bordering wood; the still life in the room, which seemed the stiller for its sober antiquated elegance, as if it kept a conscious well-bred silence, unlike the restlessness of vulgar furniture. (Ch. 12)

This is the English archetype, the English gentlemanly life. Mansfield Park. The quietness of Mansfield Park, which is such a positive value in Jane Austen. And within it you have a man who has got a tiny Maltese dog with a tiny silver collar and bell on his lap, and his hand rests on this small parcel of animal warmth. The liver-coloured water spaniel is desperately trying to get any sign of affection from him. And he torments it, by holding up the little dog. You see people do that. Yet it fills you with real horror, this scene.

> But when the amusing anguish burst forth in a howling bark, Grandcourt pushed Fetch down without speaking, and, depositing Fluff carelessly on the table (where his black nose predominated over a salt-cellar), began to look to his cigar, and found, with some annoyance against Fetch as the cause, that the brute of a cigar required relighting. Fetch, having begun to wail, found, like others of her sex, that it was not easy to leave off; indeed, the second howl was a louder one, and the third was like unto it.
>
> 'Turn out that brute, will you?' said Grandcourt to Lush, without raising his voice or looking at him – as if he counted on attention to the smallest sign. (ibid.)

It's the stillness of it. And he doesn't even care about the little dog. And the cigar becomes personified and animated – 'the brute of a cigar'. So the dogs and the cigar are all equal, and all simply appurtenances.

Gwendolen will have to be a spaniel, and will have to howl. In fact she doesn't, of course. She never asks him for anything. It's Mrs Glasher who is Fetch, I suppose, who is howling and howling, trying hard not to, but can't do anything else.

SODRE: Gwendolen is too terrorised even for that. About the cigar: what is most horrible about Grandcourt is that he isn't even alive, alight. It's absolutely cold dead sadism. Anger would be more human, kicking his dogs would be more human than the cold cruelty with which he torments them. He tortures Gwendolen to assert his power; she ought to function like an expensive clockwork toy.

BYATT: If you think of Heathcliff, who is another sort of accomplished sadist and kicks things and bangs things. He does it all with terrible passion, even if pretending.

SODRE: And of course you understand Heathcliff because you know what he has suffered. But you feel Grandcourt was by some genetic accident born this horrible cold fish and has never had a soul.

BYATT: When they're moving up and down in the yacht, Gwendolen compares them to the Flying Dutchman who is kept out of heaven and isn't allowed to die and just goes on for ever, neither in heaven nor hell but sailing eternally.

SODRE: Like the Ancient Mariner.

BYATT: Like the Ancient Mariner, and like the Wandering Jew, who was one of the originals for the Ancient Mariner, and to whom Klesmer compares himself. At the beginning of the chapter in which Gwendolen confesses to Daniel there is a quotation from *The Ancient Mariner*:

> The pang, the curse with which they died,
> Had never passed away:
> I could not draw my eyes from theirs,
> Nor lift them up to pray. (Ch. 56)

This describes the dead faces on the Mariner's ship, and his guilt, and gives Gwendolen's story an aspect of a cosmic myth about death in boats and the inability to die. And you feel that Grandcourt, like many of the characters, represents Coleridge's 'Night-mare Death-in-Life' because he's not able to live or to die. He dies with so little fuss, you don't know what he feels when he's dying at all. All the emotions that the reader is allowed to feel are Gwendolen's, except that he comes up and says, in his usual rather practical way, 'Throw the rope', and she doesn't. It's rather like him saying to Lush, 'Put the dog out.' Only he doesn't get an answer. Critics have always claimed that Grandcourt is George Eliot's depiction of the dying fall of the British aristocratic landowner, a complete dead grip as opposed to the cosmopolitan liveliness of the Jewish characters. I don't myself want to stretch him out into representing the whole of Englishness.

SODRE: I think George Eliot is portraying what she sees as the worst kind of evil: this cold sadism and absolute absence of feeling for the other person. Grandcourt is much worse than Satan because there is no passion in him; it's his passionlessness which is so horrible.

BYATT: There's no intelligence in him, his intelligence is limited. He does think away very busily, and I would argue that one of Eliot's great narrative achievements is the way in which she actually follows his consciousness and his thought processes, telling you exactly what Grandcourt thought – and it was never very much.

> Had Grandcourt the least conception of what was going on in the breast of this wife? He conceived that she did not love him: but was that necessary? She was under his power, and he was not accustomed to soothe himself, as some cheerfully-disposed persons are, with the conviction that he was very generally and justly beloved. But what lay quite away from his conception was, that she could have any special repulsion for him personally. How could she? He himself knew what personal repulsion was –

> nobody better: his mind was much furnished with a sense of what brutes his fellow-creatures were, both masculine and feminine; what odious familiarities they had, what smirks, what modes of flourishing their handkerchiefs, what costume, what lavender-water, what bulging eyes, and what foolish notions of making themselves agreeable by remarks which were not wanted. In this critical view of mankind there was an affinity between him and Gwendolen before their marriage, and we know that she had been attractingly wrought upon by the refined negations he presented to her. Hence he understood her repulsion for Lush. But how was he to understand or conceive her present repulsion for Henleigh Grandcourt? Some men bring themselves to believe, and not merely maintain, the non-existence of an external world; a few others believe themselves objects of repulsion to a woman without being told so in plain language. But Grandcourt did not belong to this eccentric body of thinkers. (Ch. 54)

That is the most subtle piece of prose, and from the point of view of the art of the novelist it's rather like the beginning of the book in that it begins with a series of questions which are asked by somebody – then these very precise answers are given. You are told what Grandcourt thought without in any way being given anything to help you share his feelings. There is a sort of Jane Austen satirical novelist working away there listing the things that annoyed Grandcourt, compared to the horror that Gwendolen feels of him. And then Eliot does what Jane Austen would never do, and takes it right out into a philosophical question: 'Some men bring themselves to believe, and not merely maintain, the non-existence of an external world.' This brings us back to your point about Gwendolen's narcissism destroying the external world. Just over the page is Eliot's statement that Gwendolen was absolutely terrified of becoming pregnant. We already know that she was afraid of being touched by men. It says a couple of pages later: 'She was reduced to dread lest she should become a mother. It was not the image of a new sweetly-budding life that came as a vision of deliverance from the monotony of distaste: it was an image of another sort.' What do you think? – this strikes me as one of the novels in which, despite Victorian English conventions about not describing sexual behaviour, we know a great deal about the relations between these two in bed.

SODRE: I think that's interesting, and very courageous. She allows us to picture their relationship very precisely. It is quite clear that they have a sexual relationship which is repulsive and frightening to Gwendolen, and that Grandcourt, who is sadistic, takes pleasure in that. The baby given to her by this monster would not be a good baby in her mind; it would be like the seed of the devil being implanted inside her.

BYATT: It's partly because she feels she shouldn't bear a child to supplant the children he's already got.

SODRE: Of course that is true, but more to do with her grown-up self. But her dread is more primitive than that, than her correct moral feeling. This is much more a horror story about being possessed.

BYATT: I think the moment when the horror is most physically present to us is the moment when she puts the necklace on.

SODRE: After the fear of pregnancy is mentioned, what follows is her becoming every moment more aware that she wants to murder him. She feels so possessed by him that the only thing that would release her is his death. She is being terrorised by this death-in-life person, who is by definition someone who won't die.

So presumably Gwendolen's violence increases as she feels he will never die, and she wants more and more to murder him. Which links to the beginning: her mind possessed by this dead face, that never properly dies, never disappears completely. In a way the Ancient Mariner also comes in, because it's this evil deed that can't be undone.

BYATT: The thing about the Ancient Mariner is that you've got one living person on a rotting deck surrounded by dead people, and the dead people do rise up again and sail the ship. So it becomes life-in-death, or death-in-life, again.

SODRE: And the other thing about the Ancient Mariner is that even after he's lost the albatross he still has to repeat the story every day to somebody. Which goes back to Deronda's horror of being the blank page: Deronda is in the position of the Wedding Guest, imprisoned by this frightening woman who wants to tell him a horrible story about murder and death.

BYATT: Mirah is very interesting, because of course she's exactly the opposite. She's somebody who ought to be alive who is trying to die, and Daniel does manage to bring her back into life. What interests me about the jewel scene, going back a little, is that just before the jewels are to be put on, Grandcourt kisses Gwendolen for the first time on the lips. Then it says 'He pressed her hand to his lips and moved away, more in love than he had ever expected to be' (Ch. 31). That is the moment when that relationship was at its most possible. And Gwendolen goes off to make herself beautiful, which makes her happy, and then the box comes with the jewels. And the message from Mrs Glasher.

SODRE: A letter full of the imagery of death – the letter's appearance is just like the panel suddenly opening.

BYATT: This wonderful line just before the letter. 'She saw a letter lying above them. She knew the handwriting of the address. It was as if an adder had lain on them.' And there is the snake, which is going to strike, a poisonous snake. Then: 'Truly here were poisoned gems, and the poison had entered into this poor young creature', and there's George Eliot again using that phrase, this poor young creature. Again, it isn't Victorian patronage, it's asking for universal sympathy.

SODRE: Oh, it's like what happens in Medea, isn't it?

BYATT: The narrator says, 'In some form or other the Furies had crossed his threshold' (ibid.).

SODRE: So wonderful. Now I remember, Medea sends the poisoned clothes to her husband's new wife, and she puts them on. I hadn't thought of that.

BYATT: 'They were like so many women petrified white'. 'The reflections of herself . . .' All the metaphors come together at this point: the snake, the jewels, there's somebody sending her a necklace from outside, which recalls when Daniel Deronda returned the turquoises to her. And then Gwendolen's energy gets stopped off again.

> In her movement the casket fell on the floor and the diamonds rolled out. She took no notice, but fell back in her chair again helpless. She could not see the reflections of herself then: they were like so many women petrified white; but coming near herself you might have seen the tremor in her lips and hands. (ibid.)

She's now a petrified white woman, but 'you' might see just a little bit of blood beating in her. Extraordinary using the second person address, actually. The reader is the only person who can see that there's any life left.

SODRE: And the reader feels absolutely brought in and captured by this amazing imagery.

BYATT: Then we get the word pallid again:

> He had expected to see her dressed and smiling, ready to be led down. He saw her pallid, shrieking as it seemed with terror, the

> jewels scattered around her on the floor. Was it a fit of madness?
> In some form or other the Furies had crossed his threshold.

It's he who has brought the Furies in fact, it is his crime.

One of the things *Daniel Deronda* is constantly doing is moving the horizon. Gwendolen is terrified of wide spaces and big horizons. Artists and works of art are associated in this novel both with wide horizons and with the full use of human energy. George Eliot is always pointing out that the world is bigger than little England, the work of art is bigger than Dorothea's art 'of the handscreen sort' or Gwendolen's postures. But whereas in Middlemarch all sorts of people have complicated professions – Mr Bulstrode's banking, and Lydgate's medicine – here anybody who *does* anything does art, which means that we have to think quite hard about what making art means to people.

I think one of the most successful and surprising characters in terms of this is Miss Arrowpoint, who ought in terms of an English comedy to be going to be ridiculous, because she's the daughter of a bad novelist and a *nouveau riche*, and an heiress, and none of these things is very promising. But she has the good sense to be a really good artist, and to fall in love with an artist. In some curious way this takes them through to the truth, and the love affair between Klesmer and Miss Arrowpoint has much in common with the love affair between Amelia and Anhalt in *Lovers' Vows*, in that this very sensible woman who is in a position of some social superiority explains that there is no value in this position, compared with her sense of the merit of what he does. And he equally sensibly agrees with her and so they get married. And George Eliot goes along with this. Given that Klesmer is given to posturing and roaring, it's amazing how much good sense accompanies the good intelligence of the art of Klesmer and Miss Arrowpoint.

SODRE: Yes. I think one of the things that is satisfying is that there is no conflict between their love for one another and their love for art. There is a convincing clarity of purpose and judgement in both of them that makes their decision feel realistic in a way that doesn't detract from their passion.

BYATT: And a bad novel about those two would have spent chapter after chapter with Klesmer not daring to confess his love because he knew he was socially inferior and trying to suppress it and be quiet like Fanny and be worried like Edmund. And in fact he comes straight to the point because he's an intelligent man and his values are in the right place. On the other hand I think he is balanced against the Alcharisi, Daniel's mother, whose problem is being a woman. Miss Arrowpoint is perfectly happy to be a subordinate artist and a good wife to a flamboyant man, who can be the great artist. It becomes more problematic when it's a woman. Mirah is more successful as an artist because she consents almost from the start to do it on a very small scale. She is a true artist, she has a true voice, but she doesn't want to appear on a big stage, she has a horror of big theatres, the same as Gwendolen's horror of being touched. But she is very businesslike and practical about singing in a drawing room where her voice is true. And all the places where Daniel expects her to be nervous, she's completely sensible because she's doing her job, which is the feeling I like about it. As a girl, I loved this sense that art was a job that you did properly.

SODRE: And that she does it sincerely out of a love for art, even though her history is having been compelled to do it by her father for bad reasons. We still believe in her sincerity and her deep love for music, and in such contrast to Gwendolen, who thinks it's all something that comes from the outside. Quite moving.

BYATT: Yes. She feels it's rather like her beauty, which of course is a sort of accident. It's also an accident that her voice isn't a wonderful voice. But it's so clever of George Eliot to make her have a voice that would be good enough if she would submit to the training – which she will not.

SODRE: But she would never be a true artist, even if she had a good voice.

BYATT: She couldn't.

SODRE: She's not able to be properly passionate about beauty, because she thinks beauty is a piece of property she happens to own. She thinks, 'I'm beautiful, and therefore I shall have what I want.'

BYATT: Yes, but there are two ways of saying 'I am beautiful'. One of them suggests that you're beautiful from within, and the other somehow that you've got something people might want to have.

SODRE: Before Klesmer arrives, as we said, she's looking in the mirror, from without. I think the question of what comes from within also links to the question of what an artist feels he or she is actually doing; a work of art comes within, but is it always experienced as entirely coming from the self, or is it sometimes experienced as something given to you?

BYATT: Interesting, because I do connect my own desire to make works of art with this problem of the use of energy, particularly in women. I don't feel wholly myself unless I am *working on something*. I have a private set of images which run quite close to Gwendolen's about being stopped off, or not being allowed to act or not being able to move. And the something, the work, is the place where the self meets the outside world. I think again, *Daniel Deronda* moved me much more than most novels about artists because it did include the *work*. You can't be a good artist if you don't have a craft. It can't just be inspiration. It has to be something technical that you can really do. There's a point where Daniel Deronda and Gwendolen have a conversation about the nature of excellence, which is both funny and fits something I feel.

> 'If you heard Miss Lapidoth' – here he looked at Gwendolen – 'perhaps you would revoke your resolution to give up singing.'
>
> 'I should rather think my resolution would be confirmed,' said Gwendolen. 'I don't feel able to follow your advice of enjoying my own middlingness.'
>
> 'For my part,' said Deronda, 'people who do anything finely always inspirit me to try. I don't mean that they make me believe I can do it as well. But they make the thing, whatever it may be, seem worthy to be done. I can bear to think my own music not good for much, but the world would be more dismal if I thought music itself not good for much. Excellence encourages one about life generally; it shows the spiritual wealth of the world.'
>
> 'But then if we can't imitate it? – it only makes our own life seem the tamer,' said Gwendolen, in a mood to resent encouragement founded on her own insignificance.
>
> 'That depends on the point of view, I think,' said Deronda. 'We should have a poor life of it if we were reduced for all our pleasure to our own performances. A little private imitation of what is good is a sort of private devotion.' (Ch. 36)

I love that, it's comic, and yet it's saying something George Eliot profoundly believes: that excellence is achieved by continually pushing the boundary out.

SODRE: And it is to do with absolutely opening your eyes to what's there and taking it in and becoming so deeply involved in it that a little bit of you then becomes like that. And imperfectly. And of course if you're totally narcissistic you can't enjoy art because you want to be its creator all the time. George Eliot shows here how Gwendolen finds it difficult to learn from Klesmer, because of her wounded narcissism, but she clearly felt people could learn to appreciate art: Philip educates Maggie and Ladislaw educates Dorothea. And these dialogues about art in the three novels are different, but in each the writer is teaching the reader something about great art; the reader who is reading this work of art is learning about the wonderfulness of being passionate about art even when you are not an artist.

SODRE: Can we talk about the fairytale aspect of this novel?
BYATT: Both the novels we have already looked at have had buried fairytales. The Cinderella story informed the whole of *Mansfield Park*, and in a sense also there were references to the 'Sleeping Beauty' and tales like 'Rapunzel' – the dreaming castle set in the wood, and people moving out into the dangerous wood from the castle. And we found all sorts of wicked fairies and alternative fairytale plots in *Villette*. I think in *Daniel Deronda* too there are all sorts of fairytale motifs. We talked about the serpents and the snakes and the fairies who want souls, and how these personifications change the way you see the people. We haven't talked exactly about the way in which the key in the locked cupboard relates to the Bluebeard myth. That is a fairy story in which a young woman is forbidden to open a certain door with a key and when she does she sees all the previously murdered wives of her husband. I think that's running around here, too, fortifying one's narrative responses. We've talked about the Ancient Mariner and the Flying Dutchman. Then there are all the powers of classical tragedy, most particularly the Furies, which connect on to the snakes.
SODRE: And Demeter, Persephone and Hades. And Medea, who gives poisoned clothes to the young bride. In terms of fairytale-ish happy ends, it is interesting that in *Daniel Deronda*, as in *Villette*, there are two sets of couples, one of which is given a wish-fulfilling 'they lived happily ever after', and one that ends in tragedy, in death. Gwendolen, like Lucy, will be alone; the end is the beginning of a life which is the opposite of a fairytale. Gwendolen temporarily believed in a fairytale future if she married this prince, who she always knew was a frog anyway, or a reptile.
BYATT: That dangerous serpent ornamentally coiled in the corner of the cabin.
SODRE: It is ultimately a story of good and evil, and a fight with Satan.
BYATT: Interesting, because it is evil on the completely believable, wholly embodied level, in the sense that Grandcourt is a rather stolid whiskered gentleman with an unmoving sort of face, who persecutes people partly because he hasn't got the imagination to do anything else, yet the metaphors and imagery turn him into a demon and into a real power of destruction. But they don't work quite like Lucy Snowe calling up demons, they're more something that the writer of this novel

is offering to the reader as a way to understand the story in a deeper way than the characters do. All the serpentine imagery about Gwendolen is somehow part of what the narrator is giving the reader. We talked about the letter lying like an adder on the top of the jewels, George Eliot's metaphor. We talked about Grandcourt being like a dangerous snake curled, ornamental in the corner. I don't think either of those is meant to be Gwendolen's mental imagery. They are *our* mental imagery, they are part of the art of the poet George Eliot who is giving us these metaphors with which to deepen our apprehension of the real meaning of these events. And she's doing it curiously, by fantasising it, which immediately makes it more real. There was no adder, there was no snake, but the moment you see an imaginary adder you see Grandcourt more clearly.

SODRE: There is one very fixed image which is definitely Gwendolen's: the 'dead face' which you know is constantly breaking into her consciousness and being pushed out again, throughout the novel; the dead face eventually creates the fear that she will become a murderer to kill it; a murderer of the dead that never quite die. And yes, I think Bluebeard is very much there, too: Grandcourt is a murderer of women's souls. But the girl in the Bluebeard story wants to find out secrets, whereas Gwendolen wants to lock the door. She doesn't want to unlock anything. It never gets properly locked. And she marries Grandcourt thinking that will lock away the past for ever and the opposite happens. He is the thing itself, the dead face. Gwendolen suddenly finds her way into the secret she does not want to know, that she wants to forget and can't. All this touches the question of horrible memory again. What is so profound about Gwendolen discovering she's a murderess, even if she didn't technically kill Grandcourt: this is the point when she finally completely knows herself. She faces her murderousness: she can't bear it on her own, she has to tell somebody – but she does know that psychological truth is real. That's different from daydreaming, fantasising, wishful thinking, illusions. In reality it's true; when she says I wished to kill him, I wanted to, and therefore I have killed him in my mind, she is discovering that if she wished to kill her stepfather, then psychologically she did kill him and that's why his dead face persecutes her for ever. It's a much deeper reworking of the incident in *Middlemarch*, concerning Lydgate's first girlfriend, the actress who killed her husband. She didn't do it deliberately – her foot slipped – but she wanted to kill him, because he was boring.

BYATT: Theatricals again: she actually killed him on stage in a performance.

SODRE: Before we reach the end of this discussion, I'd like to read the epigraph to the novel:

> Let thy chief terror be of thine own soul:
> There, 'mid the throng of hurrying desires
> That trample o'er the dead to seize their spoil,
> Lurks vengeance, footless, irresistible
> As exhalations laden with slow death,
> And o'er the fairest troop of captured joys
> Breathes pallid pestilence.

Something that belongs to the core of the novel is in this epigraph, as Margot Waddell has pointed out. It is about death, and about also the dead that don't really die, who 'breathe pallid pestilence'. A kind of horrible rotting ghost that comes back. The 'spoiled child', the title of Book One, doesn't have to only mean spoiled in the way of an *enfant gâté*, but also rotten, like a fruit.

BYATT: 'Spoiled' also means grasped and seized. Gwendolen is booty. What I love about this epigraph is how much it is a nineteenth-century version of sixteenth-century verse. One of the things which is always said about nineteenth-century verse drama by poets like Browning and Tennyson, is that they moved all the action that in Shakespeare was exterior – murders, exterior moral decisions – into interior drama and therefore their plays were not dramatic. 'Let thy chief terror be of thine own soul.' It looks like Elizabethan dramatic verse, but it's nineteenth-century, it's saying the action is internal. What we have in front of us is a perfect novel full of violent action in which a murder almost takes place, in which jewels are scattered, vengeance is taken, and nevertheless what we really most care about is what Edward Dowden described as George Eliot's great innovation – she took all the action *inside*, which fits perfectly on to what you have been saying about the internal and external worlds. She has Shelley and personified vengeance and pestilence but all these are metaphorical attributes of what is *inside*. Then the second epigraph, heading Chapter 1. Pure prose wit. 'Men can do nothing without the make-believe of a beginning.' She brings in

> Even Science, the strict measurer, is obliged to start with a make-

> believe unit, and must fix on a point in the stars' unceasing journey when his sidereal clock shall pretend that time is at Nought. (Ch. 1)

And then you get on to poetry:

> No retrospect will take us to the true beginning; and whether our prologue be in heaven or on earth, it is but a fraction of that all-presupposing fact with which our story sets out. (ibid.)

The idea of the prologue being on heaven or on earth is to do with Goethe's *Faust*, where the prologue starts with Satan talking to God, and the two of them setting up the temptation of Faust's soul. Whilst apparently writing comic prose about the difference between science and poetry, she's heading us towards the tempting of a soul. We began by discussing our sense of Gwendolen's evil. Evil is metaphysical and cosmic, yet Eliot, in this epigraph, has already introduced us into the modern scientific world, into measured time as opposed to cosmic time. Then she puts us back and says nevertheless cosmic time exists. She gives us so many points of reference at once. So many tones of voice. The epigraphs are actually a *tour de force,* all through the book, because they're in many languages, from many literatures. I think that some she says are written by Shakespeare, she actually made up. Imitation Shakespeare by George Eliot. Very post-modern, a commentary in and beside the book. They give you what Klesmer knows you ought to have, windows into other worlds and other cultures and other points of view from which you can see your life. Exactly what Gwendolen hasn't got.

SODRE: The book opens windows into all kinds of things. It opens with somebody looking into somebody else, into the inner world. As if looking from the outside. The first question is a question about what is inside this person's mind. What Freud said about the unconscious and the mind is beautifully portrayed by her, even in this short epigraph. When it ends 'No retrospect will take us to the true beginning . . .' what it is actually saying is that you can't really ever go back to the beginning, there isn't such a thing. On the other hand, at any moment, in the fraction of a second where you can get into somebody's mind, you will find the whole universe of somebody's internal world.

BYATT: This prefigures the very different world of Virginia Woolf. Which is based on the fact that you can make a moment spread into endless pages, and a narrative doesn't have to be consecutive, and time is flexible.

Chapter 4

Willa Cather: *The Professor's House*

The Professor's House (1925) was seventh of twelve novels written by Willa Cather, one of America's finest writers.

Godfrey St Peter, a scholarly, compassionate man, is a professor in Hamilton, a town in Midwestern America, close to Lake Michigan, by which he grew up. Money from a prize awarded to his eight-volume history, *Spanish Adventurers in North America*, has enabled him to buy a new house which delights his family, but leaves him feeling deeply ambivalent and ruminative. He refuses to move out of his workroom at the top of the old house, in which, despite its shortcomings and the fact that it is also used sometimes by the sewing-woman, Augusta, he feels content. When Augusta tries to take her dressmaking dummies – the 'forms' – to her room in the new house, the Professor stops her.

He thinks hard about his family, from whom he feels increasingly distant: his wife, Lillian, whom he met as a young man in France, and their two daughters: Rosamond, beautiful but spoilt, married to energetic, Jewish engineer Louie Marsellus, and the more sympathetic Kathleen, married to journalist, Scott McGregor.

He thinks also, and perhaps chiefly, of the only 'remarkable' mind he had ever encountered in years of teaching, a young man called Tom Outland who, many years earlier, dramatically entered and changed all their lives. Before tragically dying in Flanders around the age of thirty, the brilliant Outland had, with the help of a Professor Crane, developed a new gas which had led to the Outland engine. His will left any proceeds from his work to Rosamond, to whom he was engaged to be married. Since then, Louie Marsellus has 'exploited' the patent; he and Rosamond are now immensely rich and are building a new house by Lake Michigan called Outland. It pains both the Professor and

Kathleen, who is envious of her sister's wealth and disgusted by her flaunting of it, to see Tom, whom they both loved, translated into dollars and cents. Indeed, Rosamond has become quite hardened, refusing, for example, to reward Professor Crane, who is poor and ill. Despite finding him vulgar, however, the Professor can't help liking Louie, who is also generous and deeply respectful of his father-in-law.

Book Two tells Tom Outland's story in his own voice, up to the point at which he walked into the Professor's life. We learn how he became great friends with a man called Rodney Blake, and how, whilst working for a cattle company in Pardee, New Mexico, they spent the winter camping under the blue Mesa: a stunning rock over a river, thought to be unreachable. Tom, however, manages to find a way over and discovers the stunning remains of an ancient pueblo Indian settlement. They sadly lose old Henry, who has kept house for them, to a nasty death by rattlesnake, but are helped by kindly Belgian missionary, Father Duchene. The Father hazards guesses at the city's origins, but Tom travels to Washington to announce his find officially and get expert opinion. After a disillusioning wait of some days, he is met with indifference. On his return he finds, to his horror, that Blake has sold off virtually everything on the Mesa to a German called Fechtig, for $4,000. Tom and Blake argue, Blake leaves and, despite elaborate searches, never reappears. Taking the advice of Father Duchene, Tom spent the summer directly after Blake's disappearance on the Mesa waiting and studying the Spanish and Latin with which he is later to impress Professor St Peter when Tom seeks him out for a university education.

Book Three takes us back to the Professor, who has stayed at home while his wife and the Marselluses go to France for a long holiday. He has undertaken to edit Tom's diary. However, he finds himself curiously exhausted by life, to the point of seeking the advice of a doctor. When his family announce their return, he feels alarmed and unable to live with them any more. That afternoon the gas fire in his study blows out, and he takes no action to fix it, later he is woken by Augusta from a sleep which might have proved fatal. He recovers, and, although he feels he is not the same man internally, he is able to face the future.

BYATT: This novel, like *Mansfield Park*, *Daniel Deronda* and in some ways *Villette*, is about the relations between human beings and the houses that contain them. At the beginning Godfrey St Peter is moving out of his old house, in which he did his best work and wrote his important history of the Spanish adventurers, into a new house in which he's had a kind of artificial workroom built. From the beginning we see a man who is both married and obsessed with his work, trying to think out the balance between these two things. This book, by a woman, suggests that a man can be as oppressed by the domestic, as inhibited in the flow of his imagination, his life and his energy, as a woman. Fairly early on he puts it to himself that he has fallen in love and then out of love. One of the things Willa Cather does best is the long flow of human lives, the movement from the beginning of a life through to its end. For this reason she's less good at the moment when two people look at each other and think 'I am stirred to the depths of my body and soul by you.' She does always include that moment, but she includes it within a very long stretch of life – so you know what the people were before falling in love and you certainly know that there is life after love.

SODRE: Yes, I agree that one of the things that is most moving and most interesting is the way she pictures this whole movement; in *The Professor's House* she is concerned especially with falling out of love, with the way this connects very deeply with the conflict between the wish to be together and the wish to be alone. I think this particular novel is so much about the wish to be alone. It's not simply about a marriage that goes wrong, about relationships that are for whatever reason unsatisfactory. When the family moves into the new house St Peter discovers not only that he can't bear to leave his attic study; he discovers that he wants to be alone, and that this aloneness represents a togetherness with a part of himself which he feels he has lost contact with.

In the first chapter he associates this moving house with his family moving away from Lake Michigan when he was eight years old: 'No later anguish, and he had had his share, went so deep or seemed so final'. And

> When he remembered his childhood he remembered blue water. There were certain human figures against it, of course; his practical, strong-willed Methodist mother, his gentle, weaned-away Catholic father, the old Kanuck grandfather, various brothers and sisters. But the great fact in life, the always possible escape from dullness, was the lake. The sun rose out of it, the day began there. The land and all its dreariness could never close in on you. You had only to look at the lake, and you knew that you would soon be free. (Book I, Ch. I)

The 'of course' added to 'certain human figures', as well as the 'various' brothers and sisters, establishes enormous distance from his original family, which here also represents the present-day family from which he begins to separate at the moment when he realises he cannot move with them. This paragraph, which continues to describe the lake, ends with telling us how 'the ice chunks came in of a winter morning' and 'made pictures in him when he was unwilling and unconscious, when his eyes were merely open wide'. In describing the impact of his early experience of the beauty of nature – 'not a thing thought about, but a part of consciousness itself' – St Peter excludes human contact with great determination (unlike the Wordsworth of the *Prelude*, which this passage in many ways brings to mind).

But St Peter does not actively abandon his family; he simply notices, in his horror at the idea of change, that he can't bear the loss of his old self, of the past, of the attic which his imaginative self has inhabited for so many years; and that his relationship with his family is growing more and more tenuous. The attic has a very different meaning from the frightening attics of Gothic novels. It is the place were he feels most in contact with himself, where he is alone except for the occasional presence of a woman, Augusta, the sewing-woman, who is very different from his wife.

BYATT: It's an attic with one living woman, Augusta, and two phantom women, the dressmaker's forms who don't have heads or faces, and indeed don't have internal organs or legs, simply torsos. I've only just thought, of course, that he has exactly in the attic what he has in life. He has a woman and two daughters. And the inhabitants of the attic are three non-sexual beings whom he likes being with, as opposed to the domestic house where there are very sexual beings, his wife and his two daughters, all of whom he has clearly loved deeply and passionately in the past and knows very intimately. I think it's significant that he fell in love with his wife in France. She isn't part of his solitary sense of himself, as an American who grew up on the shore of the Great Lakes, and as a historian. He goes out to France, aged twenty-four, thinking that he will open his horizons, and actually when he goes 'out [of his] land' he closes his horizons, by falling in love with Lillian. It suddenly struck me as we were discussing him, when you said St Peter, that perhaps he is called St Peter because he betrayed his Christ, who in that case would be Tom Outland. The other thing that interests me about this book as an emotional experience is how little opportunity we are given to know or feel for any of the characters except the central one, St Peter. The relationships are complicated; both his wife and his two daughters are done very much with tiny little thumbnail sketches. We are offered little moments where *he* sees them and by seeing them evokes their whole history and the whole history of his relationship with them. But these moments are experienced – by him and by us – only as part of that very long flow of time that I was speaking of.

SODRE: The way Cather writes this story illustrates St Peter's state of mind at this particular moment, the way he is thinking about these relationships (they are becoming sketchy in his mind). The novel starts with something very dramatic happening to him: his daughters whom he loved so much, and Lillian his wife, suddenly become almost irrelevant. This leads him to become more solitary and longing to find his old self, his child self, which is obviously also connected to his remembering and thinking about Tom Outland, whom he is partly identified with: Tom stands symbolically for his adolescent self. So although he is aware of how passionately he loved his women in the past, in his voyage to his own 'outland', into a place in his internal world, he idealises his child self. He feels as if everything had got spoilt and he had lost his true self when he became sexually mature and fell in love with a woman.

BYATT: There's a great deal of paradisal imagery connected with childhood in this book, imagery which comes back late in life, but under threat of death. All my own writing recently has been about the connection between the pre-sexual self and the post-sexual self. Willa Cather, when she wrote this book, was over fifty. I find that after fifty there is a great shift in one's attitude to that part of life which comes from child-bearing and immediate responsibility for living people. In the thirties and forties there is a network of human relations, very strong, very intense. And suddenly when you get to be over fifty they desert you, and you desert them. And if you don't feel that you're dying, (and St Peter does feel that he's dying as well as all the other things he feels) you do feel almost a kind of jubilant glee at rediscovering the solitude my kind of person so desperately desired when young. I spent all my childhood wanting both to be part of the human community *and* to find a solitary place in which I could think. We've seen this in terms of Fanny in her room in Mansfield Park, we've seen it in Lucy finding an attic to escape to in *Villette*, we've seen a negative version of it in Gwendolen's agoraphobia mixed with her fear of the confinement of marriage.

Although Willa Cather presents St Peter's retreat from human connectedness as rather gloomy, the extraordinary skill and accomplishment with which she depicts it has an aesthetic mastery and glee which suggests that she feels it is a release as well.

SODRE: I think it is very interesting that we are now discussing not a woman who is oppressed by domesticity but a man who is terrified of it – the way Cather presents St Peter's fear of the women's house downstairs, the imagery she uses, is very striking. Do you remember, there's a bit where even though he needs oil for his lamp so he can continue his work, he prefers not to have it rather than go downstairs, and he chooses to have a horrible light bulb instead: 'he jammed an eyeshade on his head and worked by the tormenting glare of that tormenting pear-shaped bulb' (Book 1, Ch. 1).

Cather describes him feeling as if life downstairs had a kind of destructive force. The imagery about his going downstairs to get the light creates a sense of stepping down into the underworld: 'On that perilous journey down through the human house he might lose his mood, his enthusiasm, even his temper'(ibid.). He is anchored in his attic which is real, but if he steps down into the 'human house', something quite frightening happens. Contact with 'certain human figures' is deadly, it might destroy his identity. You can imagine St Peter trying to escape from the cellar with his eyes closed and not looking back, otherwise he might be imprisoned in Hades for ever.

BYATT: It is true that it is life that kills you. Life wears you out and kills you; there's a profound truth in that.

SODRE: Whereas, in a curious way, if St Peter stays in this 'not in human life' state he is somehow protected from death.

BYATT: Yes, we're back to life-in-death and death-in-life again which we were passionately discussing in relation to *Villette* and *Daniel Deronda*. What about the other characters? How far does one experience them as real people with real problems? I feel them to be very schematic. The two daughters are the two contrasted daughters of so many stories. There is beautiful unthoughtful Rosamond, who seems to have a clear relation to Rosamund Vincy in *Middlemarch*. (Willa Cather loved and admired George Eliot, this side idolatry.) Then the quieter Kathleen who, we can see, is the Professor's favourite younger child.

SODRE: And more Fanny-like as well.

BYATT: Much more Fanny-like. Kathleen seems to have been able to make a real marriage. Although perhaps the most interesting character in the book, other than St Peter himself, is Louie Marsellus, the Jewish son-in-law who has married Rosamond, and exploited (financially as opposed to scientifically) Tom Outland's discovery of the gas. The Outland money enabled Marsellus to build the vulgar house, named Outland, which is spoiling the Wordsworthian views of the shores of the lake, with its doorknobs and its disastrous architecture. But Marsellus has a real energy which you feel that Willa Cather, half-reluctantly, does come to respect. She gives him all the stereotyped oriental-Semitic characteristics of vulgarity, excessiveness, loudness, rushing in on people, not understanding the niceties of reticence and courtesy. And yet you get rather fond of him because he's full of love and inventiveness and warmth.

SODRE: And St Peter, rather reluctantly, starts liking him more and more. Louie is partly a Henry Crawford character, a charming innovator who may destroy for the sake of modernising; but he also has a robust optimism which is more good-natured and unselfish; there is some basic goodness in him which isn't there at all in Rosamond.

BYATT: One wonders what has destroyed Rosamond. You feel that at some point she also was alive in paradise, when paradise was the narratives of Tom Outland to the two little girls in the garden. You feel that the little girls, when they were living in fairy stories in their pre-sexual state, and wanted to go out and find Tom's lost companion, Roddy, were alive, and that Kathleen has kept some of this.

SODRE: But do you think Rosamond actually had some kind of terrible mourning for Tom? I had the feeling that Rosamond was in fact always narcissistic and that Tom didn't notice this, because he only saw that she was more beautiful than Kathleen, and he had an idealised, paradisical image of her.

BYATT: Rosamond is actually a descendant of George Eliot's Gwendolen, as well as of Rosamund Vincy, a person whose beauty has not been good for her. My own theory – and I'm interested that Willa Cather planted this in my mind and doesn't allow me to sort it out – my own theory is that Rosamond discovered too late that Tom Outland really loved the other sister. And this problem was solved by death. And this is a story which doesn't interest St Peter so Cather's approach to the reader is very oblique. But I think tiny little clues are laid, because everybody has a feeling that something has frozen Rosamond, something has put her in a glass case, something *made* her selfish. You don't get the feeling that she always was.

SODRE: I had the feeling she always was, that she was spoilt, like

Rosamund Vincy; I thought she was meant to be that sort of a character, the daughter who was seen as the most beautiful and was therefore narcissistic, that she had taken after the narcissistic aspect of Lillian, as opposed to the more loving and more connected aspect which came out in Kathleen. Louie's Rosamond, like Lydgate's Rosamond, is 'like a basil plant that grows in a dead man's brain'. But Louie is more cheerfully ambitious and less idealistic than Lydgate; he is thicker-skinned, and can survive her. I thought Kathleen was more the Fanny Price figure, who ought to have been loved by Tom, who didn't notice her and preferred the more externally attractive woman, like Edmund preferred Mary Crawford, or Graham Bretton preferred Ginevra in *Villette*.

BYATT: It raises the whole problem of the propriety of the novelist in raising a lot of questions in the reader's mind which she then doesn't answer. In life you may meet people, speculate about histories and motives, and come to no conclusion. A novelist can create that uncertainty in her readers' minds if she tells a story very consistently from only one point of view.

SODRE: Taking up your point about the novelist 'planting' questions in the reader's mind that are left unanswered: I suppose this can leave in the reader's mind two different kinds of gap. One can ultimately be satisfying, if it is the sort of gap that allows the reader to play imaginatively with different answers, so that the whole story does not have to be completely contained between the two covers of the book, but may have bits that develop at the fringes, as it were. The other is an unsatisfactory gap that just leaves the reader with a sense of frustration, or of being misled.

SODRE: In relation to 'Tom Outland's Story', Cather fills a 'gap' in an extremely interesting way, by allowing Tom, who is idealised by several characters in the novel, to tell his own past history. Through his 'story' she explores the themes of idealism, idealisation, and self-idealisation. One of the most moving scenes is the one between Blake and Tom on the Mesa, when Blake points out that Tom is not perfect, that he has 'spots of commonness', to use George Eliot's words about Lydgate. Blake leaves as Tom is making what Blake calls his 'Fourth of July' speech about how he loved the ancient Mesa artefacts that Blake sold and therefore will never trust Blake . . .

BYATT: I love that bit, yes.

SODRE: The only thing that Tom says to stop Blake going is 'I notice the river's high. It's dangerous crossing' (Book 2, Ch. 6). And Blake answers sarcastically, 'I'm surprised at you, using such common expressions! . . . *Dangerous crossing*; it's painted on signboards all over the world!' (ibid.). Tom is self-righteously holding on to his idealistic persona, claiming to be entirely faithful to the beauty of old things, and Blake is saying 'That's not entirely true, there is some other aspect of you.' Blake feels betrayed, and wants to make Tom see that he is more ordinary than he thinks he is. I thought that perhaps Tom's falling for Rosamond was in a way Tom falling too much for external beauty, not really connecting –

BYATT: It's youthful romanticism, in a way – it's also what people *do*. Indeed *Daniel Deronda* begins with the question 'Was she beautiful?', and Gillian Beer has most brilliantly argued that this is related to Darwin having just written his speculations about sexual selection, in which he sees beauty as part of the mechanism which controls the generation and development of species. In all fairy stories you select the most beautiful, and the most beautiful is also the most good, but in life it isn't like that and you have to learn that there are other criteria for selecting. And Tom is in a way too young and too idealistic, and his commonness and his idealism work together.

When Tom arrives, he is the stranger who comes in from the outside and transfigures everybody's life. Such figures in literature tend to walk in and then to walk out. You could argue that Godfrey St Peter's family, including Godfrey St Peter, attempt to domesticate this wanderer who comes from somewhere beyond their comprehension or apprehension. In so far as he does, he's very much an *American* mythic figure – he has to be for Cather, and she manages just about to pull it off. He has to be both the cowboy whose blanket still smells of horses after his death, and the discoverer and explorer of the unknown. Because this is what it is to be a 'great American'; they push the frontier out and find the very ancient in the very new. But he also has to be an intellectual discoverer, a scientific discoverer, and discover his gas and work out the principle for the vacuum which leads to a revolution in engineering. It interests me very much that she didn't make Tom Outland into a great literary scholar or a great historical scholar. In a sense he should have been that – his past history made him Godfrey St Peter's heir: both of them were working on the discovery of the ancient structures of the American land. But not at all, he discovers something more universal and even more primitive, which is a gas.

SODRE: But do you feel that this entirely works? I am not sure, I sometimes feel this is a bit artificial. Perhaps this impression comes from the reader's lack of first-hand knowledge about Tom the scientist. The Tom we know first hand is absolutely in love with the past and he himself links it to the fact that he lost all his family; he says about the pots and pans that he discovered on the Mesa, 'I'm not so poor that I have to sell the pots and pans that belonged to my poor grandmothers a thousand years ago' (Book 2, Ch. 6).

This Tom is the American hero, as you said, but he is also a boy who hasn't yet grown up. His voyage into the 'outland' of the undiscovered territory and of the historical past of his country is also symbolically a voyage to the 'inland' of his internal world, an adolescent voyage of self-discovery. The adult Tom who invents the gas is different, born from the disillusion of the adventurer Tom; to some degree it is from his loss – of the Mesa, but also of his more ideal self through his betrayal of Blake – that this new Tom the scientist is born. Is there something about his making a will and then dying in the war which connects with his painful experiences? Does his invention, which gets corrupted and commercialised, come from a part of him functioning at a level which isn't so real and so connected? The gas is not a work of art, it is a scientific invention that can be used creatively or destructively. Gas has so much to do not just with St Peter's near-suicide, but also with the war that kills Tom: poisonous gases as weapons. I wonder if Cather is making a point about the difference between inward creativity and something more of the nature of an invention of the wrong kind, which isn't entirely creative, and therefore leads to a negative kind of progress – which is something she is preoccupied with, isn't she, in several of the novels? A different version of this problem comes up in the Conquistadores, in whom St Peter is so interested, who are also rediscovering the past.

BYATT: They do tend to destroy it, as well. No, I think that is probably very much what she thought – she did value the wholeness of the culture which was tied together by ties like religion and cookery. She was afraid of science in a way I personally find tiresome. Scientific curiosity is as much part of our nature as our sexuality is. If artists just flit about saying science is bad and dangerous they're actually letting down the human race. In a way you could turn the Conquistadore metaphor the other way – Outland discovers his gas, something which can be used as a weapon of conquest, although his interest in it was purely intellectual. When Outland first sees the little town on the Mesa, both Cather and her character insist on the extraordinary beauty of the air – and the air, I think, is the opposite of the killing gas. The symbolism is precisely and deeply worked out. The little town is preserved in the dry, pure air on the Mesa.

We ought to talk I think about Tom's relationship with Blake, which you touched on. One of Willa Cather's most explicit remarks, as various people have said and I have thought, about homosexuality, comes early on when Tom Outland is describing Blake's motherly relation to him.

> It was that winter I had pneumonia. Mrs O'Brien couldn't do much for me; she was overworked, poor woman, with a houseful of children. Blake took me down to his room, and he and the old Mexican woman nursed me. He ought to have had boys of his own to look after. Nature's full of such substitutions, but they always seem to me sad, even in botany. (Book 2, Ch. 1)

Here is Cather, a homosexual woman talking about how a man assisted by an old Mexican woman made a better mother and a more loving parent to another man, than a woman with a house full of children. Even at that point, the parallel between Tom and the Professor is suggested. Mrs O'Brien couldn't help, because she was involved in all the implicitly 'dangerous' life of the house. Blake, who was male and outgoing, could help, and nursed him back to life.

SODRE: But Blake had also been betrayed by women. So he may have given his active heterosexuality up and gone back to something more homosexual in which he can be identified with an ideal mother, different from the betraying women he actually met. And then of course Tom betrays him too. Tom accuses Blake of being interested in money rather than in culture and art, when in fact Blake is only guilty of misunderstanding. And Tom's is the real betrayal of friendship. Blake was never interested in commercialism; he wanted Tom to go to university.

BYATT: Blake's 'betrayal' was selling while Tom was absent. At the moment when Tom was being betrayed by all the directors of the Smithsonian who refused to be interested in the creatures in his Mesa, Blake had lovingly sold them to a German who had carried them all away. And when Tom gets back he berates Blake for a sort of aesthetic betrayal of an ideal which hadn't even entered Blake's mind. One of the best moments of the narrative is one of the most simple ones, when Tom shouts at Blake, and comments:

> This painful interview went on for hours. I walked up and down the kitchen trying to make Blake understand the kind of value

> these objects had had for me. Unfortunately, I succeeded. He sat slumping on the bench, his elbows on the table, shading his eyes from the lantern with his hands. (Book 2, Ch. 6)

This is when you really love Tom, because he knows what he has done and how destructive his high moral indignation was. But it reverberates out into further betrayals, it reinforces the feeling that Marsellus has betrayed Tom.

SODRE: This also links to Professor St Peter's emotional betrayal of Lillian, and Lillian's emotional betrayal of St Peter many, many years ago. There is this painful moment when they are sitting in the opera and he sees how moved she is, and she sees how moved he is, and he says 'We should have been picturesquely shipwrecked together when we were young' (Book 1, Ch. 8). They realise that they have both betrayed their original love for each other. He had imagined her to be completely self-involved, and then she says something that makes him realise that she had been deeply wounded. Do you want to quote that bit, as it is so important?

BYATT:

> 'We should have been picturesquely shipwrecked together when we were young.'
>
> 'How often I've thought that!' she replied with a faint, melancholy smile.
>
> 'You? But you're so occupied with the future, you adapt yourself so readily,' he murmured in astonishment.
>
> 'One must go on living, Godfrey. But it wasn't the children who came between us.' There was something lonely and forgiving in her voice, something that spoke of an old wound, healed and hardened and hopeless.
>
> 'You, you too?' he breathed in amazement. He took up one of her gloves and began drawing it out through his fingers. She said nothing, but he saw her lip quiver, and she turned away and began looking at the house through the glasses. He likewise began to examine the audience. He wished he knew just how it seemed to her. He had been mistaken, he felt. The heart of another is a dark forest, always, no matter how close it has been to one's own. Presently the melting music of the tenor's last aria brought their eyes together in a smile not altogether sad. (Book 1, Ch. 8)

SODRE: Beautiful.

BYATT: We'll come back to the dark forest, but this fits on to what you were saying about the difference between his love for Lillian and his love for Tom.

SODRE: Lillian thinks that it was his love for Tom that came between them, and so does St Peter, in a way.

> Lillian had been fiercely jealous of Tom Outland. As he left the house, he was reflecting that people who are intensely in love when they marry, and who go on being in love, always meet with something which suddenly or gradually makes a difference. Sometimes it is the children, or the grubbiness of being poor, sometimes a second infatuation. In their own case it had been, curiously enough, his pupil, Tom Outland. (Book 1, Ch. 3)

But St Peter says he had two love affairs, an affair of the heart and an affair of the imagination. Which I think is beautiful as well. So it is only partly true, as it is also for the love of the world of imagination that he abandons her; his relationship with Tom symbolically represents this world – it isn't simply Tom the person.

Tom represents the love for imagination because St Peter is so identified with him; this relationship provides emotional access to what he then calls his true self, his child self. But I think we know – and he knows too – that he had abandoned Lillian before he met Tom, not just for the Conquistadores but because of his wish for solitude. We should quote the passage where he fully realises this:

> That night, after he was in bed, among unaccustomed surroundings and a little wakeful, St. Peter still played with the idea of a picturesque shipwreck, and he cast about for the particular occasion he would have chosen for such a finale. Before he went to sleep he found the very day, but his wife was not in it. Indeed, nobody was in it but himself, and a weather-dried little sea captain from the Hautes-Pyrénées, half a dozen spry seamen, and a line of gleaming snow peaks, agonizingly high and sharp, along the southern coast of Spain. (Book 1, Ch. 8)

This is a reference back to the moment when the whole conception of his work suddenly comes to him as a whole, as sharp and clear as the mountains are.

BYATT: And the little town in the Mesa is to Tom Outland –

SODRE: Yes, of course, the Mesa appears to Tom exactly like that, suddenly, as if out of nowhere, in its entirety and splendour. It is a crucially important moment of aloneness, when he discovers his wish to be alone and deeply involved in something creative. It is just like St Peter's revelation of the design of his book:

> All day long they were skirting the south coast of Spain; from the rose of the dawn to the gold of the sunset the ranges of the Sierra Nevadas towered on their right, snow peak after snow peak, high beyond the flight of fancy, gleaming like crystal and topaz. St. Peter lay looking up at them from a little boat riding low in the purple water, and the design of his book unfolded in the air above him, just as definitely as the mountain ranges themselves. And the design was sound. He had never meddled with it, and it had seen him through. (Book I, Ch. 8)

So beautiful; the same experience as Tom's: the whole design of Tom's life is changed by seeing this complete thing, the Cliff City, above him in the air:

> I wish I could tell you what I saw there, just *as* I saw it, on that first morning through a veil of lightly falling snow. Far up above me, a thousand feet or so, set in a great cavern in the face of the cliff, I saw a little city of stone, asleep. It was as still as a sculpture – and something like that. It all hung together, seemed to have a kind of composition: pale little houses of stone nestling close to one another, perched on top of each other . . . (Book 2, Ch. 3)

BYATT: Almost like seeing the Holy City. It reminded me suddenly when you were speaking of that wonderful passage in *Middlemarch* where George Eliot talks about how many novels are written about the passions of this young man for that young woman, and how he finds her beautiful, but much more rarely is anything ever written about those equivalent passions of the mind where somebody falls in love with a high idea and follows it through. Eliot is talking of Lydgate feeling a pure passion for science. I feel that may be behind both Tom and the Professor, George Eliot's knowledge that to be in love with the life of the mind is as powerful a driving force in human life as to be in love with another human being. And of course the two loves do get across each other.

SODRE: Yes, they can be felt as to be integrated with each other, or they can be felt to be in conflict, even though they originate in the same life force.

BYATT: Scott McGregor says to St Peter, 'You know, Tom isn't very real to me any more. Sometimes I think he was just a – a glittering idea' (Book 1, Ch. 10). Tom becomes an emblem of the life of the mind. I think actually Tom is like Daniel Deronda, he often stands for Christ, who is both a human being and an idea – the spiritual force incarnate.

SODRE: I want to read a passage from Tom Outland's Story which relates to the question of imagination and the inner self, to an experience of being closest to oneself when entirely alone. Solitude in this context is absolutely connected to life, and yet it is also connected to death; in the solitary state of mind of the Professor near the end of the book, death is felt as a welcome solitude, and life as a really difficult state, in which you are constantly invaded by things which are extraneous to you. Solitude as an ideal state is most strikingly described in Tom Outland's Story when he has lost Blake. For a moment, when Blake decides to go, Tom has the impulse to hold him in his arms to stop him, and immediately becomes aware that something internal powerfully prevents him from doing so. What holds Tom back is not resentment about being betrayed, it is the knowledge that he wants to be alone and have the Mesa and the Cliff City all to himself. He then goes to sleep, and wishes never to wake up. A moment where Tom is suicidal, like the Professor, but from which he recovers into a very elated state in which he is the sole possessor of this magical place. He doesn't feel lonely for the loss of Blake: this is an ideal state of solitude. But what I thought was extremely interesting is that he seems to want closeness and to want remoteness at the same time:

> The moon was up, though the sun hadn't set, and it had the glittering silveriness the early stars have in high altitudes. The heavenly bodies look so much more remote from the bottom of a deep canyon than they do from the level. The climb of the walls helps out the eye, somehow. (Book 2, Ch. 5)

Helps the eye to feel remote, not to feel close. Which I thought was extraordinary – a description of intense pleasure in aloneness. The entire universe belongs to him, the sun and the moon are both there at the same time. But of course on another level closeness comes into it too, because if in his fantasy he is the sole possessor of this ideal object, in his inner world this must symbolically represent a union with a perfect other, the lost Mesa city which is now, with the disappearance of Blake, his alone, representing presumably the lost mother of his infancy.

This blissful experience goes back to an idealisation of his own ancient past, just like St Peter idealises his childhood self merged with the beautiful lake. That passage continues:

> I lay down on a solitary rock that was like an island in the bottom of the valley, and looked up. The grey sage-brush and the blue-grey rock around me were already in shadow, but high above me the canyon walls were dyed flame-colour with the sunset, and the Cliff City lay in a gold haze against its dark cavern. In a few minutes it, too, was grey and only the rim rock at the top held the red light. When that was gone, I could still see the copper glow in the piñons along the edge of the top ledges. The arc of sky over the canyon was silvery blue, with its pale yellow moon, and presently stars shivered into it like crystals dropped into perfectly clear water. (ibid.)

He is this solitary island and simultaneously he is merged with this perfect, beautiful thing.

BYATT: As a piece of writing this is wonderful. Because having given you this vision – and Cather is one of the most skilful describers (always in this crystalline way) of landscape – she then gives you the whole meaning of it in the next paragraph. Because Tom says 'that was the first night I was ever really on the Mesa at all – the first night that all of me was there', that is, he is one person in one place. Then – 'It all came together in my understanding, as a series of experiments do when you begin to see where they are leading' (ibid.).

His work is his vision of the landscape, exactly as Professor St Peter's was.

> Something had happened in me that made it possible for me to co-ordinate and simplify, and that process, going on in my mind, brought with it great happiness. It was my possession. The excitement of my first discovery was a very pale feeling compared to this one. For me the mesa was no longer an adventure, but a religious emotion. I had read of filial piety in the Latin poets, and I knew that was what I felt for this place. It had formerly been mixed up with other motives; but now that they were gone, I had my happiness unalloyed. (ibid.)

It is a sense of the coherence of himself, the world, and his work. But it's also religious and also to do with filial piety. And he connects to the human family at this huge distance exactly at the moment when he's not connecting to any individual people. Which is how you feel about St

Peter the historian – he feels himself connected to the human family – he feels a filial piety to the Conquistadores, and indeed the Crusaders. But his wife and children and sons-in-law are somehow stopping him having this sense of what it is to be human. Now I know this feeling myself well enough to know that Willa Cather hadn't invented it. It's deep in our nature. Interesting.

SODRE: This experience is the central core of the novel, I think. The Professor's house, where he can feel 'all of himself is there', like Tom's experience in the passage you just quoted, is not the whole house, but just the small attic where he writes and the French garden he created entirely by himself. In this novel the small, restricted, cluttered external space represents the large inner space where creativity can take place and individuality can be preserved; in marked contrast with the rest of the house which is felt as a place of intrusion, where otherness impinges in a very destructive way. The new house adds to this sense of destructive otherness in a way that reminds us of the 'innovators' ' destructiveness in *Mansfield Park*. This is about a horror of a woman's house, of a woman's inside, which is felt to imprison the man in a deadly state.

BYATT: Yes, trapped, or a tomb. Willa Cather had a very double attitude towards houses. As a young woman she wanted to be a boy called Will Cather, she signed everything 'Will Cather'. I think the boys in the story about the Enchanted Bluff, who want to go off and be explorers, are one side of Willa Cather, and she certainly had a very strong sense of herself as an ambitious male person who wished to conquer the world. But the other side of her is the praiser of civilisation and the praiser of the arts of housekeeping. She is interested in cooking pots, in growing herbs – there are herb gardens, carefully tended herb gardens, protected against the weather, in almost all her books. In the house on the rock of Quebec, in *Shadows on the Rock,* two French émigrés, father and daughter, manage to keep a pot of parsley alive in order to cook civilised food, all through the winter. Cather sees this domestic carefulness as deeply part of civilisation. It comes up in *Death Comes for the Archbishop,* and it comes up in the moment when Tom Outland says 'what I really love about old vanished civilisations is the smoke and dust on the bottom of their cooking pots'. And he describes the perfect forms of the cooking pots. Now before Cather describes St Peter's distaste for his new house, she describes the French garden that he'd made. The garden is between the house and the outer world and everything is perfectly designed:

> There was a bed for salad herbs. Salmon pink geraniums dripped over the wall. The French marigolds and dahlias were just now at their best . . . St. Peter had tended this bit of ground for over twenty years, and had got the upper hand of it. In the spring, when home-sickness for other lands and the fret of things unaccomplished awoke, he worked off his discontent there. (Book 1, Ch. 1)

Cather both loves and hates houses, I think.

SODRE: Yes, I remember how striking the gardens are in *Death Comes for the Archbishop*. As you say, St Peter's garden is a place in between the house and the outer world, a place of imagination, the space in which he could concretely create the world as he wished it to be. This particular garden is both real and not real, because it's a French garden, not entirely in the real American world; part of his pleasure is in re-creating something which is familiar to him from his past, and also foreign in that it does not match current external reality; it is, as it were, a fiction.

BYATT: She does refer to it as art; making gardens is art. But gardens also of course go with paradise imagery, and I notice that Tom Outland's story of his journey into the wilderness starts 'When I was a call boy in Pardee, New Mexico' (Book 2, Ch. 1), which I'm sure is to do with paradise. And the human home and the human family take many forms. When the Professor lies wishing to die he thinks of a poem of Longfellow:

> For thee a house was built
> Ere thou wast born;
> For thee a mould was made
> Ere thou of woman camest.

This is man's last home, man's last house. It always reminds me of Emily Dickinson's wonderful 'Because I could not stop for Death', where Death takes the poet to a similar place.

> We paused before a House that seemed
> A Swelling of the Ground –
> The Roof was scarcely visible –
> The Cornice – in the Ground –

All the houses and homes represent the human condition in a way.

SODRE: I was wondering, in relation to the French garden, if perhaps we should see it not as a work of art in itself, but again as representing the space of imagination that is potentially available to human beings, which they may or may not be able to inhabit. The relationship with art, as a creator or just as somebody who experiences it, is connected to one's relationship with the central core of oneself which is a dark, not entirely known place which one can explore. But it also has this intermediate area where you can imaginatively re-create yourself. The Professor thinks of his real self as being the young boy who should never have left the beautiful lake; but we must not assume that this boy is exactly how Godfrey was as a real little boy; he is a transformation of Godfrey the boy via his experience of his relationship with Tom Outland. So he is also an invented boy. This invented boy is not a work of art, but it is a work of the imagination; St Peter has re-created that boy, not just as a memory but as an imagined part of himself, which is deeply meaningful to him. In his mind he has become a more wonderful boy. But this is also a 'walled garden', because it excludes his wife and children, and one of the possible outcomes for this turning inwards could be death.

BYATT: I think Cather is an artist deeply concerned with death. Death as a very natural thing. In her other books, some characters die violently and horribly, but others simply one day begin to fail, the energy goes out of them and they begin to die. And this process interests her. She's interested in the coming of energy and the power of energy in human beings, she's interested in the slow fading of the fire. I think she's one of the most accurate describers of that. You feel that the attic in which St Peter decides to start to die is the place where he also did his most creative work. In a sense that inadequate lamp and the gas which is leaking and killing him, are images of that energy which was once the light and warmth of creativity and is now slowly destroying him. And the sinister 'forms' in a sense are forms of death. They are hard and they are inanimate. And Augusta presides over the scene, with her stories of people's funerals, which are very lively stories. I think Cather also manages to suggest that only people who have lived very energetically experience very precisely and fully this desire to die. That a powerful life makes for a powerful death.

SODRE: And the desire to die is so much to do with him being in the grip of his horror of this change in his life, moving to a new house, which stirs up the wish to go back to his older self and to be alone. So that to be alone is to move back into the past as a way of being in contact with things which are internally more alive, but simultaneously also a wish for something which is akin to death, a total solitude which he feels grateful for.

BYATT: The little poem by Longfellow suggests that in a way, because it suggests 'from earth thou camest, into earth shalt thou return'. It's a home.

SODRE: To die is to return to the place where you belong, like a return to the womb.

BYATT: It's interesting, in terms of that, that in the little town that Tom Outland finds, at first they find only one human being, and she has been murdered. She has been killed, there is a big wound in her ribs that suggests she was knifed. And round this all sorts of stories of adultery and bride sacrifice are built by Father Duchene and Tom. Nobody actually knows how she died. But it's somehow significant that this dead body, this damaged body, is out in the air, whereas the others have somehow gone back to the earth. All the other inhabitants have vanished.

SODRE: But also Father Duchene imagines that the woman may have been killed for the adultery caused by her husband leaving her: he imagines she has taken a lover because she is lonely. It is suggested that loneliness leads to an attachment to life which is life-threatening. And this story in hinted at in a novel where marriage itself is life-threatening: St Peter feels the marriage to Lillian to be a death trap for his true self, whereas he longs for a different, idealised kind of death in which his sense of self would be preserved.

BYATT: It's amazing how much early novels were about events leading up to marriage, and marriage made everything happy ever after, but the moment the novel went beyond the threshold of marriage and started describing it, the predominant image is of a death trap really; marriage is in novels death traps and death. You said that *Mansfield Park*, which is the nearest thing to a fairytale novel we have talked about, was profoundly anti-marriage. Lucy Snowe has a desperate desire to be in a marriage in the sense that she doesn't want to miss out on human life, and yet she also recoils from it. Happy marriages in novels tend to be very much on the edge. Then you get Tolstoy saying all happy marriages resemble each other.

These themes are interesting in the context of Cather's own life. One does get a sense in *The Professor's House* that this highly accomplished artist is reworking some very personal material in a way that is hard for the reader to follow. She meant it to be hard to follow – her letters are embargoed in perpetuity, no one may ever quote them. But it is known that she was passionately attached to Isabelle McClung and that she did have a room in the McClung parents' household – a sewing-room converted into a study for her – she had a typewriter on the table where the sewing machine was and was a journalist, and was happy. And then in 1916, at the age of thirty-eight, Isabelle married an energetic Russian-Jewish violinist, Jan Hambourg (who is generally thought to have been the origin of Louie Marsellus) to whom Willa Cather dedicated the first edition of *The Professor's House*. Later she set up house with Edith Lewis; they lived intensely privately. You feel that if she identifies with anybody in this book it is the Professor, very strongly. She had just won the Pulitzer Prize for *One of Ours*, which was her war novel, that is, her novel about the death of Tom Outland, about the young men who went out and fought in France in the 1914–18 war and died. Like the Professor she was wondering whether her major work was at an end. Like the Professor, she might have felt expected to live on her laurels.

SODRE: And he equates this living on his laurels to a kind of death, but I suppose it would be also a betrayal of himself, a betrayal of his creative self, who is alive in the world of the imagination rather than in the world of beautiful new houses.

BYATT: As though great success either destroys you or creates an urgent need to recover your solitary self.

SODRE: But it also brings with it a kind of mourning for an earlier, younger aspect of yourself – as if through this gain you are in danger of having lost your desire to create something new. It brings a longing to recover a state of mind in which you were full of eagerness, full of the wish to create and to possess.

I am wondering about how much the idea of death itself is connected in this novel to the death of love, which is the death of the self who once was passionately in love. St Peter says that the saddest thing in the world is to fall out of love. And Blake says, when Tom betrays him, 'I'm glad it's you that's doing this to me, Tom, not me that's doing it to you' (Book 2, Ch. 5) – confirming that the worst loss is the loss of the part of yourself which is capable of loving. Which is in fact what happens at the end of the book; St Peter has to learn how to live without joy and delight, to live bereaved of his passionate self.

BYATT: Yes, he's died a small death. It's very interesting that Iris Murdoch always talks about falling out of love as a sort of visionary revelation of the truth just as exciting and interesting as falling in it. Which I think is partly what I feel. I'm not distressed for the Professor, for some reason – I think it's because of Willa Cather's technical mastery of her novel. I feel he is so much her – she was going on to write better and better. This is a temporary fifty-year-old blip, and the Professor has survived. He does survive death; Augusta does save him.

BYATT: I think the 'forms' are oddly the most memorable thing about this book. All critics discuss them. They have been made into bad fairies or guardian angels. They are figures of death, negative figures apparently of female sexuality. The first is a headless torso.

> It presented the most unsympathetic surface imaginable. Its hardness was not that of wood, which responds to concussion with living vibration and is stimulating to the hand, nor that of felt, which drinks something from the fingers. It was a dead, opaque, lumpy solidity, like chunks of putty, or tightly packed sawdust – very disappointing to the tactile sense, yet somehow always fooling you again. For no matter how often you had bumped up against that torso, you could never believe that contact with it would be as bad as it was. (Book I, Ch. I)

The second is apparently more frivolous, a glittering cage on which a ball dress might hang before going off to the ball. It has a 'sprightly tricky air'. What do you as an analyst make of them?

SODRE: Clearly St Peter wants to hold on to them because they are an integral part of the attic he cannot bear to be separated from; but they also represent bad aspects of women, like the essence of his internal bad objects, bad relationships in his inner world. They are both deceitful: one because of its traumatically unexpected hardness, the other because she is an unprincipled seductress. St Peter is desperately attached to these forms, as if he needs constantly to keep an eye on the enemy, as it were, represented by these dead 'forms'.

BYATT: They never come to life like Lucy Snowe's nun. 'At times the wire lady was most convincing in her pose as a woman of light behaviour, but she never fooled St Peter. He had had his blind spots, but he had never been taken in by one of her kind!' (Book I, Ch. I). I'd never thought of it that way before, but they actually reduce the threat of the female. They stand there and he feels quite safe with them.

SODRE: It's like when somebody says, 'I had a terrible dream, but thank God it was only a dream.' Well, you know very well that there isn't such a thing as 'only a dream', yet you are able to distance yourself from this particular experience. The form represents something horrible, but it is 'only a form', with no power over him. Not the real thing.

BYATT: It's interesting, because in so many fairy stories, in the attics you find the witch with the spindle, and you prick your finger, you go into the room in the house where people don't go and there is the witch, or the ghost, or there is the demon. And here are these two forms and Augusta, who sews. Sewing and clothes have come up in all the novels. There was Fanny making her little boxes in her attic. We've discussed Lucy Snowe and Paulina sewing things, Paulina pricking her fingers, and Lucy making a brilliant watchguard for M. Paul. Sewing is one of the persisting metaphors for female creativity. You were saying earlier that what Augusta makes is clothes, which are then put on to real women.

SODRE: The clothes have different meanings, to dress and to conceal, or to beautify, or to masquerade. They are very important in several scenes we have discussed, in particular in *Villette*, where Lucy Snowe is disguised as 'Lucy Snowe'. Here they remind St Peter of his attachment to his lively, delightful little girls – the pretty party clothes move from the forms to the real girls, in an image clearly connected to benign femininity – and to his distance from them, from the women in his life, who are gradually becoming just forms. They are symbols which contain complex meanings; in the fairytale dimension Augusta is the fairy godmother, who is dressing them as princesses; whereas Rosamond's fur is a malignant piece of clothing which stirs up such envy in Kathleen that she becomes green with envy.

BYATT: She becomes green like a snake. Which is exactly how Gwendolen is seen.

SODRE: Rosamond with her fur projects such envy that Kathleen becomes temporarily bad – poisoned by this evil thing. There is a sense of horror when St Peter sees her green face, distorted by envy; he sees ugliness in her, and recoils. I think this also links with Medea and the poisoned clothes (which we also discussed in *Deronda*), and the idea of being psychologically poisoned by evil feelings. There is a moment when he is feeling that his children don't need him any more, and he would like them to be the fragrant, lovely little girls they once were, because he possessed them then. He thinks:

> When a man had lovely children in his house, fragrant and happy, full of pretty fancies and generous impulses, why couldn't he keep

> them? Was there no other way but Medea's, he wondered? (Book I, Ch. 10)

He becomes aware of a destructive fantasy: 'If I can't have them fixed in the way they used to be, I'll kill them.' It is very violent and terribly surprising. But it is also not real, as it belongs to this mythical world.
BYATT: That's *very* interesting. Now I look, it's clearly stated just before those lines.

> Oh, there had been fine times in this old house then: family festivals and hospitalities, little girls dancing in and out, Augusta coming and going, gay dresses hanging in his study at night, Christmas shopping and secrets and smothered laughter on the stairs. (ibid.)

But I think there is a positive aspect to the forms too. What most struck me and most moved me when I first met them was actually the word itself. A writer feels both that she is giving form to a series of apparently unconnected thoughts and observations, and that she is *discovering* some deep form in things, that was waiting to be found. When I first read Plato, as I'm sure Willa Cather did, I got very excited about the idea that the philosopher sees the true forms of things, the form of the Table which gives rise to all tables, the form of Tree which gives rise to all trees. And there is a sense in which that word can be related to those visions which both Tom Outland and Godfrey St Peter have, of the form of their work when they suddenly see it. Iris Murdoch has said that there is a moment all writers both long for and dread when the form of a work of fiction settles and cannot thereafter be changed. And that's exactly what St Peter was talking about. In one sense the forms in the attic are forms of fear, forms of terror, of ghosts: you would read in a Gothic novel: 'I saw a terrible form advancing towards me.' But Cather's forms are also the raw material which is to be formed, which is why the word putty is important, the clay out of which things can be moulded but which in itself is dead. And they are the rough stuff, the rough shape, before you have done it. And if you're saying all that, that they are the forms in Plato's shadowy Cave, that they're unformed human beings, that they are ghostly forms, you're also saying that they are what exists before creation, before life, before work. In so far as they are forms of fear, they are forms on which women's art, the making of dresses, masquerades, hiding places, will be put. In so far as they are rough forms of art, they're the guardian angels which accompany St

Peter's work. And if ever there was an artist who really cared about the form of her work, which she then disguises as easy formlessness, it was Willa Cather.

SODRE: You can also link the forms to psychoanalytic ideas of archetypes and of innate preconceptions, 'forms' in the mind that then get filled in with content and particularity. Consider for instance the idea of the Oedipus complex: as Freud discovered, we are born with some very schematic, primitive knowledge of a parental intercourse that excludes ourself as the child, and that may produce other children; this is like a 'form' in the mind that gets filled in with the particularity of each person's attachments and relationships and impulses.

The other psychoanalytic idea (which connects to things we've been discussing in relation to *Deronda*), is the question of the form being an object with some characteristics but not very detailed, so it is also like the blank page. Daniel Deronda dreaded being the object to which the transference could be attached, a basic form that is there to be dressed up with somebody else's fantasies, an object that is needed for projection. Gwendolen needed Deronda as this kind of 'form'. The need is not only for somebody to *listen*, but for somebody to *be* in a particular way.

BYATT: Absolutely brilliant. And of course that fits in with what we've been doing in our conversations. We have discussed the accidents and the particularities and the realism of the characters first, then we've moved on to the conscious meanings, and then we have moved on to the bit which we always most enjoy, which is the structuring with forms like Oedipusness, or here suddenly the Medea myth bobs its head up, or the myth of the fairy and the needle pricking. And every time anyone tells you such a tale as a child, you form a visual image of it. Every child throughout the centuries has formed a visual image; no two of them will be the same, and yet all of them are the same. That is what it is about the archetypal stories which we tell ourselves, and I think all these novelists have known how to evoke and stir up in us those ancient forms which we then clothe as one does in one's life, with flesh and blood. And of course the final form is the corpse in the bed of clay, which St Peter is heading towards.

We could also think about the words 'inform' and 'information'. They derive from Neoplatonic ideas that the mind, or spirit, or 'nous' enters into matter or 'hyle' and gives it life and form from within: *informs* it. Milton speaks about the serpent in the Garden being '*informed* by Satan, inmate bad', as if Satan has given the snake its form of being a snake.

SODRE: To start with the snake is described by Milton as an innocent form, and then Satan slides into it, and it becomes evil. This reminds me of the gas as a poisonous substance that can penetrate and invade every single bit of the body, or symbolically of the mind. Like the 'bad air', the atmosphere in the gambling room in *Deronda.*
BYATT: Or the mephitic and gassy atmosphere of Pandemonium in *Paradise Lost.* How interesting. You are saying that the first scene of *Daniel Deronda* combines poisonous gas and the serpent – for Gwendolen is an 'innocent' form of snake. And there is a kind of almost buried, almost inactive Christian myth in *The Professor's House* as there is in *Daniel Deronda.* I mentioned that Elinor Shaffer said that Deronda is a secularised, agnostic image of the Messiah, the incarnation of an idea in a human being. And St Peter has a very mythological name, he's called Napoleon Godfrey St Peter.

SODRE: You talked about the significance of names in your introduction to *The Professor's House.*
BYATT: All St Peter's names are names of Conquistadores or conquerors of some kind. Napoleon conquered Europe, and Godfrey is Godfrey of Boulogne, the Crusader who took Jerusalem when the other Crusaders failed. St Peter was Petrus, the Rock on which the Church was founded. Which I think is very ambiguous, I've only just thought of it that way. Godfrey 'St Peter' is the rock on which the Church is founded, he's the mountain on which these visions of order, both his and Tom Outland's, rise. Although as I said when we were talking about treachery, Peter was also the one who turned his back and renounced Christ when he was pressurised and threatened. In an essay called 'The Kingdom of Art', Cather compares the Crusaders with the artist:

> There were other crusades many centuries ago when all the good men who were otherwise unemployed, and their wives and progeny, set out for Palestine. But they found that the holy sepulchre was a long way off, and there was no beaten path thereto, and the mountains were high and the sands hot, and the waters of the desert were bitter brine. So they decided to leave the journey to the pilgrims who were madmen anyway, without homes; who found the water no bitterer than their own tears and the desert sands no hotter than the burning hearts within them. In the kingdom of art there is no God but one God and his service is so exacting that there are few men born of woman who are strong

> enough to take the vows. There is no paradise offered for a reward to the faithful, no celestial bowers, no houris, no scented wines; only death and the truth.

And the whole of this wonderful paragraph does connect St Peter and art to the image of the Conquistadores in a beautifully complicated way. And to the Crusaders. The myth of the conquering Crusaders who went to the East to try and rescue the Holy City is as powerful as the myth of the Conquistadores who went west and discovered the New World and the old paradise. St Peter's pageant is relevant here: 'Not long ago, when the students were giving a historical pageant to commemorate the deeds of an early French explorer among the Great Lakes, they asked St. Peter to do a picture for them.' He poses his two sons-in-law as Richard and Saladin before the walls of Jerusalem. The narrator remarks it 'amused him very much, though it had nothing to do with the subject.' But Cather's mind, and perhaps the Professor's unconscious, equates the early explorers of America with the Crusaders who went out to try and retrieve the Holy City. Tom Outland comes from a town called Pardee, to find the secret town in the Mesa; in a sense he finds the original walled garden and the original Holy City. In Walter Scott's novel *The Talisman*, from which this pageant must be taken, where Richard Plantagenet –

SODRE: – where the Jewish question comes in –

BYATT: The Jewish question comes in – oh yes, I'd forgotten that. Richard and Saladin fight. The British king fights with a heavy Crusader's sword, in armour; the Eastern Saladin is volatile and swift, and has a sword which can slice through a cushion because it's so subtle. He is in many ways very feminine, because he has a skirted garment. Marsellus the Jew is being typecast as Daniel Deronda was, as a type of the Orient. And, using the same typology, Charlotte Brontë compared the Jewish actress, Vashti to Saladin. 'Place now the Cleopatra, or any other slug, before her as an obstacle, and see her cut through the pulpy mass as the scimitar of Saladin clove the down cushion' (*Villette*, Ch. 23). It's interesting in this context that the ship on which St Peter's family finally return from Europe is the *Berengaria*. Berengaria was Coeur de Lion's queen, who made a long romantic journey to marry him, and appears to have found he was in love with his job as a soldier and in love with the male soldiers, with the minstrel boy who finally rescued him, according to one romantic novel. And so when the whole of St Peter's family is coming back to him on the *Berengaria*, they're coming back from Europe to the land of the Conquistadores on a ship which bears the name of a neglected queen with a possibly unconsummated, deeply unhappy marriage. I suppose a woman rather like the one in the myth Father Duchene makes up – left behind when the men went out to fight or explore.

SODRE: The murdered woman on the Mesa. But it is rather beautiful that the novel ends with the *Berengaria*, because of its ambiguity. Lillian of course is the abandoned wife, and St Peter comes to realise that he has abandoned her a long time ago; but he also feels abandoned *by* her, because she isn't who he thought she would be. The *Berengaria*, with its connection to neglect, to long distances that may or may not be bridged, appearing as the final 'sight' in a novel which is so centrally about the question of remoteness and closeness, is a brilliant idea.

I think Willa Cather conveys something very complex about the Professor's state of mind in the last chapter: she implies that he has changed and matured, and that a part of him died, and that he is in a state of mourning; but she also implies that there is something remote and narcissistic about him. This is from the last paragraph of the novel:

> His temporary release from consciousness seemed to have been beneficial. He had let something go – and it was gone: something very precious, that he could not consciously have relinquished, probably. (Book 3, Ch. 5)

At the centre of the novel is this process of mourning, of having to give up something precious; but the word 'probably' suddenly throws the whole thing into question! Is it really true that he needed to have been near suicide? Is this an idealisation of the state of near-death? Perhaps this whole painful process wouldn't have been necessary if he had understood himself better. Our understanding of St Peter's process of growing old and maturing and dying is thrown by this 'probably'. He then says 'He doubted whether his family would ever realize that he was not the same man they had said good-bye to; they would be too happily preoccupied with their own affairs' (ibid.). This is very sad, because we know that he isn't the same man, we know there is now an enormous gap between himself and his family that will probably never be bridged, he will be alone for ever. We also know that what he lost is the capacity for joy, his passionate self has died. And then, 'If his apathy hurt them, they could not possibly be so much hurt as he had been already' (ibid.). Now, this is a terribly narcissistic thought to have. Why do we have to side with him in assuming that he is the most hurt person in the world?

His wife was hurt, his children were hurt, Tom was hurt. He moves from a psychological position of having achieved some insight into a position of self-pity. The passage ends, 'He thought he knew where he was, and that he could face with fortitude the *Berengaria* and the future' (ibid.). But we are left unsure whether this is real fortitude that comes from self-knowledge.

BYATT: That phrase, 'He thought he knew where he was', is as important as the 'probably'.

SODRE: It leaves you with an end that opens something up.

BYATT: Yes it does.

SODRE: It's not final, the end. You are free to have different kinds of thoughts about the characters and about life and death.

BYATT: If you think of Willa Cather's other work, both in *Death Comes for the Archbishop* and *Shadows on the Rock* she manages to give an immensely sympathetic portrait of the people who are bringing Christianity, which means civilisation, which she values, to an uninhabited country or a wild or savage country, and in both cases also she does imaginatively enter into the life of the civilisation that was already there (which Saladin would represent also). At the time she wrote this novel, she was moving towards her final membership of the Church, because she needed the structure and belief and the form, I think, very deeply, of that sort of relation to the whole of human culture. Augusta is important here. Her name represents Roman civilisation: the Augustan age was the age of innovators and civilised people which followed the heroic age of Julius Caesar. The Augustan age is the silver age in both English culture and Roman culture. It's the age when Virgil wrote the *Aeneid*, which is what Tom is reading in the Mesa. Cather saw her own talent as Virgilian and civilising, bringing the arts of peace to a rough culture. Augusta combines the classical and the Christian, when she says 'Our Lady sat down and composed the Magnificat'. And that word 'composed' is as powerful as the word 'forms', because it suggests that the Virgin Mary, who is traditionally depicted as a breasted mother, was actually an artist who wrote this perfect poem. It's wonderful. It is another vision of the Form of art. And it is Augusta, with this very practical vision of the Virgin Mary as poet, who pulls the Professor by his feet out of his death back into life, and more or less tells him he ought not to die, he ought not to do that. So she is a kind of muse, like the two forms that stand beside her in the sewing place, and she is the witch because she has the needles.

SODRE: But she also says to him that he is ignorant – and what he's ignorant of is a different aspect of woman, not the woman he dreads and has to run away from, but woman representing creativity.
BYATT: That's it.

Willa Cather wrote about her excitement about realising what you could do, by putting a short story or a novella into a novel, by telling a story within a story in a different form, in a different light. She used a metaphor which moves me greatly, of the window in the back of a Dutch painting of an interior, making a house which opens on the sea and the open air. So that in the innermost depth of the picture you've got this window on to the outer world, which perspectively is the most inner thing of all. And metaphorically the outer world is the inmost thing, because the inner life is the outer life, the sea or the forest, which you see through the window. I think I wouldn't love the Tom Outland story so much if it didn't always carry for me immediately this image of a window in the interior creating an interior exterior, which fits on to everything you have been saying about the inner and outer life.

SODRE: And Cather's descriptions of landscape are so marvellous in the way they allow you to see external and internal reality, touching simultaneously profound experiences of contemplating beauty and relationships with particular objects in the mind. But I think the other image that goes with the one of the Dutch painting – there are several metaphors of things enclosed in things – is in the epigraph, supposedly Louie Marsellus's words, about the bracelet Tom gave Rosamond: ' "A turquoise set in silver, wasn't it? . . . Yes, a turquoise set in dull silver." – Louie Marsellus'. It is so interesting to have as an epigraph a quotation from one of the characters, making him into a completely real human being! A metaphor for the preciousness of Tom and for the fact that the novella is the turquoise inside the dull silver, but also for the question of what is in the centre of things, like the tower in the centre of the cliff dwelling. I'm referring back to what you were saying, the question of moving inside to some central point which can also be located in the outside which is the internal landscape. The eye converges to this particular point, the heart of light rather than the heart of darkness.

BYATT: Yes, and the image Tom uses for the Mesa is the fly set in amber: the creature whose whole life exists inside this quite other form and this quite other material. In the novel, with the story, Cather manages to do all that. Of course the whole thing is within her book, which is within her mind and now within our minds. You were saying before we began talking: you can lift this book up from the table, it is a real object, but it is a whole world. If you have two narratives, in a way you cast both of them into doubt and make them both more real, by this act.

SODRE: In the end, underneath it all, there is also something fascinating about the use of the male narrator, and about the texture of the novel.
BYATT: What one should say about the narrator, perhaps, is that here we have a woman novelist telling a story from a male point of view, because even when she moves outside the point of view of Godfrey St Peter she only moves as far as the son-in-law, really. She doesn't move into the consciousness of any of the women. They are always seen from outside. But what she does do is move into the first person, the idealised male boy who does male things, two sorts of male things, one very active, riding horses and exploring, and the other very mental, finding out things about science.
SODRE: But we don't have a narrative of the story of the scientific discoveries, we only have Tom Outland's Story until he meets the St Peters.
BYATT: But we have him at the moment when he's describing seeing the Mesa, comparing it to the excitement of making the discoveries in science. Which makes me happy because it stops the science being a purely negative concept. The other thing is, it is traditionally felt that first person narrative is more immediate and you feel closer to the teller. I think this novel is a perfect example of how this is not true: you feel infinitely closer to Godfrey St Peter than to Tom, and you feel closest of all at the moment which you described at the end, when she inserts little words that could be hers or could be his. Like 'probably', and 'he thought'. That is where Willa Cather is present, most unobtrusively. That is where you feel closest to the thing she's describing. Whereas Tom Outland feels like somebody met at an enormous distance – as he saw the stars – you hear his voice, but you know him much less. All Cather's novels have a loose, fluid surface. The writing seems to move along quite quietly with no force or direction. Underneath are the very powerful forms, and some sort of very strong undertow of things happening, inexorably and violently. You were saying earlier that there are times when suddenly the language becomes violent.
SODRE: Yes, I think the passage I quoted about Medea is one of those. We are given the lovely sense of the family, and suddenly this woman who murdered her children is thrown in front of us.
BYATT: The other thing Cather does is encapsulate a whole terrible vision of things in very small episodes, for instance when Harry gets

killed by the rattlesnake. The description of the killing of this old man is very brief, but the reader is made to visualise the whole thing, exactly how his body blew up and how long it took him to die, and exactly where the snake came from. Hermione Lee in her biography of Willa Cather offers this as an example of folksy speech and roughness – it isn't only that, it's absolutely elegant, a sure-footed capacity to make something just long enough for you never to forget it.

SODRE: But it's also such a good example of the novelist, through her way of telling the story, causing the reader to have an experience which is similar to that which she is describing in the characters. Something suddenly appears totally out of the blue, which is so striking and violent and immediate that it makes you feel that a serpent comes out of the page and hits you in between the eyes. It is written so brilliantly and so concisely that it 'strikes you square' in your mind. The Medea line is exactly that: a horrible knife pierces your vision of delightful little girls.

BYATT: It's interesting how many of these moments in all the books are to do with snakes. We were talking about the serpent being informed by Satan. The snake that bites Harry is a real snake in a real paradise, but it is death and it does strike. It takes me back to Gwendolen and all her snakes, and the adder on top of the letters, and beyond that to Brontë's Paulina with her needle like the head of a golden serpent. It's amazing how a culture can be both completely realist – there would have been snakes there – and yet rely on the myth of that culture to produce a kind of over-reaction, a violent and complex reaction, in your own mind.

St Peter himself has this mythic and real doubleness. When he is first described, he is described as a cross between a man and a demon and a statue – a form. The narrator says he looks like a Van Dyck painting, and has a hawk nose and hawk-like eyes. She continues: 'His wicked looking eyebrows made his students call him Mephistopheles'. So we're in the realm of myth in a light-hearted way. Then

> His daughter Kathleen, who had done several successful studies of him in water-colour, had once said: – 'the thing that really makes Papa handsome is the modelling of his head between the top of his ear and his crown; it is quite the best thing about him.' That part of his head was high, polished, hard as bronze, and the close-growing black hair threw off a streak of light along the rounded ridge where the skull was fullest. The mould of his head on the side was so individual and definite, so far from casual, that it was more like a statue's head than a man's. (Book 1, Ch. 1)

Now, the word ridge connects with the mountains, as though you had a mountain peak. More than that, he is a form, an artificial form. We're talking about a person who has a love affair in his head in the attic, in the top of himself, a love affair with form. And in a way you feel he is a mythic being, but a mythic being partly solidified. The male head (which takes us back to the old Neoplatonic dichotomy which I dislike between woman as matter and man as mind), has solidified mind into a statue of itself. And the women are the busts with no heads and no viscera. A few chapters later, you get another image of St Peter's head as being partly a work of art and partly human:

> He wore on his head a rubber visor of the kind he always brought home from France in great numbers. This one was vermilion, and was like a continuation of his flesh – his arms and back were burned a deep terra-cotta from a summer in the lake. His head and powerful reaching arms made a strong red pattern against the purple blue of the water. The visor was picturesque – his head looked sheathed and small and intensely alive, like the heads of the warriors on the Parthenon frieze in their tight, archaic helmets. (Book 1, Ch. 5)

It says he's intensely alive, but he's alive because he's like a frozen statue that's dead. And he's using his energy at the full, because he's swimming in the water with this red face and red visor, like a warrior. Yet again there's this sense that he's also become a statue, and a statue has a longer life than a human being that will moulder away into the ground. So again it's ambiguous whether he's dead because he's partly artificial or much more intensely alive because he's partly artificial.

SODRE: I think it is an extremely rich image, very phallic, also serpent-like. Part of his head being more 'like a statue's head than a man's' links up with your point: does this statue-like quality, which is linked decidedly here with individuality (it makes him more defined and particular, rather than more general) make him more, or less, human? In a novel where creativity is so closely interconnected to the capacity and the need to be alone, this is an extremely important question. On the whole, as we have noticed, creativity and involvement with the human family stand in opposition to each other. But Cather also shows with considerable psychological depth that this opposition may not be a universally necessary one, but may be part of St Peter's way of rationalising his own difficulties. We know that he feels Lillian has become hardened, and that he has fallen out of love because of that.

> He could not live with his family again. Not even with Lillian. Especially not with Lillian! Her nature was intense and positive; it was like a chiselled surface, a die, a stamp on which he could not be beaten out any longer. If her character were reduced to an heraldic device, it would be a hand (a beautiful hand) holding flaming arrows – the shafts of her violent loves and hates, her clear-cut ambitions. (Book 3, Ch. 4)

Lillian the chiselled surface is as much a statue as he is, or more so, he claims; and yet, is she? or has she been 'reduced' by him, in his mind, to this hard surface? The constant oscillation in his capacity to be aware of his own distorting contributions to his perception of his wife is brilliantly conveyed by Cather.

The novel ends with a marvellous ambiguity about this perfect 'form', about its opposing lifelike and deathlike qualities: she is intense and positive, and yet as a stamp or a die she moulds him, forms him in a horribly powerful way; she is too hard to touch, and yet it is in his mind that she is transformed into the frightening, beautifully violent 'heraldic device'.

Chapter 5

Iris Murdoch: *An Unofficial Rose*

An Unofficial Rose (1962) is Iris Murdoch's sixth novel.

Characters have gathered together for the funeral of Fanny Peronett, wife of Hugh Peronett, who reflects upon his marriage, during which, he had a passionate love affair with Emma Sands, now a famous detective-story writer. Musing upon his wife, he at one point thinks that he may have married her for the Tintoretto, a painting of Susannah and the Elders given to her by her art-dealer father in his will, which he keeps in their London flat and loves. At the graveside are also his son Randall, creator of a beautiful rose nursery: a charismatic man, who, since the death of his son Steve, has turned to drink and has increasing displays of violence and bad temper, feeling himself to be trapped in a claustrophobic, impossible marriage with his meek wife Ann, whom he irrationally blames for their son's death. Still living is their precocious, strange, adolescent daughter, Miranda, who, despite her age, still keeps a host of dolls. Also present for the funeral is Penn Graham, Hugh's fifteen-year-old grandson from Australia, who finds life with his English relatives alienating, although Ann is kind, and discovers a fabulous knife with a white swastika on it that belonged to Steve. He also falls for his difficult cousin Miranda, and they have one encounter which is disturbing. Douglas Swann, the local rector, also perhaps loves Ann in a way 'a tiniest bit more than pastoral', despite being married to Clare, and Nancy Bowshott, the gardener's wife, a background figure, turns out to be secretly in love with Randall.

The other family involved in the story is the Finch family: Humphrey, a homosexual civil servant who has his eye on young Penn, and whose career came to an abrupt end after an 'incident' in Marrakesh, his clever wife Mildred, who has loved Hugh ever since he kissed her many years ago, and Colonel Felix Meecham, Mildred's younger brother, a gentleman, in love with Ann and involved with a French girl, Marie-Laure Auboyer, who is in Delhi.

Emma Sands appears at the funeral with her assistant Lindsay Rimmer, with whom, it turns out, Randall is passionately in love. The sight of Emma inflames Hugh's old feelings, and Hugh turns down a trip to India with Mildred and Felix, thinking he will revive their relationship. Randall engineers a terrible row with Ann, and takes off to London where he visits Emma and Lindsay, with whom he has a curious triangular relationship. Hugh also visits Emma again, but finds her unfathomable and detached. Lindsay says she will leave Emma for Randall if he can get enough money to support them both in style, and Randall asks his father to sell the Tintoretto. Hugh is torn between horror and being impressed by his son's daring, and asks Mildred's advice. Mildred sees that if Hugh sells the Tintoretto, she herself will lose Hugh, who will be able to gain comfort from the deserted Emma, but her brother Felix, with Randall out of the way, may gain Ann. On her advice, Hugh sells the painting, and Randall elopes with Lindsay. Ann does fall in love with Felix, but despite everything, and with the added complication of discovering that her controlling daughter Miranda had been in love with Felix from the age of five, she cannot accept the 'freedom' he offers her. Hugh finds that Emma will not redeem the past, and has simply replaced Lindsay with a new companion, Jocelyn. She then reveals to him that she is in fact seriously ill, and has left her money to young Penn. Having been released from Emma, Hugh is able to go to India with Mildred and Felix, who, now all is lost with Ann, is returning to Marie-Laure. Ann simply gets on with her old routines, half waiting for Randall who may yet return and anyway, not knowing any other way to live.

BYATT: I think we could start by agreeing that the characters in a rather formal way divide into the good and the dangerous, into those who proceed through life in a state of unconsciousness, unknowing muddle, and those who think of themselves as, or appear to be forceful, decisive, making patterns in other people's lives. We might start by talking about Ann and Hugh, who belong to the first category.

SODRE: What occurs to me, before saying anything specific about Ann and Hugh, is that it is interesting to notice how 'goodness and not knowing and being in a muddle' comes as a cluster of qualities that belong to the 'good' group of people, while cleverness and activity and being in control belong with the 'baddies'.

BYATT: It has always been said that it's much easier to depict an evil character than a good character because good characters tend to be boring, and they tend on the whole to be negative, to be saying no to things. This may be partly the Christian vision, where renunciation and not giving way to temptation and not impinging on others are seen as a form of virtue. I think *An Unofficial Rose* is a very Christian book in one sense. It does take off very precisely from *Mansfield Park*, and possibly also from Lionel Trilling's essay in which he says that the virtues of Fanny Price are those of the poor in spirit, those of the Christian heroine who was rather sickly and faded and unassertive. I don't think Ann is any better a character or more interesting than Fanny, but she was created by a novelist who had met a long line of self-sacrificing heroines, and understands our ambivalence about them. Iris Murdoch calls the goodness in question; she doesn't just say Ann is good, she says that Ann has these forms of behaviour which have in the past been characterised as goodness.

SODRE: In your book on Iris Murdoch, *Degrees of Freedom*, you say – and I agree – that Ann and Hugh are the most strongly created characters, more worked through and real than the others; so although on the whole 'baddies' may be easier to depict than 'goodies', it's not true of this novel, because here the 'good' characters are more alive and built in depth than the others. But one thing that occurs to me, in contrast with *Mansfield Park*, is that in that novel the central virtue for Jane Austen is self-knowledge. She often defines the moral nature of her characters in terms of their capacity for self-knowledge. In *Mansfield Park*, it's the 'baddies' who are muddled. Fanny is insightful, Mary Crawford is likeable inasmuch as she is insightful and not likeable inasmuch as she is psychologically blind, and Austen discusses their capacity or incapacity to think of their motives. Mrs Norris, who is a 'witch', is totally devoid of insight. So the way the characteristics are distributed is very different, even though there are so many parallels in the two books.

BYATT: That's very true, and helpful. I suppose what has come between Austen and Murdoch is both Henry James and E. M. Forster. I think that Ann in *An Unofficial Rose* springs partly from the work of Iris Murdoch's husband, John Bayley on love and virtue, in his book, *The Characters of Love*. He does an intricate and impressive analysis of the self-renouncing American heroine of *The Golden Bowl*, Maggie, who regains her husband from the powerful enchantress figure Charlotte (who was his mistress and tries to be his mistress again), by pretending *not to know* what is happening. She fights in silence, keeping the surface conventions of their lives intact, and in this way she preserves the structure of the marriage. And you can see, I think, that Iris Murdoch has been meditating on this use of the convention of pretending not to know in order to hold a structure intact.

I agree with you that Ann is in a way less likeable than Fanny; you get terribly exasperated with her. She's holding on to a series of precepts, Christian precepts about how to behave. 'You must not assert yourself', 'the assertion of your own desires, the taking of anything from anybody else is always wrong, always wicked'. She is held by convention, which is not virtue, but which John Bayley says can stand in for virtue and can hold you to virtue because it's been constructed for that purpose. Ann is held by convention, and convention says she is Randall's wife and must keep the house and forever wait for her husband who in fact wants to leave her and tries to demonise her. Convention says – and I think there's a difference between holding on to Randall and rejecting Felix – convention also says that she must reject this good man who is very similar to her but knows exactly what he wants.

She says yes to Felix, against her nature, in a conversation with Mildred. This is a very satisfying moment in this novel, because it's both very comic and very schematic, in the sense that you feel all the machinery of Iris Murdoch's ideas and the very structure of your own moral consciousness, both working fiercely. But dramatically it's perfectly natural and right, everything coheres.

> Mildred stood her ground. She barred Ann's way and said very quietly, 'You know that Felix is terribly in love with you?'
>
> Ann was silent, and it seemed afterwards that she had passed a vast time in reflection. What she said and did now was crucial, not so much for Mildred as for herself. Mildred had led up to her moment of theatre, but she must be cheated of it and sent away empty. There must be no drama here, no possible foothold for the imagination. What Mildred was trying to conjure up must be made nonsense of, must be made somehow not to exist. The thing must be laughed off briskly. Mildred must be clapped on the shoulder and taken to her coffee. There must be no admission of knowledge or interest, no confused looks, nothing. Again it was no and nothing.
>
> 'Yes,' said Ann. (Ch. 14)

SODRE: This passage is wonderful.

BYATT: I love that. It does bring up the idea in conjunction with Ann that the imagination is dangerous and is perceived by the good people, particularly Ann and the more ambivalent Douglas Swann, as a force that can lead to disaster and terror. This is true also in Murdoch's earlier novel *The Bell* (1958), where the saint in the book, a man called James Tayper Pace, in effect tells Michael the homosexual would-be priest, 'You mustn't even think about this illicit relationship, you mustn't think about helping this boy that you are in love with and shouldn't be in love with, you must simply not think, not imagine, and in this will lie virtue.' He implies: 'The moment you start making a spiritual drama out of it evil can creep in.' In *An Unofficial Rose* Ann is trying to be good by keeping to the rules because the rules actually contain goodness in them, because goodness made the rules. And she says no. Where do you think Iris Murdoch is in relation to that? Do you think she feels Ann should have said no, or should have said yes? Or is it simply dramatic?

SODRE: My impression here is that it is dramatic, and it works, it surprises the reader; it also reveals that when Ann is more aware of how she functions, she can, for a moment, be less trapped in herself. But Ann should eventually be able to say yes, when it would be conventionally all right; the fact that she ultimately doesn't shows in what way she is different from Henry James's quietly determined Maggie. Maggie's silence is her strength; Ann's, her weakness. Ann's 'yes' is only momentary; ultimately, for psychological reasons, she is compelled to say no. First, she has to be bound by conventional thinking because she is muddled and lost, and for her convention is structure, a solid reality; she needs 'form', just like Randall says he wants 'form'. Secondly, Ann is so terrified of her own potentially violent passions, she has had to repress so much, that whatever puts her in contact with her own desire immediately becomes a threat to her stability. Felix says, I can take you to Greece, I can take you to a different universe of love and sexual passion, and she answers, that will be impossible. And even when it's not wrong any more for it to be possible, when Randall leaves, it's still impossible because she's so afraid of anything 'dark' in herself. Hugh says Ann has no darkness, he and Randall married women without shade. But of course there isn't such a thing as a person totally devoid of darkness, it's just that Ann is too frightened of it. This is part of her relationship with Randall; when she finds that she is not able to let go of him she half realises, I think rather beautifully, that it's not just convention and Christianity that bind her to Randall, it's also that she has a dark passion for him, which she can only know about when he is gone; unconsciously whatever is dark in her personality is projected into him, thus making their characteristics so extremely polarised. Randall functions as a boundary for her too, as if having become shadeless and formless she needs somebody with an edge; his disappearance disturbs her sense of identity:

> For the fact was that, keeping pace demonically with her love for Felix, there had developed in her a dark new passion for Randall. It was as if one were the infernal mirror image of the other; and at times when she woke from a troubled sleep, not sure which of the two she had been dreaming of, she almost felt the loves to be interdependent. Being in love with Randall in this way was something entirely painful and with a brutality of its own, as if such a love could not but hurt its object. It was quite unlike her old romantic love for the young Randall, or her steady married love for her husband. She was not sure indeed how she recognized it as love at all. It was a kind of mutual haunting. It made her frightened; and because she suspected at times that it was simply her resentment and jealousy run mad, she tried not to indulge it. She began to need help. (Ch. 28)

But Felix can't help her, he is too kind, he lacks Randall's cruel edge.
BYATT: It's wonderful that Felix is a soldier. Because soldiers too represent violence, violence which has been completely ordered and controlled by convention after convention. Felix is not shapeless although he is virtuous, but he is inhibited by his sense of what it means to be an officer and a gentleman. *An Unofficial Rose* was written in 1962, just when everybody was thinking about liberation and breaking all bounds and annihilating convention – and Iris Murdoch asks her readers to think hard about what it really meant to be somebody who believed in oaths they had sworn and structures they were upholding. It was written when everyone was vehemently anti-military, marching and demonstrating against the Bomb. I find that intensely moving.

Do you think that the relationship between Ann and Randall is so sado-masochistic that it's actually hurting both of them? She's forcing him to be the torturer and he's forcing her to be more shapeless and victimised than she need be, and Felix wants her to be equal and she's forgotten how. Or never knew. Do we know?
SODRE: I think she probably knew once and then forgot how, because there are points when you see she can momentarily stand up to Randall,

as if she had remembered a firmer identity which she then loses again. The roles have been fixed in this sado-masochistic mode, so that the firmer part of Ann has got lost, projected into Randall, whose softness resides now in Ann. There is a wonderful image about the projection of blame, when Ann sees the process happening, as if she 'sometimes a little resentfully thought, since the others wanted to blame someone and she did not, she made a vacuum into which their blame ran'. (Ch. 14)

BYATT: Yes, there is the moment when she reflects that in some curious way she has become the person who is guilty of the death of her son, because Randall absolutely has to blame somebody, and she is there to be blamed. And yet you feel also that because Randall can blame Ann he isn't suffering the death in the way he would have done if he, like her, just suffered it. Iris Murdoch is interested in a kind of automatic structure in which a blow is passed on from one person to another person to another person until it meets a pure victim where it simply stops, because it isn't passed on. She takes this out of Simone Weil's religious ideas in *Gravity and Grace* and other places, where Weil says that true virtue is to accept the blow and not pass it on. But the gap between this kind of goodness and masochism is a hair's breadth, and if you look at the life of Simone Weil it's very difficult to know which is which.

SODRE: Yes, there is a very small gap between the two. Ann falls into this gap and this is where she is muddled: she can't tell the difference between love and masochism. What happens between Ann and Randall is entirely credible – their marriage is real, even if Randall himself is not always entirely believable. As their qualities become polarised in their marriage, you might associate them with maleness and femaleness, although they obviously don't need to be.

BYATT: No, because it works the other way between Emma Sands and Hugh.

SODRE: Exactly. It's interesting that she makes these contrasts, and makes sure that one doesn't think that a woman is necessarily all floppy and a man all edgy.

BYATT: I wanted to say, before we leave this topic, that the scene in which Randall engineers the row, which allows him to leave because he has finally caused Ann to shout at him, is absolutely beautifully dramatised, because it has a slightly mechanical structure. People go into rows knowing that there are certain sequential stages in a row which you have to go through, and then when you come out the other end you will have got what you want. And Randall begins the row knowing this. He shouts at Ann, knowing that in the end she will have to reply. And when he has finally forced her to reply he can blame her and go off to London. Iris Murdoch is at her best when she demonstrates this almost ritual or dancing structure of human behaviour, which you can almost abstract from the two individual people who are doing it, and say 'yes I recognise that, that is a *form* of human life'. I love that.

SODRE: Yes. She does it beautifully; this is one of my favourite scenes in this novel. Randall knows he will succeed, he knows eventually he will be able to make her feel guilty. Hugh, who is a witness, can see perfectly well what happened, but Ann can only stand up for herself for one second, then she falls into the muddle; she doesn't know what he's done, even though it's obvious to Hugh and he tells her. Randall consciously means to do it, he builds up that little scene, and it's completely deliberate. What is not entirely conscious in Randall, but works so well, is that he is terrified of Ann's capacity to make him feel guilty. So he tries to avoid this by making *her* feel guilty and then quickly closing the door on her and running away (thus symbolically preventing his projections coming back into him again). But she haunts him through her (unconscious) capacity to make him feel guilty: her formlessness and her softness and her vulnerability to guilt, paradoxically make him feel guilty. He can't bear the suffering Ann, so he makes her suffer more and then he has to get away. Which I think works very well.

BYATT: This is the psychology of the scapegoat. That's both the psychology of a sado-masochistic marriage and the psychology of the scapegoat. Which poor Ann is.

SODRE: I think this is a good point to think about Hugh, because he plays a part here. Hugh isn't being his usual stupid self, he knows exactly what's going on, but he is suffering from one of his problems: he very quickly becomes selfish. The scene ends with Hugh feeling concerned for Ann, who reminds him of Fanny and of his guilty past. He tells Randall to stop being so horrible, he tries to get Ann to understand what has happened and tries to console her, and then he gloomily realises that he 'now would have to stay at least until Thursday', and that he does not want to – like Randall, he wants to get away. Hugh's complacency and selfishness make him entirely real.

BYATT: The interesting thing about Iris Murdoch's novels is that there are always so many characters whose fate is interesting. One of the things I really like about this novel is that it opens with Hugh mourning or not mourning or wondering exactly how far he is mourning the death of his wife, with whom he has lived in bad faith for years and years because he should have perhaps gone off and lived with Emma Sands, who reappears dramatically at the graveside. I think Hugh and Mildred work so well because they are both representatives in a way, in so far as we the readers identify with them, of the *homme moyen sensuel*. They are trying to get through life and make sensible decisions, and all their decisions wound them slightly, incapacitate them slightly, and they go struggling on and they manage to survive. Whereas Randall and Ann and even Felix are in a state of extremity which almost pushes them into a tragedy. And Hugh and Mildred remain in a comic realist novel where what you do can have apparently appalling consequences but nevertheless the ordinary run of life goes on. This feeling of 'the ordinary run of life' (which after all is only a concept) going on is part of what you just said about Hugh appearing to be stupid and selfish. Iris Murdoch says more than once, when one of her characters is in mourning, that after a while 'the ordinary claims of the ego' will reassert themselves. (I am thinking particularly of the central characters of *The Bell* and *The Good Apprentice*.) She feels this to be both natural and saving. I think she puts the ordinary claims of the ego against the unnatural unselfishness of people like Ann who nevertheless have a higher idea of virtue than people like Hugh. I think both Hugh and Mildred are decent people with fairly strong egos. Does that make sense?

SODRE: I think Mildred is more decent, and has a much stronger ego, than Hugh. Hugh is lovable, but he is weaker. Murdoch doesn't describe him as capable of going through the mourning process and then coming out of it; she shows him finding ways of getting away with not going through this process. Hugh suffers from a kind of moral laziness! He muddles because he makes so many excuses for himself which Mildred never does; she does the opposite, she sees her position with total clarity. The whole question of Mildred's moral choice is interesting: paradoxically, she chooses *not* to act in a particular way, because it would benefit her if she did.

BYATT: She's quite surprised as well. Mildred is the link between the two parts of the book and the two sorts of characters, because Mildred would quite like to behave like Emma, who sees herself as a *metteur en scène*, and believes she can control people's lives and organise them like the plot of a detective story which she writes. She would like to be a *deus ex machina*. Mildred has a little go at pushing people's lives: she tries very hard to cause both Felix and Ann to stand up and act independently, and she fails.

SODRE: But she's very good at working it all out, terribly clever. Except she can't do it when it's to benefit herself.

BYATT: No, and within the machinery of the comic novel this means that in some curious way she can be recompensed and get what she wanted, because she has made the act of renunciation. George Eliot would have deeply disapproved of this. Eliot's wonderful essay 'Silly Novels by Lady Novelists' was prompted by her scorn for the idea of Compensation, '[a doctrine] which I detest, considered as a way of life'. Eliot believed strongly that those who renounce anything should do so for nothing; you shouldn't expect to get anything given to you. Otherwise it isn't a renunciation. But this is a comic novel, like a Shakespearean comedy, so in a sense it is appropriate that Mildred should be rewarded for her virtue. And she's rewarded by the machinery of other people behaving much worse, really. Such as Miranda. It is wonderful how everybody's moral nature is *shown* to interact with everybody else's moral nature. If Murdoch had only three characters, or even as few characters as there are in *A Severed Head*, you wouldn't get such a complicated moral patterning. Mildred relates not only to Hugh but to Humphrey and to Felix.

SODRE: And even to Emma.

BYATT: And to Emma, and to Ann. And you can see her thinking about all these people. Iris Murdoch says in her essay, 'Against Dryness', that what is required in the moral world and so in the novel is a picture of the moral world as complicated and full of lots of other people all with their own structures and intentions.

BYATT: Should we discuss the 'bad' characters?

SODRE: I find Randall not entirely believable, not properly drawn into complete reality. I think Randall in relation to Ann works, I think the marriage works; and as Emma the enchanter's puppet, a fairytale character, he is fine. But once you have Randall on his own, he doesn't sound true; the machinery behind the writing shows too much. I don't like it when Randall says he needs 'form', because 'form' is Iris Murdoch's own word.

> ' "Poor Randall," they say, "he's hardly there any more." I need a different world, a formal world. I need form. Christ, how I fade!'

> He laughed suddenly, turning to face Hugh, and took the rose out of his hand.
>
> 'Form?'
>
> 'Yes, yes, form, structure, will, something to encounter, something to make me *be*. Form, as this rose has it. That's what Ann hasn't got. She's as messy and flabby and open as a bloody dogrose. That's what gets me down. That's what destroys all my imagination, all the bloody footholds. Ah well, you wouldn't understand. *You* managed all right without fading away. What's it matter. Would you like a drink?' (Ch. 3)

Why can't Randall say he needs hardness, or opacity or just structure? When he says he needs form, you feel the writer hasn't done enough homework.

BYATT: That's a very good way of putting it. It is precisely her own word, and Randall slips into a kind of language which is very like her own philosophical writings on aesthetics, her remarks on Plato, or on Simone Weil's valuing of formlessness.

SODRE: And 'necessity', also a word Randall uses.

BYATT: Yes, this happens throughout Iris Murdoch: you get characters suddenly talking a kind of Murdochian shorthand.

You could argue that Randall is as he is because of Hugh's relationship with Emma. He feels that his father perhaps *should* have gone away with the person he desired. And so he repeats his father's behaviour, and the person he desires is attached to the person his father desired. This then follows through in Randall's child, who desires the man her mother desires. Freud did point out that such terribly rigorous structures of behaviour do actually pertain in the structure of human families – people do desire their father's mistress, children follow in their parents' paths of desire. You can imagine that when you *think* about the characters here, but you don't actually believe in it emotionally when you read the particular scenes in which these patterns are enacted.

SODRE: I think that's right. And also it depends, I think, on what the writer is creating at that particular point in a novel, on what is meant by each sentence and scene; if at that moment we are reading a comedy, as you said, we don't need to entirely believe it, because what the author is producing is type and pattern and relationship looked at from the outside. What I love about *A Severed Head* (which is an extremely funny, terribly clever send-up of psychoanalysis!) is the way in which these brilliantly crafted 'types' are immediately recognisable, how they relate to each other like comic verbal cartoons. You never want them to be real people! But when the characters are completely seen from the inside, like Ann and Hugh here, their psychology has to be fully worked out. Randall is sometimes looked at from the outside and sometimes from the inside. And when something is too thin, you feel the author is letting you down – frustrating your need to know more.

BYATT: The inside bits go wrong. Randall has an outside seen by other people –

SODRE: Randall as the Oedipal boy works perfectly well as an idea. It's the actual Randall in his relationship with Lindsay, for instance, that you don't entirely see in flesh and blood.

BYATT: This is partly a technical problem. I think all of Iris Murdoch's novels are – I want to say belaboured, but – beset by the problem that she does genuinely see human relationships and human society as extending infinitely, and she does try to make little threads of relationships out into the void, so that the characters have meaningful relationships with people who are not described in the bit of their life that is within this novel. She tries to create worlds that are not closed, even if they're highly formal structures. And what has happened to Randall, I think partly, is that all of his relationship with Lindsay, which could have made a whole novel for another writer, has had to be crammed into two or three tiny scenes, and indeed into two or three tiny symbols, because what one remembers most of Lindsay is the long lengths of her blonde hair. When she is introduced Murdoch describes the coils of hair at least three times in three or four pages, as in this example:

> She was, whatever her other short-comings, undeniably beautiful, with a pale complexion, very rounded head, long golden braids of hair, large brow and great expressive light brown eyes. She resembled Diane de Poitiers, and had round small breasts which would have delighted Clouet, and with which Randall's acquaintance had been but brief and tentative; since Emma intervened. (Ch. 7)

This is a trick you can learn from Dickens as a writer: if you haven't got room to make a character, if you give him or her one totally memorable physical characteristic, the character becomes symbolic and stands for itself. I've tried this, partly because I learned it from Lindsay Rimmer, and it's always worked. Somebody will always come up and say to you, that is an absolutely wonderful character you created with that great big plait down her back. In fact the character consisted only of the plait down her back, she had no other character. But it was memorable. I think Iris Murdoch has tried that with Lindsay Rimmer: she says she's the earthly Venus, and she says she's a bit of a slut. And with those very powerful statements she tries to make her be a character. But she remains 'flat', as Forster would have said.

SODRE: But I don't think Lindsay needs to be a real character, whereas I think Randall does; what matters is his attachment to somebody beautiful and bad who, as you pointed out, is in his mind connected to his past. The other thing about Lindsay's hair is that it is just like Susannah's hair in the Tintoretto, it's all plaited round her head, so she is also linked with Hugh's other great love. So, literally, she's that simple.

BYATT: It's difficult for a real character to go to bed with a symbol. In fact Murdoch almost pulls that off too. Because there is a wonderful moment when Randall – the first description I had ever read in fiction of a man being unable to perform a sexual act when he actually gets into bed. I thought, my God, of course that happens – but I've never read it in a novel before. And then he thinks his sado-masochistic thoughts about doing down Emma, and finds after all he can penetrate Lindsay. That's brilliant. The moment of not being able to get it up.

> Lindsay was lying full length on the undone bed. Randall knelt and looked. Then he looked into her face. It was as if their eyes had become huge and luminous so that when they gazed they were together in a great cavern. Slowly he pulled himself up to sit upon the edge of the bed. Then he turned away from her and hid his face in his hands.
>
> 'What is it, dear, dear?' murmured Lindsay. She caressed his back.
>
> 'I'm not going to be any good,' said Randall. 'God! I was afraid of this.'
>
> 'It doesn't matter. Embrace me.'
>
> He stretched himself out almost stiffly and buried his face against her. His arms pinioned her with violence.
>
> After a little while she said again, 'There. Relax. It doesn't matter.'
>
> 'It does. I wish I hadn't talked so much about Emma. I'm poisoned.'
>
> 'Emma's not important here. She's not important any more.'
>
> 'Ah – not important any more. You know, Lindsay, I don't think I really like Emma.'

'I don't think I like her either. In fact I think I dislike her.'

'I dislike her too.'

'In fact I think I detest her.'

'And I detest her. Oh Lindsay –'

It was a few minutes later that he said, 'Do you know, I think it's going to be all right after all.' (Ch. 15)

SODRE: It's brilliant because of course Randall is completely entangled in the fairytale created by Emma, and although he is dreading Emma being around, Emma is central to his whole fantasy about Lindsay, to his erotic pull towards Lindsay. One of the complications about having a fairytale atmosphere for some of the story is that it is hard to make the transition to concrete reality. This is also Randall's problem:

> Now that he was passing, as he thought, out of fantasy into reality, the real world seemed a region even more fantastic than the dream palace he had inhabited before. He felt like a favourite slave who has been kept on cushions and fed on sherbet and who is suddenly put at the gate and told he is free. Such stories end with the sword. (Ch. 15)

Taking your point about his impotence: the 'real world' threatens Randall with castration, terrible things happen if you act out your Oedipal fantasies. (This makes me think again of the theatricals in *Mansfield House* as an enactment of forbidden sexual fantasies, and of Sir Thomas's return with a metaphorical 'sword'.) The author has put the reader in the ambiguous position of being 'enchanted' by the fairytale atmosphere surrounding Emma whilst simultaneously being told that, whilst Randall needs to believe in Emma's magic powers, you always know she is just a very clever, manipulative old lady. He looks for the 'witch' concretely under the bed:

> Randall knelt down and lifted the coverlet. His heart was beating violently as if he really expected to see the form of Emma crouching in the darkness. There was nothing there except several pairs of shoes and a suitcase. (Ch. 15)

BYATT: And then the voice comes on the tape recorder. The witch can actually speak, be in two places at once and can be heard.

> Randall watched her open-mouthed, his hands hanging. He was prepared for anything, for a strange darkening of the room and the appearance in luminous effigy of a magical Emma and Lindsay.

Lindsay pulled the tape recorder out from where it was nestling under the frill of Emma's chair. Crouched above it she examined it and adjusted the tape. Then she set it going. With hypnotic slowness the two wheels began to revolve. She turned her eyes, sombre and stern, upon Randall. After a moment the silence of the attentive room was broken by Emma's voice.

'If you're going to do it it's got to be now. There's no time for theory now, no time for ifs and buts. You're in the dark, and you must go forward in the dark.' (Ch. 15)

SODRE: That's wonderful: Emma at this point is dictating her crime story, but what she says fits in exactly with Randall's fear of her magically knowing he is about to make love to Lindsay. He can't make love without bringing Emma in as a hateful witch, and he can't have an erection if he is too afraid of her castrating sword . . . The best thing about Randall is his being caught in the complicated world that exists between pure fantasy and ordinary, adult reality.

BYATT: Another interesting part of the weaving pattern of repeating relationships between the rapacious and the patient, is Fanny. It is important that Randall should have married a woman who so resembled Fanny and that Hugh always thought of Ann as simply being a repeat of Fanny until right at the end when there's this vision, which I love, of Fanny going through life carrying a little flag upright.

SODRE: Or half upright: 'It was as if at the end he had recognised in her a dignity which she had had all along but had kept humbly lowered like a dipped flag or a crumpled crest. He was glad, after all, that he had stayed with her. He was glad that he had been good to her.' (Ch. 36) I think Hugh is again being complacent. Emma has suffered and paid for Hugh's act, and so has Fanny.

BYATT: I think, despite Emma saying she has suffered, the reader is wholly on Fanny's side. Do you think?

SODRE: I don't think so. Even though Emma is not entirely realistically portrayed, I think it is believable that she has suffered. And I think again Hugh in his general cloudiness of mind doesn't have ever to completely grasp the fact that Emma and Fanny have both suffered. You referred to the beginning, to Hugh at the funeral resenting Fanny and not being able to mourn her and think of her positively, and to Hugh in the end, having worked something through, so that he has more respect for Fanny. But the point you make is that there's something that he missed out on. I think what he missed out is that he wasn't good to Fanny. He is slightly contemptuous of her. When he thinks of himself as virtuous, he's not being virtuous.

BYATT: Except that he is staying within the bounds of the conventions which are a form of virtue, as John Bayley says about the conventions of marriage in *The Golden Bowl*. His instincts are not to hurt where it is right not to hurt, and he can't bring himself to hurt Fanny. And I think this is fair, he isn't a man who could hurt people intentionally – he doesn't live with Fanny out of inertia, even though he may at times accuse himself of this. He is confused in the way Randall is confused, but much more profoundly confused, I think, because you feel that he was more genuinely in love with Emma, than Randall is with Lindsay. Randall is compelled by something, either a phantom of beauty, or some kind of demon. The word demon is frequently used to describe Randall and what is driving him. Whereas you feel that what Hugh did feel for Emma was love – in the way falling in love overtakes you and overwhelms you and makes you a completely different person. And this is another thing, the machinery of which interests Iris Murdoch very much, the way in which the blow of love can transfigure a human being so that everything in them is changed between yesterday and today.

SODRE: I like the way Murdoch describes what happened between Hugh and Emma. Hugh had always thought of Emma as a rather absurd friend of Fanny's, and then one day he looked again. She describes this moment:

> From the moment when, in Emma's dark over-furnished flat at Notting Hill, he had with a burst of illumination which came quite suddenly, and with a deep prophetic groan, taken her into his arms, until the moment when he had walked away down the long corridor in a coma of misery, had been a space of two years. It sometimes seemed to him that that time had been his only real life, and what began and ended it his only real actions. (Ch. 1)

So there isn't a conscious decision at that moment, there couldn't be, which I think is a point she's making clearly. I agree that Hugh did not want to hurt Fanny; he has, nevertheless, hurt her, but to be able to survive, not to feel too guilty, he has to make her all right in his mind. Iris Murdoch says in her essay, 'On "God" and "Good" ' that you can't fall out of love by a jump of the will, which is true: 'Deliberately falling out of love is not a jump of the will, it is the acquiring of new objects of attention and thus of new energies as a result of refocusing'.

BYATT: You can fall out of love suddenly, which she understands and many people don't. You can fall out of love the way you fall in it. You can have the negative vision equally powerfully. Suddenly one day you look at the person and realise it's gone, whatever it was.

SODRE: I think Murdoch makes it clear that Hugh's moral failure is complacency – which links to the question of inattention. Hugh is sometimes capable of understanding the other person, but he does not sustain that if it costs him too much effort and pain. She describes it clearly, in relation to his mourning for Fanny. Hugh knew that he felt this pain acutely, but he also knew how he could find ways in his mind not to miss her so much, and he only partly approved of this. She does describe this so perfectly; you can see the movement, described with accuracy and economy, when complacency and turning a blind eye take over in Hugh, and he mentally moves away.

BYATT: A survival instinct, a kind of automatic . . .

SODRE: Yes, and it's possible to sympathise with him; he is human in a way that feels real.

BYATT: He's just not good, and there are characters in Murdoch's novels who *are* good who would have stayed with imagining it, because they felt they must.

SODRE: Ann imagines Randall too much, which ends up being self-destructive. Mildred imagines exactly right. The 'good' character whom I intensely dislike (I was going to say, as a person!) is Douglas Swann. I find him a believable, but horrible, character.

BYATT: Swann is very interesting, because he requires an almost abstract, absolute virtue from others. The whole structure of convention I've been talking about, which holds people to being good parents and good wives, and to not suddenly stabbing each other – the whole structure depends on the authority of a Good which Swann claims to know. So he doesn't really even have to look and see what Ann is feeling, he simply *knows* what Ann ought to do, and what it is his duty to hold her to. Ann and Felix are both more human than Swann in their attitude to morals. They would accept the same moral structure as Swann but they would also believe that they had more room to question it or make moral decisions within it.

SODRE: Ann knows that Swann's position is too simple to encompass all her experience. A passage I find entirely convincing is when Swann says to Ann that she must always wait for Randall and always love him. It is because Swann is so cardboardy good at that moment that Ann can get herself together and think for herself; she senses something perverse in him: 'It was as if he wanted to break her down. Perhaps he did, even if unconsciously, want her to break down so that he could console her' (Ch. 14). She's beginning to realise that her attachment to Randall is not just made of pure love, that there is something more destructive involved. Douglas Swann may be giving her advice which would lead her to something destructive.

BYATT: Yes. I always set that beside Hugh saying that he has performed an act which was too high for him. He did the right thing, he stayed with Fanny, but it has not made Fanny happy and it hurt Emma. In a sense Swann is simply telling Ann to perform an act which is too high for her; she hasn't got the saintliness of spirit for this kind of renunciation to be meaningful. In that context Hugh is a better character than Ann because he is nearer – I don't know if I really mean this – Hugh's instincts are nearer right in some curious way; Ann's muddle is much worse because she's nearer to Swann.

SODRE: Hugh's selfishness is saner than Ann's unselfishness. You have to be self-protective, which Ann can't be: she must never have what she wants, she is self-destructive, which Hugh isn't. There's nothing unvirtuous about self-preservation, which is the word you use. Ann is incapable of it, because she's too caught up with Randall, which is precisely what torments Randall. Felix tells Ann that she holds on to Randall out of spite, which is a bit simplistic, but he is right about there being something perverse in Ann's possessiveness of Randall, which terrifies him; it makes him feel guilty and claustrophobic.

I just want to add something about Swann's goodness, which I think is suspect. I think Ann senses that there is something in his 'saintliness' which is not to do with love and goodness, when he suggests you should love Hitler; children of this new generation shouldn't be taught to hate Hitler.

> 'I can't agree,' said Hugh. 'It's a matter of practical politics. You speak as if we were in fact all saints. As the world runs, evil soon makes tools out of those who don't hate it. Hatred is our best protection.' (Ch. 6)

I think Hugh is right, I think he knows, like Ann knows, that there is something in Swann's position that leads to corruption; aggression is not focused on what is bad. This is an important point I think, that Iris Murdoch makes about evil.

BYATT: Yes – she makes it in a way that is very complicated, and does do justice to the Swann position. Because what he says is not stupid. And just before the bit you quoted from Hugh:

> 'Are you suggesting that we should love Hitler?' said Hugh. He felt irritated with Swann and wished he would go.
>
> 'Not exactly,' said Swann. 'That would be, from the point of view of our generation, an impossible task, except perhaps for a saint. But there can be, even for Hitler, a sort of intelligent compassion. Involuntary hatred is a great misfortune, but cultivated hatred is a positive evil. The young have escaped the terrible compulsion to hate which has been our lot. They should be left uncorrupted and judged lucky.' (Ch. 6)

Now that is not a stupid remark.

SODRE: Well, yes and no. It's not a stupid remark because he is a clever man, making a general point about loving your enemy, which is a good Christian point. But what Hugh senses is that there is a way of misusing this that will allow evil to have the upper hand. Loving 'Hitler' in this particular context means Ann should love everything that's bad in Randall, which of course she should not. Randall is the cruel tyrant in Ann's life.

BYATT: But Swann doesn't say love, he says we should have an intelligent compassion. There is a possible argument that 'a sort of intelligent compassion' rather than cultivated hatred is a better moral position to be in, but it does cause immense stress and strain. But also you feel that Swann hasn't quite earned the right even to claim that. You feel his own self-knowledge isn't complete and that his feelings for Ann are not something he wholly understands either. But of course that wouldn't necessarily invalidate what he says. I don't think he's claiming sanctity, there are characters who are much more vertiginously on the edge of sainthood in Murdoch's books than Swann.

SODRE: I think he is rather seductively suggesting that Ann should be saintly, even though he doesn't say it explicitly. It makes him into somebody who is misusing 'truth' (like Palmer Anderson, the psychoanalyst in *A Severed Head*).

BYATT: Yes, this is interesting, because Swann in a sense stands with all the poor in spirit and the Fanny Price and Edmund side of *Mansfield Park*, and yet he is perceived as manipulative and enchanter-like and pushing and trying to arrange people's lives in a way that although it doesn't exactly appear to resemble that of Emma Sands and Mildred, is not so different. And he is trying to shape Ann's life for his own ends, because he would like her to stay where she is, as well as because he genuinely believes that marriage ought to be respected. But you don't feel he's anywhere near as good a man as Felix, who appears to be much more muddled because he doesn't know what to do about his French lover.

BYATT: Thinking about what one can feel about Hitler leads to thinking about the the German dagger which was given by Felix to Steve, the son who is now dead. Penn loves the dagger with deep passion; Penn thinks it's absolutely beautiful, with a swastika on it, whereas his seniors feel all the horror and complexity of terror that goes with it, with a swastika on it. And Swann says, ' "The young are not touched by this." "No, I suppose not," said Ann, "it's a rather disconcerting aspect of their innocence." ' (Ch. 6). How far do we believe in the innocence of Penn and Miranda?

SODRE: We don't, of course, have any grounds at all to think Miranda is innocent, but we believe in Penn's innocence. What makes Penn so excited by the knife is that it seems sinister to him, and like all the other 'good' characters, he has an attraction for the sinister side of things. These sunny characters who are so good have something in them that is missing, something that needs to be completed by the 'dark' characters. I feel the knife is not quite real, though, not a symbol that is fully used, although it makes sense in terms of Penn's excitement in relation to what he feels is dangerous and incomprehensible; Miranda's mysteriousness and incomprehensibility are essential components of Penn's erotic attraction to her.

BYATT: And the only moment when she responds to him is when he hurts her. He hurts her quite badly and ignores her instructions not to touch her, and this makes her appear to be very pleased, and she of course is already part of the structure of passing on pain which was started by Hugh's love of Emma, at least in this book, and moved itself into Randall's desire to hurt Ann.

SODRE: And to be hurt by Lindsay.

BYATT: And to be hurt by Lindsay. And this moves into Miranda's desire. Miranda has been rather clever because she's fixed on Felix as an object of love, a man who is simultaneously a soldier and hurter, and a good man, an officer and gentleman. I love the scene in which Penn and Felix have the competition to see who can throw the stone the furthest, and Penn has this moment of pure balance when he knows that he can out-throw Felix's last throw absolutely. And Iris Murdoch makes him into a visionary Australian cricketer who can throw a boomerang miles on the plain. Then he sees Miranda and the throw goes short, and you see he's been trapped in something.

SODRE: I think it's Miranda's knee again – he is aware of falling in love with her when he sees her knees, when they are visiting Steve's tomb:

> Penn thought, I can beat that. It was almost as if his will alone could carry the stone bird-like and drop it out of sight in the middle of the reed bed. He loosened his shoulders and drooped his arms for a moment as his coach had told him to do. He moved into action. But just as his hand was coming forward he saw Miranda, who had advanced to the edge of the beach a little beyond the group, and with apparent unconcern was taking her shoes and socks off. Penn's stone fell a little short of his second throw and well behind Felix's. There were groans of commiseration. (Ch. 26)

BYATT: It's very believable, all that. But there's something wrong with Miranda herself.

SODRE: I think it's the passion for Felix. I think that it needn't be there. I suppose that's me trying to rewrite the book, but I think Miranda could be truthfully caught between a passion for her father and a passion for her mother; she's terribly competitive with Ann, but also possessive, and therefore would want to take Ann's man away from her, whoever he was. It would be possible for Miranda to invent, defensively, a pseudo-passion for Felix, but the reader would have to know about its falseness. The reader is invited to believe in this love, when it would be much more convincing to suppose that Miranda is an extremely controlling child who wants to split the parents from each other and from any other relationships, so that each parent is made to relate only to her. She consciously plans to get rid of Lindsay, so that she can live alone with Randall; she could also be unconsciously identified with the Randall that wants Ann to be alone and waiting for ever, in her negative Oedipus complex.

BYATT: In fact what you're saying makes clear to me something I hadn't understood. It is that the daughter/mother relationship isn't one, that is why it doesn't work. Perhaps it takes the psychoanalyst to see this. The way in which Miranda manipulates Ann is partly the way any manipulative child manipulates its parent. But what is not there is the terrible need for Ann and the love for Ann which at some level must have motivated this manipulating. The child appears to be detached and scintillating like a separate star, and yet her behaviour is that of somebody deeply implicated in her relationship with her parents, but you don't feel it. Nor do you feel that she is so damaged that she doesn't relate to them, you feel that it just isn't in the book and it should have been. Do you think that's right?

SODRE: I think that's right: it almost works, because up to a certain extent one knows she's deeply involved with her parents, but there is something not entirely realised, and the introduction of her love for Felix in the end falsifies it. The dolls, her little princes, work in the sense that through them she acts out her absolute wish, which is a driving passion, to be omnipotently in control of her parents. Miranda would like to be an Emma to her parents, to treat them as puppets, and her playing with dolls is a symbolic way of being in control. But the dolls are a powerful symbol which one does not entirely understand. Are they princes because she wants to manipulate men, or maybe because they stand for her brother? Perhaps Miranda, in her relationship with her mother, would like to be a boy, Ann's little prince in addition to Randall's princess. All this is possible, would make sense psychologically, but it doesn't entirely click.

BYATT: You don't think it's to do with the family romance? One of the things I feel about the dolls is that what is stressed about them is their watchfulness, they represent Miranda's watchfulness multiplied. And I always connect them, though this may be far-fetched, with the idea of the multiplication of the snakes on the Medusa's head, which Iris Murdoch, in her book on Sartre, quotes Freud as saying represents 'the female genitals feared not desired'. She says in the same paragraph that for Sartre the Medusa's snakes represented our fear of being watched, overlooked. I feel that the dolls represent family life feared not desired, or something. There are too many of them, they proliferate, there are babies all over, and yet the babies are not children. The dolls are not babies. For most little girls who have a doll, it's a baby. Miranda neither is nor has a baby. She has this watchful company of enchanters, which Mildred knocks over one by one with her umbrella in one of the best scenes in the book, and all their eyes close and they have to stop watching.

> She turned to go, and nearly tripped over the dolls. 'Isn't Miranda getting a little old for dolls?' She regarded the little figures. Then she began to knock them over gently one by one with her

> umbrella. As each one fell backward on the floor its waxen eyelids closed. (Ch. 14)

SODRE: This is a very good psychological point, because Miranda is a child who cannot leave the parents alone, she has to control them all the time. Any relationship between the parents is feared and hated, not ever desired, as you say; the appearance of Felix could symbolically re-establish the hateful parental sexuality (and they might have a new baby, which, as you imply, Miranda would hate).
BYATT: In a way we're saying that we think Miranda's character is more convincing than we thought it was, in the sense that we can give a perfectly good description of why Miranda is as she is. Yet, all the same, you don't feel she's quite real, do you?
SODRE: No.

BYATT: In one sense this is the novel of a moral philosopher about the nature of good and evil. It's a novel by a moral philosopher who believes that you can and should discuss the meaning of good and evil. It is the novel of a moral philosopher, to put the argument briefly, who believes that our ideas of what is good and our ideas of what is evil in the society in which we live have always been provided by religion, and that we have now become a society which is no longer religious. Murdoch believes that we have not wholly understood that our ideas of what is good and what is evil have been formed by what our society has thought in the past, and has ceased to think. Our sense of Good depends upon the sanction of a God in whom we no longer believe. If we do understand that, we lay ourselves open to a Nietzschean vision of chaos and absence of value, and of words themselves – such as good, and evil – being meaningless.

She also believes that Freud accurately described human energy. She says that the psyche is a mechanism whose attachments and sexual ambivalence are hard to understand, and that it constantly deflects you away from your intelligent attempts to understand what goodness is. Many of her characters aren't even making an intelligent attempt to understand what goodness is. But I think she believes that morality partly consists in intelligently seeing what is going on and attempting to understand it.
SODRE: Yes; I'll read her analysis of Freud's view in her essay 'On "God" and "Good" ':

> Freud takes a thoroughly pessimistic view of human nature. He

> sees the psyche as an egocentric system of quasi-mechanical energy, largely determined by its own individual history, whose natural attachments are sexual, ambiguous, and hard for the subject to understand or control. Introspection reveals only the deep tissue of ambivalent motive, and fantasy is a stronger force than reason. Objectivity and unselfishness are not natural to human beings.

But of course psychoanalytic theory does have implicit in it a very clear sense of good and evil, in the concept of the life and the death instincts; 'the ego is not master of his own house,' as Freud put it; the question of not being able to know your own mind and being dominated by impulses and forces that are beyond consciousness, and that therefore the idea of free will is constantly having to be played against this sense of powerful unconscious and therefore unknowable forces. On the other hand, the question of the struggle between life instinct and death instinct is very much a moral question. Love and hate are always present, each trying to take the upper hand; concern for others is constantly disrupted by the wish to be at the centre, by envy and greed.

The concept of a death instinct comes up in the way Murdoch thinks out the psychological functioning of her characters; for instance, in the characters who have no shade but are attracted to something that is dark in others. When she shows how Ann is attracted to a darkness in Randall, she implicitly puts forward the idea that destructive impulses operate, unconsciously, in Ann. There is always the sense of determinism, but there is also a sense of being able, through insight and self-knowledge, to negotiate with oneself a position of taking responsibility for one's destructiveness, and trying to modify it; Klein calls this 'the depressive position', where concern for one's loved ones predominates. Murdoch brings these conflicts to life in her characters, in marvellously complicated and interesting combinations in this novel.

BYATT: It is possible to diagnose fantasy even if you can't hold on to knowing what your own fantasies are. Indeed Murdoch's characters do from time to time diagnose it in themselves and in others. They move in and out of consciousness and they move in and out of being purely driven by the dark forces. They have lucid moments.

SODRE: Moments when they are able to have in their mind a clear, truthful picture of what they're up to. Yes. Mildred is her most lucid, and therefore most mature, character in this novel.

BYATT: Another thing Murdoch says in her essays, which is important in all her novels I think, is that moral decisions are not made blindly in a leap, but are the product of a lifetime's habit of attention or inattention. If you have always paid attention (a word of Simone Weil's) to what was going on, you will almost automatically do the right thing when you come to it, or at least do the thing which your mode of attention has led you to.

SODRE: Of course George Eliot so beautifully describes that. One of the things she's so magnificent at is describing states of mind connected to the struggle for self-knowledge against the part of the self that prefers consoling lies. This struggle is brilliantly illustrated in the story of Dorothea's progress from psychological blindness to self-knowledge and knowledge of the other and their 'equivalent centre of self', in *Middlemarch*. And in *Deronda* Gwendolen moves from narcissistic self-idealisation and ignorance to acknowledging her destructiveness. George Eliot's main philosophical sense is to do with moral Good being understanding of others and sympathy – sympathy is the word she uses, to mean insight leading to the understanding of mental processes in other human beings.

BYATT: Even Hitler. Yes, you feel that George Eliot would have been interested in the question of whether you can feel intelligent compassion for Hitler. At the moment when Gwendolen decides to marry Grandcourt there's this wonderful image, 'quick, quick like pages in a book' she flicks through her life and feels that her life has impelled her to make this decision as she does make it. It's very like Ann trying to work out whether she can or can't marry Felix. Both novelists depict a moment of choice which is in fact determined by a whole history, which the readers are aware of. But the same mixture of freedom and control is working in both cases.

BYATT: This is also very much a novel about what's artificial and what's natural, what's art and what's nature. The enchanter figure who attempts to make other people's lives into a work of art is Emma Sands. She attempts to write Hugh's life, Randall's life, everything that goes on at Grayhallock, as though it was a detective story by Emma Sands. There are at least two other forms of art – the hybrid roses which are partly nature and partly art, and of course, the Tintoretto. I think Iris Murdoch does think of art as a form of knowledge, and also of good art as a form of pursuit of the Good.

SODRE: She says it quite explicitly in her essay 'The Idea of Perfection', doesn't she?

> I would suggest that the authority of the Good seems to us something necessary because the realism (ability to perceive reality) required for goodness is a kind of intellectual ability to perceive what is true, which is automatically at the same time a suppression of self. *The necessity of the good is then an aspect of the kind of necessity involved in any technique for exhibiting fact.*
>
> One might start from the assertion that morality, goodness, is a form of realism. The idea of a really good man living in a private dream would seem unacceptable. Of course a good man may be infinitely eccentric but he must know certain things about his surroundings, most obviously the existence of other people and their claims. The chief enemy of excellence in morality (and also in art) is personal fantasy: the tissue of self-aggrandizing and consoling wishes and dreams which prevents one from seeing what there is outside one. Rilke said of Cézanne that he did not paint 'I like it', he painted 'There it is'. This is not easy and requires, in art or morals, a discipline. One might say here that art is an excellent analogy of morals, or indeed that it is in this respect a case of morals. We cease to be in order to attend to the existence of something else, a natural object, a person in need. We can see in mediocre art, where perhaps it is even more clearly seen than in mediocre conduct, the intrusion of fantasy, the assertion of self, the dimming of any reflection of the real world.
>
> Art and morals are, with certain provisos . . . one. Their essence is the same. The essence of both of them is love. Love is the perception of individuals. Love is the extremely difficult realisation that something other than oneself is real. Love, and so art and morals, is the discovery of reality. What stuns us into a realisation of our supersensible destiny is not, as Kant imagined, the formlessness of nature but rather its unutterable particularity; and most particular and individual of all natural things is the mind of man.

BYATT: Here is Murdoch's rich and ambivalent description of the Tintoretto:

> Most of all the Tintoretto glowed upon her with a jewelled beneficence. It lighted the room now, like a small sun. It was not a very large picture: it represented a naked woman and was almost certainly an earlier version of the figure of Susannah in the great Susannah Bathing in Vienna. Only it was no sketch, but a great picture in its own right and justly of some fame: a notable segment in the vast seemingly endless honeycomb of the master's genius; and well might a spectator think of honey, looking upon that plump, bent, delicious, golden form, one leg gilding the green water into which it was plunged. A heavy twining complication of golden hair crowned a face of radiant spiritual vagueness which could only have been imagined by Tintoretto. Golden bracelets composed her apparel, and a pearl whose watery whiteness both reflected and resisted the soft surrounding honey-coloured shades. It was a picture which might well enslave a man, a picture round which crimes might be committed. (Ch. 10)

What do you feel it represents?

SODRE: I feel different things, I'm not really sure about the Tintoretto. As a great work of art, it represents the possibility of having something that symbolises the Good, and that also transcends ordinary life. It is also in opposition to life, because it can be perfect, whereas life is extremely imperfect. One can think of it as symbolising goodness for Hugh – aesthetic beauty and moral beauty being identified with each other in his mind, and in his internal world representing his wish to preserve and protect his good objects. But the painting is also Hugh's object of desire, in opposition to his love of Fanny (who is said to have been afraid of the Tintoretto as a rival), and in that sense it represents a pull towards idealising something which causes a withdrawal from his ordinary relationships. It also represents the more imaginative, more passionate world that Hugh temporarily inhabits with Emma.

One more thing about the Tintoretto: the picture depicts Susannah and the Elders, and I thought that one of the things that's interesting in this novel, and which I like very much, is the fact that it centres so much on elderly people falling in love with other elderly people, which makes them very different from the horrible, lecherous elders in the Tintoretto. There is something very hopeful and very gratifying about the fact that love and life go on, as people aged seventy fall in love in equally passionate ways.

BYATT: I think they probably do. The old faces in the complete picture of Susannah and the Elders are ambivalent because they're partly grotesque and their desire is predatory. Tintoretto's Susannah is a beautiful naked woman who is the object of intense sexual desire, but also of pure aesthetic contemplation, if such a thing can exist. Looking at the painting is looking at the Good, because this is a really good painting and a really good painting in Murdoch's view is the truth. There's a wonderful scene in *The Bell* where Dora walks through the National Gallery and feels that the terrible things in her life are calmed by what she thinks of as the authority of the paintings, and she actually says to herself, 'there is something good and outside myself in the world'. I think good paintings always carry this implication for Iris Murdoch. Nevertheless the Tintoretto is a painting of dark desires and people driven to destroy by desire for something very beautiful.

SODRE: There is a marked contrast between Randall's love for Lindsay, who looks like Susannah – her hair is described just like the hair in the painting – a love which is rapacious and too lustful, and Hugh's love for Emma, who is described as now physically being almost as witch-like as Madame Walravens in *Villette* – her skin is like an alligator's and she has a stick; she looks much older than she is – but Hugh's love for her is totally believable and very moving. He looks at her alligator's-skin hand that smells strongly of nicotine, and he's dying of desire for that hand. He smells it before he kisses it as if he wants to completely take it in. This contrasts beautifully with the narcissistic, exhibitionistic nature of Randall's love for Linsday. It corrects the idea that sexual love has to belong entirely to pretty young things.

BYATT: Yes. And at the end, when Hugh and Mildred are on the ship and move out into the Indian Ocean, there is an almost Indian religious sense that God and sexual love and life are all the same thing, really, in which case the Freudian 'machinery' is part of something much bigger that is all really one. Iris Murdoch did once say, 'I have a tendency towards monism myself.'

Like our other novels, *An Unofficial Rose* is a realist narrative inhabited by mythic and fairytale narratives. We've already suggested that Emma Sands represents the bad fairy, or possibly the good fairy, with her stick, or wand.

SODRE: The interesting thing about the fairytale atmosphere in Emma's flat is its ambiguity, as there are two levels working at the same time: Emma the detective-story writer delights in 'inventing' herself as a witch (a sort of Madame Walravens, but more seductive) to emprison Randall in her plot; but the way Murdoch describes the flat with its green door and treasure cave inside, and most of all the unsettling moments like the 'voice in the tape' one that we mentioned, deliberately carry the reader into the fairytale. So that we have Emma the character as a puppetmaster, and Iris Murdoch as Emma, creating a magic world for the reader too.

BYATT: That transports the reader into the world of fairytale where everything has a meaning, out of the world of real life where things can be shapeless and formless and an act might go one way or another. All acts acquire meaning and importance and sense of destiny if you get into a fairytale. It suddenly struck me as you were speaking that the fairytale of Emma and Lindsay is 'Rapunzel'. Emma is the witch, who imprisons the woman with the immense amount of yellow hair which the woman may or may not secretly let down to allow the prince to come in to take her. And of course the witch may kick the prince out and blind him, or castrate him as in the older stories.

SODRE: Emma does symbolically castrate Randall; when he says 'You stole my action', he feels castrated by her. Exactly that. He had thought he could triumph over Emma by being potent and taking control of his life, but he finds he is her puppet.

BYATT: Which is frightening. Whereas the fairy story that goes with Grayhallock is really 'Sleeping Beauty'. You feel that Ann is the Sleeping Beauty inside and she's surrounded by this great fence of relatives.

SODRE: Grayhallock is also described like a *fake* fairytale castle, because of the added towers that don't belong to the original architecture, and are presumably grotesque; Murdoch is here taking up the theme of the bad innovators, like the Crawfords. We've talked about houses in each of the novels, starting with *Mansfield Park* – and what Iris Murdoch does is to create a negative picture of Mansfield. Grayhallock is described as a 'bad' house:

> The sense of unhappiness at Grayhallock had been, since his return there, almost intolerable to him. The house was a melancholy one at the best of times, and had always seemed to him, if not exactly hostile to Ann and Randall, certainly indifferent to them. It had never, he felt, taken them altogether seriously. It had known quite other things, and there were times, especially at night, when one could feel it thinking about them. (Ch. 2)

The house acquires a fairytale feeling through Penn's eyes: Penn

clearly is terribly impressed by the towers and the staircases and the slightly labyrinthine feel of the house.
BYATT: Of course it is also the case in *Daniel Deronda*: country houses are fairytale castles in which you prick your finger. Somebody does, don't they? . . . Ann, yes. Swann plasters her up.
SODRE: Oh, yes, in the scene with Emma when Ann gathers the roses. Emma is in her witch role when that happens. The telephone rings, and Ann pricks her finger. Ann recites the names of all the roses. Like an incantation:

> Ann spoke their names: Agatha Incarnata, Duc de Guiche, Tricolore de Flandre, Sancy de Parabère, Lauriol de Barny, Belle de Crécy, Vierge de Clery, Rosa Mundi. (Ch. 16)

BYATT: It's a most beautiful scene:

> 'What lovely stripes,' said Emma, 'just like Miranda's dress. And what names! I really must write a murder story in a nursery garden. But there, how shocking! All I can think of when I find something beautiful is how to make it an occasion for violent death.' (ibid.)

Now this is a description of herself as the evil fairy, and also of the detective-story writer. Ann goes on talking about the roses: ' "These old roses are more beautiful," said Ann,' and then you get Lindsay coming through on the telephone and Ann turns into a rose –

> She felt herself blushing with a sudden mixture of anger and fear. It must be Lindsay Rimmer. With this there came back to her that sensation of being encompassed and plotted against with which she had first met the news of Emma's coming. (ibid.)

'Encompassed' evokes the besieged or surrounded or enchanted castle. And then Emma gets up and goes to the phone, helped by Ann. 'The roses clung by their thorns to Emma's dress. Ann picked them off and pricked herself in the process' (ibid.). Then later on, Ann stands listening and hears it, looking with fascination at the little bead of blood that had appeared on her finger. What is interesting of course is that the bead of blood wakes her up.
SODRE: Oh, right, yes. Instead of putting her to sleep.
BYATT: Reverses it.
SODRE: I think Emma starts by putting her to sleep in this scene: Ann at the start of Emma's visit is so hostile to her and Emma enchants Ann into feeling closer and closer to her – one feels that when she has asked for the

roses and she says 'Now you shall tell me the names of these', as if she wanted to hypnotise Ann. Ann then repeats these names like a spell, which is broken by the telephone.

BYATT: Earlier when – it's an interesting structure, first Emma appears and then – this is one of the lovely things about a novel being able to tell you what it likes in whatever order – Emma appears and you get this long description at exactly that moment of how Ann has always known that Felix loved her.

SODRE: Emma really is able to find out all that's happening. There is the Emma who invents and creates people (like the novelist or detective-story writer, and like a witch or enchantress), but also she is able to completely understand what everybody is doing to everybody else. She also has the other side of the writer, who is not inventing but is taking everything in in great detail (like Fanny on the sofa!). You feel that in one afternoon Emma has understood this entire world; she has this quality which is attractive to Ann, who has never understood. There is this interesting oscillation in which Emma seduces Ann and then the spell is broken by the thorn and the phone call, and then she gets near Ann again. That's when Emma discovers about her loving Felix. Emma does not really want Ann to be Sleeping Beauty for ever; she wants her to wake up to a new life: ' "You loved Felix," said Ann.' . . . ' "Ah," said Emma.' And then she puts her arm round her shoulder: ' "There there, my child" ' (ibid.). And of course Ann so needs somebody who will do exactly that, who would hold her and tell her what she's feeling: ' "You have been patient with an inquisitive old reptile." ' But she's being a good witch here, a good fairy.

BYATT: I was thinking that as you were speaking. Many of Murdoch's enchanter figures, such as Julius in *A Fairly Honourable Defeat*, are male figures, who somehow accrue to themselves the horror of the concentration camps and the violence of the Second World War; they are people who know that from the inside. And Julius likes – almost as a game – to destroy the lives of all the people in *A Fairly Honourable Defeat* because really nothing matters to him. And he fights Tallis, who is a character very like Ann in the sense of being formless and messy and trying to be virtuous.

SODRE: Tallis is really good.

BYATT: Yes, but in the most awful mess. And Tallis loses and Julius wins. Julius is a vengeful victim, and Emma's witchiness also partly comes out of her own hurt. In a way she overcomes that and becomes good and when she decides to leave all her money to Penn because he's a nice and good boy, you feel that this gesture of reconciliation is intelligent, because she hasn't left it to Miranda whom she doesn't like. She's left it to Penn who is a good person to hand something on to, a good aspect of Hugh.

SODRE: When she embraces Ann, Emma is doing some sort of reparation for whatever she did to hurt Fanny in the past. Emma goes to Grayhallock not only to decide about the money, but also to find out if there is a chance for Ann to survive. She will let Randall run away with Lindsay but will make this all right by making sure Ann has Felix.

BYATT: Felix's name is perfect there, he represents happiness. People are always trying to give him to somebody. Nobody can have him.

SODRE: It's so sad. But Emma clearly means Ann to be happy, she is not spiteful in any way towards Ann, she's a good fairy godmother here.

BYATT: Yes, she is, and both she and Mildred try to organise Ann into being happy but fail. Though Mildred gets nearer. In a sense it's like there being three fairies: Emma, Miranda and Mildred. And Miranda is the bad fairy.

SODRE: If you think about *Villette* and the fairytale part, you don't want to know the deep psychological intricacies of Madame Walravens, she's there as a witch, a fairytale character, she's there to be seen through Lucy's eyes as a fairytale character, so the reader doesn't have to know if she is bad because her mother was evil to her or whatever, that's not necessary. I think it must be terribly difficult for the writer when these worlds are intersecting and you have realistic characters and fairytale characters, or a fairytale scene with realistic feelings from some characters – like when Randall has to make love with Lindsay and therefore is now part of a 'real' story.

I read *A Severed Head* just before I read this, and I thought, in that novel, it doesn't matter that everything is contrived, it's meant to be contrived, to be caricature and cartoon, all funny triangles, comic and farcical. There, psychological depth is not the point; cleverness about detailed type is, so details matter, since a good cartoon has to be drawn with tremendous accuracy, a detail should be able to convey the whole story. You're not interested in the profound inner life of such characters. Whereas in this book you are, so when something fails and it's two-dimensional, it doesn't work for the reader.

BYATT: Yes. In a way all our books have mixed all the levels. In *Villette* Madame Walravens is juxtaposed with Lucy, who is both the heroine of a Gothic romance making Gothic noises and, simultaneously, a profoundly wise study in hysteria and repression and the desperate desire to preserve a threatened autonomy. Iris Murdoch tries to allow the reader to respond in both ways at once. In the scene when Emma is kind to Ann and then the telephone call comes and Ann pricks her finger, we aren't entirely in the fairytale world, I think – it is also two real women meeting, and when one hears Ann's thoughts particularly, one is listening to an intelligent person trying to think out her life.

I love too the way in which she has a world so full of so many characters, so some of them are simply perceived by other people wandering away at the very edge of the narrative like Mildred's husband Humphrey, who exists to take Penn on a good holiday to London. And we know that there has been an incident in which he has lost his job at the Foreign Office because of an incident with a boy in North Africa. We also know that Mildred says that Penn will be quite safe, and we know that Humphrey has excited feelings. That's all we know. Iris Murdoch once said to me, 'What I would like to do when I have finished a novel is take one of the very minor characters and rewrite the whole novel again from his or her point of view.' There is a novel to be written in which Humphrey is the central character. One thing I love about Iris Murdoch is that she knows that, because egocentricity as a writer is alien to her, and it's against her principles as much as it was against George Eliot's. And of course what they both do is switch the centre of sympathy to the reader, frequently enough for the reader actually to go through the moral process of realising the different people are real to each other in different ways, which is very moving. Hugh, for instance, is somebody we mostly see through his own eyes. We don't exactly identify with him, we can even judge him, but we see through his eyes. But then when we suddenly see him through Mildred's eyes he's diminished and slightly more mysterious.

SODRE: But quite lovable as well, because one does identify with Mildred's love for him, even though Mildred knows she's embarking on something a bit fairytale-ish. Yet Mildred is also a tremendous realist, the most insightful and realistic person, she knows exactly what she's doing.

I was wondering if there was a link between Emma Woodhouse and Emma Sands; Jane Austen's Emma is not as clever as Iris Murdoch's Emma, but she also uses people as puppets.

BYATT: Yes, she does, and she learns not to. Whereas Emma Sands is in a fairytale so can be a witch. One way of using fairytales in a novel – which has been done since writers became interested in the ideas of psychoanalysis – is to make the characters appear like symbolic creatures in a way, out of dreams. I think for instance of Bettelheim's interpretations of the fairytales. His interpretation of 'The Sleeping Beauty' is that it is about the wakening of the adolescent girl; adolescent girls go through a period of drowsy withdrawal from the world, he says, and awake to sexuality.

SODRE: Which makes a lot of sense, but there must be other meanings and levels in such a powerful story. Even when you are looking purely from a psychoanalytic point of view there must be more than one interpretation.

BYATT: And there's also what you make of it in your own individual history.

BYATT: Another thing I'm interested in – and I'm never quite sure what I feel about this – is Iris Murdoch's use of symbolic structures and objects to pattern a narrative which is about psychological thoughts. We've talked about what she does with the Tintoretto. We haven't talked about the roses, which are very beautiful, very obtrusive, and recur like patterns in a tapestry all the way through the narrative.

SODRE: The symbols that are interesting surely must be those that are multi-determined, the ones that do stand for several different things; maybe the German dagger is supposed to mean one thing in a defined way –

BYATT: What is the one thing it is supposed to mean?

SODRE: I don't know if I know that. I thought, for a moment, that it just means 'evil'. As a reworking of the knife which Susan and Betsey quarrel over in *Mansfield Park*, it would be connected to sibling rivalry; here, it mainly stands for Penn's attraction to the sinister, to darkness:

> The German dagger, at which he had been gazing unseeingly, suddenly took possession of his consciousness in a painful way. He thought at first that the pain was simply the realization that he must shortly part with it to Miranda. Then he realized that it was a special pain compounded of this, and of a thrilling alarming consciousness that this would make an excellent pretext for mounting the other tower to her room.
>
> *'Foul infidel, know*
> *You have trod on the toe*
> *Of Abdul the Bulbul EMIR!'*

> He picked up the dagger and drew the beautiful thing lightly through his fingers. It was sharp, polished, dangerous, marvellously integrated and sweetly proportioned. He could not remember when he had loved an object so much. It was even better than the visionary revolver which he had once desired. He caressed its smooth black hilt and traced the enamelled swastika with his fingertip. He would never see its like. (Ch. 9)

What Penn perceives as 'an excellent pretext for mounting the other tower to her room' (followed by his sensuous attachment to this 'dangerous' but 'sweetly proportioned' object) reflects his growing awareness of the mysterious, for him incomprehensible, violence of sexuality.

I think it is true to say that the more meanings a symbol has, and the more intricately they're woven into the narrative, probably the more interesting and thought-provoking they are. If the symbol means just one thing, it restricts and is too concrete.

BYATT: I think the dagger is overdetermined partly because of the swastika on it. It is burdened with having to represent the whole war and the whole of male aggression.

SODRE: But that's restrictive, really –

BYATT: It is experienced as restrictive, and it is experienced in some way as leaching the life out of the characters, when they handle it, rather than conferring an extra dimension on them. When Madame Walravens appears as a witch, it adds something to Lucy, that she sees her. But when Steve has to hand the knife to Miranda and Miranda wants the knife but Penn has got it, and it came from Felix, this is all too patterned, too neat. On the other hand the roses, I think, are rather beautifully done, because a rose is a very generous symbol, and the title is beautiful – *An Unofficial Rose* – and the little couplet from Rupert Brooke which is used as an epigraph makes Ann into an archetypal English unofficial rose, the single rose, a dog rose. This connects her with Fanny – the good Englishwoman in the countryside, a perennial English character, like E. M. Forster's Mrs Wilcox, in *Howards End*. Then the garden with the roses is the paradise garden.

SODRE: Described in fact as such in the last scene.

BYATT: Yes, when Randall says goodbye to Nancy Bowshott.

> He felt like a sorcerer who has created a vast palace and adorned it with gold and peopled it with negroes and dwarfs and dancing girls and peacocks and marmosets, and then with a snap of his fingers

> makes it all vanish into nothing. Now when he turned his back upon it the Peronett Rose Nurseries would cease to be as completely as if they had been sunk in the Marsh. Here was the slope where he had first planted his roses, against much wise advice, in the face of the sea winds from Dungeness. Here he had created Randall Peronett and Ann Peronett, names to keep company with Ena Harkness and Sam McGredy, and also his darling the white rose Miranda. They would live on, these purer distillations of his being, when their namesakes were only so much manure. (Ch. 22)

Then he asks if he'll ever do it again, and then he talks about making floribundas and hybrid teas –

> the endless tormenting of nature to produce new forms and colours far inferior to the old and having to recommend them only the brief charm of novelty. What was it all for, the expulsion of the red, the expulsion of the blue, the pursuit of the lurid, the metallic, the startling and the new? (ibid.)

Lindsay is always metallic.

> It was after all a vulgar pursuit. The true rose, the miracle of nature, owed nothing to the hand of man. (ibid.)

Now the rose stands there against the Tintoretto, which is the work of the hand of man, and they're both an image of perfection, an image of the Good.

SODRE: But I think there's the conflict between art and nature and there's the conflict between old and new, which aren't exactly parallel. If the rose is art, then the rose is like the Tintoretto. But as it is described here, in the contrast between the old and the new roses, it's much more like the Mansfield contrasts between constancy and innovation: Lindsay the lurid rose is an invention of Randall's, who is a Henry Crawford who innovates and modernises in a way that attacks the good, beautiful, virtuous things of the past.

BYATT: He's being closed out of paradise quite clearly, and of course he names the things in paradise, he names the roses, he is like Adam in the Garden, naming the plants, naming the creatures. And he has sinned and so he is going.

SODRE: Thinking in terms of the imagination as opposed to wish-fulfilling fantasy, there is a real question about Randall's creativity. We are to believe that he is an artist, he created this beautiful garden and he has invented these new roses as works of art. And we are also to think of Randall as fantasising rather than imagining. Going for the lurid and metallic Lindsay, he's seduced into a world of fantasy which never feels real; we don't think he really loves Lindsay, the actual person, although he loves, as Emma says, he loves the symbol. Randall even fantasises about possessing other women, and we can see that what he thinks is his freedom is in fact a descent into drunken self-destructiveness.

Here is Randall in the Garden of Eden saying goodbye to his roses:

> Moving slightly in the breeze the intense little heads surrounded him and drowned him in their odour. Lifting a few towards him he looked with his ever new amazement at the close packed patterns of petals, those formulae that Nature never forgot, those forms that were the most desirable of all things and so exquisite that it was impossible to carry them in belief and memory through the winter; so that every year one saw them as if for the first time, and as they must have looked in the Garden of Eden when in a felicitous moment God said: let there be roses. So Randall moved on, deeper into the rose forest, between the tall thickets with their crossing and interlacing boughs, and as he went he picked them, snipping off here a faintly blushing alba and here a golden-stamened wine-dark rose of Provence.
>
> A woman started up suddenly . . . (Ch. 22)

– which is very much Nancy Bowshott as Eve –

> A woman started up suddenly, appearing on the grass path between the bushes with the sudden illuminated presence of a Pre-Raphaelite angel. He turned with a gasp of fear. But it was Nancy Bowshott. (ibid.)

BYATT: She might not be Eve, she might be the serpent. It says the woman is like a Pre-Raphaelite angel, and the Satan is a fallen angel. If one is to believe Iris Murdoch's account of Freud as understanding why we cannot possibly contemplate the Good, this colours Randall's embrace of the woman in the garden. Sex has deflected his attention from the innocent contemplation of the Good and the Beautiful – the roses.

SODRE: I had thought of her as Eve in the Garden.

BYATT: I was suggesting that because it says she is an angel and doesn't say she's a woman, she might be the Satan, or more plausibly the flaming angel since she's got red hair, who actually closes him from the Garden, because it is his sensuality which is closing him out of the Garden.

SODRE: But it's also greedy, rapacious Randall who seduces Nancy. He is rather cruel to her, she will be in love with him for ever, so I suppose Randall could be the serpent too.

BYATT: It's one of these wonderful moments when you see that the 'bad' really are not attentive, because it's clear that Nancy's always had passionate feelings about him, to which he has never paid any attention. When he notices them, he pays exactly the wrong kind of attention, making everything much worse for her. Iris Murdoch doesn't even have to say that it is making it infinitely worse, we are allowed to make that moral judgement.

BYATT: I felt when I first read it that this novel is Iris Murdoch's reaction to thinking again very hard about the English novel, but particularly about the virtues of Jane Austen and particularly *Mansfield Park*. Her earlier novels were not realist in the way this one is. They were in the tradition of Beckett or the French, Sartre and Queneau, and as you have said *A Severed Head* is the most beautiful artificial comedy of manners, whereas this tries to go deeper. In what ways do you think she is like and unlike Jane Austen?

SODRE: I can see why you think she is quite deliberately reworking *Mansfield Park* here. Which is both about feeling a tremendous affinity with Jane Austen, but also wanting to work from something already there and established and loved, to transform it, to work out different solutions; like negative or different triangularities, and different ways in which the characters in the first novel can be transformed, and have different destinies. For instance, Hugh is like Edmund Bertram but he's also being like Henry Crawford when he has a love affair; and Felix is like Edmund but this new Fanny, Ann, and this new Edmund, Felix, don't get together because of the particular circumstances of the novel, and the psychological make-up of the characters. Thus Fanny Price's 'constancy' becomes Ann's total inability to give up her old relationship for a new one, even when the old one has given her up completely; a traditional virtue becomes self-destructive. Freud has a description of melancholia that very much applies to Ann, as well as to the melancholic side of all of us:

> Reality-testing has shown that the loved object no longer exists,

> and it proceeds to demand that all libido shall be withdrawn from its attachments to that object. This demand arouses understandable opposition – it is a matter of general observation that people never willingly abandon a libidinal position, not even, indeed, when a substitute is already beckoning to them. (*Mourning and Melancholia*, 1917)

Iris Murdoch deliberately refers to – and also nearly quotes – Jane Austen. Hugh sends Jane Austen's books to Miranda from Hatchards, and Miranda is only interested in the fact that the covers are soft. And then Murdoch deliberately starts one chapter writing like Jane Austen: 'The news that Randall Peronett was off, that he had left his wife and gone away, positively and definitively gone away with Lindsay Rimmer, was greeted with almost universal satisfaction' (Ch. 23). This is obviously done on purpose, and it's rather delightful to feel that you, as a reader, have a sort of complicity with the writer.

BYATT: *Pride and Prejudice*: 'It is a truth universally acknowledged, that a single man in possession of a good fortune, must be in want of a wife' (Ch. 1). The sense of who it is, who is universally thinking it, is different in these two books, and yet also the same.

It interests me that Iris Murdoch hasn't actually created anybody in this novel as successfully evil as Austen's Mrs Norris. This is because she has made all her evil people intelligent and self-questioning, there isn't anybody who produces a kind of automatic malevolence. The nearest is Miranda. This caused me to think about something we were saying when reading *Daniel Deronda*. I quoted Bradley on Shakespeare saying that after Hamlet he decided it would be more interesting and manageable to do stupid tragic heroes, rather than intelligent ones. I think all our novelists are absolutely wonderful at depicting the limitations of people's intelligence. And the characters one loves in all the novels are the ones who see so much and no more. One loves Fanny Price, who as you say comes to self-knowledge, and who sees more than anybody else in that novel, but nevertheless both the writer and the reader see a lot more than Fanny, I think. Gwendolen is a most wonderful tragic heroine precisely because she isn't very intelligent, and I think we love Hugh in this book, and even Ann, because we think they aren't very intelligent. I don't know exactly why, but I always want to connect this with something else we've observed throughout all the books: that all the people are afraid of marriage as though it's going to take away from them what little autonomy they have. The fairy story says life is full of hazards and horrors and terrors and then you will be married and you will live happily ever after. The novel says life is full of energy, then you will be married and you will live unhappily ever after, or at least you will *think* you are living unhappily ever after, and you will never understand anything again. Iris Murdoch talks so intelligently about the brute sense of connection between married couples, which she says survives any real sense that the people love each other and want to be together.

SODRE: As Randall says, 'We are so horribly connected.'

Chapter 6

Toni Morrison: *Beloved*

The narrative technique of *Beloved* (1987), Toni Morrison's fifth novel, is deliberately non-linear and complex.

It is 1873 in America. Sethe, a former slave, lives at 124 in the free North, with her daughter Denver and the ghost of her dead baby girl: two sons, Howard and Buglar, have run away, her mother-in-law, Baby Suggs, whose house it was, is dead, and Halle, her husband, disappeared without trace. The book opens with the unexpected arrival of Paul D, one of the five men with whom she had been enslaved on a farm in Kentucky, Sweet Home. Much to the chagrin of Denver, Paul D moves in with them and as they face the past together, slowly, their tragic story unfolds. Meanwhile, on return from a fair, they meet a strange girl who calls herself Beloved – the only word Sethe was able to secure for her dead baby's tombstone – and invite her home. She does not speak of a past, but they imagine that she has suffered so much abuse at the hands of white people that she cannot talk of it. Denver and Beloved become firm friends. Beloved, clearly no ordinary girl, who somehow remembers incidents from Sethe's history, disturbingly, becomes Paul D's lover in the storeroom, something he hates himself for and doesn't understand.

Sweet Home had been run by benign whites called Mr and Mrs Garner. There Sethe had been allowed to have children by – but not to marry – Halle. After the death of Mr Garner, however, an ailing Mrs Garner sells Paul F, and brings in her brother-in-law, Schoolteacher, who is sadistic, to run the place. Paul A is killed, the slaves go hungry, and plan to escape North. But plans go very wrong. Paul D and Sixo, unknown to Sethe, get caught. Meanwhile, she herself is held down and has her breast-milk taken from her by Schoolteacher's two nephews.

Her children, sent on ahead, get to safety, but Halle never turns up. Sethe, imagining herself abandoned, takes off anyway, nine months pregnant and on foot. With the help of a white girl, Amy, she gives birth to Denver *en route*, before finally crossing the river, with the help of Stamp Paid, to safety. From Paul D she learns the terrible truth about that night: Sixo had been burned to death, he himself put in a collar and bit, then sold to a chain gang from which he eventually escaped, and her husband Halle had not abandoned her, but, having witnessed Sethe's indignity, had lost his mind with grief and anger.

Running parallel to these revelations is the truth of Sethe's own story: having arrived at Baby Suggs's house and having reunited her four children, she is, for a short while, happy with them. Baby Suggs is a much-loved centre of the religious community, but then disaster: after a massive feast, Sethe sees Schoolteacher arrive, and, traumatised at the thought of having her children taken from her again, in a state of hysteria she slits the throat of her oldest baby girl. After this, she is sent to prison and ostracised by all, a state of affairs which has continued up to the present; Baby Suggs dies.

Paul learns of Sethe's murder through Stamp Paid, and leaves. After this, it becomes clear to Sethe, as it has to us, that Beloved is no less than her dead baby. At first Sethe is delighted that the strength of their love has brought her back. However, they become too intensely entangled and the relationship begins to pall. Sethe loses her job. Denver goes to the white schoolteacher to whom she was close before the murder separated them, and tells them of the troubles at home. The teacher and villagers respond with sympathy, and send food. Eventually, they herd together and encircle 124 and exorcise the ghost for ever. In a frenzy of fear, Sethe has a fit of madness and tries to attack a man on horseback called the 'bleached nigger', who she thinks is Schoolteacher come back.

In three sections of poetry, the meaning of 'Beloved' is explored; 'Beloved' becomes more than just the baby's ghost, personifying the ghosts of all dead and suffering slaves.

After much reflection, Paul D comes back to Sethe. Sethe is still ill, but there are signs that with Paul D's help she will recover, and Denver will grow up healthy.

BYATT: *Beloved* starts:

124 was spiteful. Full of a baby's venom. The women in the house

> knew it and so did the children. For years each put up with the spite in his own way, but by 1873 Sethe and her daughter Denver were its only victims. The grandmother, Baby Suggs, was dead, and the sons, Howard and Buglar, had run away by the time they were thirteen years old – as soon as merely looking in a mirror shattered it (that was the signal for Buglar); as soon as two tiny hand prints appeared in the cake (that was it for Howard). (p. 1)

I think that's a brilliant beginning technically, because it's introduced a house immediately characterised in one adjective and one adjective only, which is 'spiteful'. So it says this is a novel about spite. Which is a strange thing for a novel to be about. Not love, not hate, but spite. And then it introduces a whole series of characters, Sethe and her daughter Denver, and the grandmother, Baby Suggs who is immediately said to be dead.

SODRE: The house is the first character, the second character is the baby. You don't know who the baby is, but you do know it's a tremendously powerful baby, in control of the house.

BYATT: It does magical things, like crack mirrors and put hand prints in cakes. And this is partly comic, the tone of it has a kind of robust comic energy. The narrative is describing terrible things, but it isn't exactly meant to send a chill down your spine. The tone is also matter-of-fact: this house was like that, therefore these people did this.

SODRE: It brings you immediately into this completely different world – you step into 124 like the characters will do, from the ordinary outside world into the strange world of 124, a world dominated by this baby ghost. It is written in a way that makes you feel pulled into 124.

BYATT: But it doesn't give you atmospheric terms, it operates with facts. The broken mirror, the tiny hand prints and the fact that the two boys simply ran away, because they couldn't stay.

SODRE: This is a non-Gothic ghost story, in which the ghost is completely matter-of-fact and concrete; so that there is no question of terror of the unknown, and no possibility of 'not believing' in the ghost.

BYATT: The ghost is a baby, and the baby is full of spite. There is a wonderful image when Baby Suggs is contemplating colour. (We'll come on to colour.)

> Winter in Ohio was especially rough if you had an appetite for color. Sky provided the only drama, and counting on a Cincinnati horizon for life's principal joy was reckless indeed. (p. 4)

The tone of this narrator is robust and full of energy. And then you get Denver and Sethe fighting the house: 'For they understood the source of the outrage as well as they knew the source of light' (ibid.). And that makes the black and white, the light and dark, absolute, before you've got three paragraphs into the book, which is very strong and sets the tone for the rest of the book, which moves from chick peas to the source of dark and light, completely solid and matter-of-fact. George Eliot, in *Middlemarch*, speaks of Casaubon having yet to learn to imagine with feeling: 'an idea wrought back to the directness of sense, like the solidity of objects'. Her own ideal as a novelist was to make her ideas solid, incarnate. And Toni Morrison can supremely do this. 'The sideboard took a step forward but nothing else did' (p. 4). Precise, exact.

> 'For a baby she throws a powerful spell,' said Denver.
>
> 'No more powerful than the way I loved her,' Sethe answered and there it was again. The welcoming cool of unchiseled headstones; the one she selected to lean against on tiptoe, her knees wide open as any grave. Pink as a fingernail it was, and sprinkled with glittering chips. Ten minutes, he said. You got ten minutes I'll do it for free. (pp. 4–5)

And then there is the first shocking double-take, because you realise that she has given him ten minutes' sex, to have the word 'Beloved' put on the tombstone, and this word is all that could be put on, because it was all there was time for.

SODRE: The first time I read it I don't think I understood that, not immediately. I had to reread it, even though now it seems quite obvious. As if there was a reluctance to take it in completely.

BYATT: If you look at the word rutting, 'rutting among the headstones with the engraver, his young son looking on', you do have to read every word. And you don't immediately take the force of 'her knees wide open as any grave'.

SODRE: That's right; when you get to that point, then you can see. But it is so compact that I had to take a step back to see it completely.

BYATT: So it's a shocker paragraph, yet the whole thing is tied together with this immense matter-of-fact narration. But what is being dragged into the matter-of-fact narration is appalling. Emotions. And you begin to realise that. Then you get another wonderful line: 'Counting on the stillness of her own soul, she had forgotten the other one: the soul of her baby girl' (p. 5). Which is a very profound observation about one's relations with the dead, or Sethe's relations with Beloved. 'Who would have thought that a little old baby could harbor so much rage?' (ibid.). With Toni Morrison you need to read every word. A little old baby is colloquial language, and yet the moment this baby is dead it becomes the ancient of days, it becomes the whole history of its own race. And in a sense the dead are old because they're part of the past and the ancestors, everything that's gone.

SODRE: You feel that at some level Sethe thinks about the death of the baby all the time, even when she isn't conscious of it: it is just a millimetre beyond consciousness, ready to pounce on her: 'and there it was again'. It takes you absolutely by surprise, the suddenness of it. Every time she becomes fully conscious of it, she feels assaulted by her thoughts, by the memory coming back with the tremendous violence of reality.

BYATT: The characters in this story are in such a state of extremity that they have to suppress all emotions, all normal responses because their lives have been so terrible that mere survival becomes central and you only survive by not feeling. And yet precisely because every feeling they have has been pushed under, they have a power and a dignity and a force and ferocity which the feelings of ordinary people in ordinary novels don't have. This novel is the history of a race, a people, as well as of its characters. And you feel that's woven into the gritty texture of the prose in the first scene.

SODRE: These are people who have gone through such unbearable experiences that they have to be constantly engaged in fierce battles with their own minds. Like Baby Suggs, who gets to the point where the only thing left to be safe with is colour, and even then only one colour at a time, as if to exclude any possibility of conflict. The central question of the book is memory: how to deal with the past which is present in the mind, how to negotiate these intolerable experiences; a book written so that the past is not forgotten, about people who desperately want to forget.

Each of the central characters deals with this in a slightly different way. For instance, Sethe is all the time trying to 'disremember' the events of the past, but she never loses her love, so she has intense relationships with the dead. Her love has to be kept alive for Denver and for the boys, just as when she was running away from Sweet Home to the North she knew she must not die, she had to hold on to life for her children. And she has to be constantly reassuring the dead baby that she loved her and still loves her. She has to do this complicated thing, in which she keeps her emotions intensely alive, whilst at the same time trying to keep another part of her mind, which contains unbearable memories, as dead as possible. So Sethe is involved in a tremendous acrobatic feat in her mind. Her mind is an object she thinks about and talks to and struggles against; she refers to her brain as an enemy.

BYATT: Something about Baby Suggs, I might just add. You said there she was contemplating colour, minimally, one colour at a time. When you first read that sentence you have an image of somebody comfortably lying in bed who has retired from the world, even if persecuted by the ghost of a baby, and likes to look at colour. You don't realise the weight the word colour is going to carry through the book. In fact you probably do know that colour goes with coloured people because of the recent conventions of black writing. But you don't think too hard about it, at least if you're a white reader. And you don't have any idea, even though you know there's a spiteful demon in the house, of what it is that has broken Baby Suggs, you don't feel her at that stage as broken.

SODRE: You not only feel that you don't know about a lot that's being referred to, but your imagination may run to the wrong place temporarily, to be corrected later by other bits of information; Toni Morrison writes in such a way as to have this particular effect.

BYATT: Yes, I think she allows you to run on little easy journeys; easy is the wrong word, but she allows you to suppose that you feel –

SODRE: Comfortable with what you know?

BYATT: – and then she tells you something so much more terrible that you see you didn't know, you were morally inadequate. We'll come back to that.

BYATT: Let's talk about Sethe. The novel is based on a true story of a woman who killed her child in order that it not be returned to slavery. This is a story so repugnant and frightening to any woman, any child, any person, that it is extraordinarily daring for a novelist to take a person who has committed such an act as a protagonist and then to make you love her, identify with her and sympathise with her. She does it by inventing a woman whose powers of love are extremely strong and in whom other powers are also extremely strong. Do you find her psychologically convincing?

SODRE: Entirely convincing, and I find that my sympathy for Sethe is absolutely unwavering throughout the book, which is extraordinary, considering what she has done. You never react against her, as you find out the truth – that she has killed her own child. You react to the intensity of her pain and the horror of the tragedy, but never for a moment against her, because you entirely believe in her motives. Sethe herself never mistrusts her love either. And you don't have the feeling that she is trying defensively to deny a secret hostility. Her sole preoccupation, what she agonises over, is that the baby misunderstood her, and is angry because she feels unloved. The ghost stays with her for ever, obviously because she lost her child and wants her back, and it is unbearable that she can't undo what she has done. When she is trying to convince the baby of her love for her, it's always because the baby doesn't believe it. It pains her horribly that her baby doesn't know how much she loves her. That she wouldn't ever not want to be with her. She killed her, and meant to kill the other children and herself, so that they could all be together 'on the other side'.

BYATT: It's interesting, because here we have a woman who hasn't known either of her own parents, and who broods a lot about that fact, who is allowed to have a husband (though not allowed to marry him because it's felt not to be important), by kindly white people who make a home for her, a sort of home, where she is actually allowed to bear four consecutive children to one man, which makes a family. We tend to think in terms of the nineteenth-century European novel, which is about tensions of family, and people trying to break out of families – here we have a novel which is about people to whom this very basic human structure, a man and a woman and their children, is denied by the social structure within which they live. So in a sense it's almost mythological to Sethe that she should be a mother of several children and love and look after and nurture them all. She doesn't have any of the responses you might imagine; you might suppose she might feel she had to reject her parents because she didn't have them, they hadn't fed her with their milk, nurtured her. She doesn't even know who her father is.

SODRE: But she does know something important about her father. She knows that her father was the only man whom her mother loved. Of course it's true that, logically, one could think that Sethe should have been a neurotic person, full of hatred, but what's so extraordinary about the book is that something quite unusual is conveyed with such imaginative truthfulness. I do completely believe it here, that it *is* possible. Sethe does have the image, given her by Nan, the woman who looked after all the children in the farm when Sethe was little, that her mother had loved her father, that she had 'put her arms around him', and had named Sethe after him; Sethe is the only baby that her mother didn't throw away (as she had done to all the babies she had had by white men). Now this brings another question: presumably there is also somewhere in Sethe's mind a nightmarish story of babies who were thrown away; so that she has to prove her love against this psychological background, to prove to her ghost baby that she hadn't done that to her.

BYATT: The slave-women reduce these half-white babies to something that can be simply treated as not quite human. Which is wonderful, because it plays against the conventional white man's image that black people are nearer to the animals, which is so powerful and appalling in this book. One criticism that has been made of *Beloved* is that the black characters are idealised and turned into heroic figures. I wondered if you felt that this was at the cost of any psychological verisimilitude? It could be said of both Baby Suggs and Paul D that they are persons whose experiences have been so foul that you feel they should harbour very bad feelings. And this book says that they are persons more than usually full of good and positive feelings.

SODRE: Well, two thoughts occur to me: one, that they are not good in a saintly, idealised way; they all have hatred and spite and other bad feelings, so this obviously gives them reality. The other is that there is a quality which doesn't detract from the sense of psychological reality, but is an added dimension, which is a mythical quality. They are described in great detail as individuals, but they also represent their past and race. This makes one judge them and think about them as part of a different universe, like in Greek tragedy: they are larger than life.

To make a psychoanalytic point: each person's relation with their internal objects, in psychic reality, depends on the way in which external relationships have been internalised. It is possible to conceive that Sethe could have held on firmly to the picture of her parents getting together and creating a baby whom they would certainly have loved.

BYATT: Toni Morrison has made all this plausible; she has put the young Sethe into a 'kindly' background where the whites who own her, allow her to hold on to this image and don't kill it off, they allow her to have children whom she can treat with love, because she has an internal image of a woman who is good to her children. And one believes in her autonomy, and the resourcefulness with which she gets the children away and manages to take them through the cornfield and get them in the wagon so that they all, except the one inside her, can get to Baby Suggs, whom at that stage she doesn't know. Just as you believe in her complete use of the amount of dignity that the shapeless space of her marriage allows her. She wants to marry in a wedding dress, and Mrs Garner says she can't see why she wants a wedding day, though she expects she'll have a baby in due course. So Sethe steals things and makes a wedding dress which is completely ridiculous; she even knows it is, but that doesn't matter to her – there has to be a ceremony, a marriage, she has to have significant objects, ceremonial things out of an ordered society in order to live a 'real' life. Sethe is in a way a cross between Medea and Dorothea, in *Middlemarch*, an idealist in a hostile world. I also feel that the author feels a moral need to be kind to the characters, and a moral need for there to be mythic figures in terms of internal objects to whom both author and readers can relate and feel good. And I believe that she has completely succeeded in making figures that she can love and we readers can love, who have come out of a background out of which lesser writers would have made much more twisted beings. Medea and Sethe are both desperate child-killers but Medea is more twisted than Sethe – Sethe is a good mother, and that is why what she did is so terrible. And it's also why she's so vulnerable when the child decides to strangle her.

SODRE: Sethe has never been able to recover from the horror of what she has done, and from the pain at the loss of her child, and this is why she is vulnerable. Her strength, on the other hand, comes from the solidity of her ties with her lost loved ones.

BYATT: It occurred to me, as you spoke, that Toni Morrison has talked frequently about her own parents, and the power of their Christian belief. It is as though her black parents, who she says were not allowed to swim in the lake next to where they lived, had in their minds this wonderful story of suffering and dignity which empowered them. Morrison draws on biblical and Christian language in *Beloved*, as she does in all her work, but I see her use of these stories in a new way as we talk, because the Christian story too presents large mythic suffering figures from whom you can take strength, rather than feeling that they require you to undertake persecution or vengeance. And that leads me to Beloved's name, which comes from the Song of Solomon: 'My beloved is mine, and I am his' (Song of Solomon 2: 16). The ghost in her late monologue (p. 210) begins 'I am beloved and she is mine.' Many of the themes and the images of the novel are in the 'Song'.

> I am come into the garden, my sister, my spouse: I have gathered my myrrh with my spice; I have eaten my honeycomb with my honey; I have drunk my wine with my milk: eat, O friends; drink, yea, drink abundantly, O beloved.
>
> I sleep, but my heart waketh: it is the voice of my beloved that

> knocketh, saying, Open to me, my sister, my love, my dove, my undefiled: for my head is filled with dew, and my locks with the drops of the night. (Song of Solomon 5: 1–2)

And also of course 'I am black, but comely, O ye daughters of Jerusalem' (ibid., 1: 5). The Song of Solomon has been read mystically, as an account of the marriage between Christ and his Spouse, the soul or the Church. In that context of course, Paul D is also the beloved. I think the image of the good suffering person, whom you can hold on to to make yourself good, underlies what Toni Morrison can do with a novel and European novelists have lost, in making good people. Dostoevsky could do it, in Alyosha and Myshkin, and Iris Murdoch tries to make a Christ figure in Tallis, in *A Fairly Honourable Defeat*. The relation of Toni Morrison's writing to Christian stories and images is very powerful. Black slaves and their descendants took Christianity and made it into the religion of their suffering, and it gave them strength, and music – and other arts – came out of that.
SODRE: Strength, and hope, which is part of the strength. You were talking about how Sethe is convincing in her resourcefulness; she's got faith in the possibility of an entirely good relationship, which is why she can entrust her children to strangers, to be put in a wagon and taken to another part of the country. She doesn't waver, she knows these children will get to this good mother, Baby Suggs. There's no doubt in her mind. It's not just the horror of where she is, it is not despair. It's the holding on to the certainty that goodness exists, against the evidence of so much evil. This certainty is what Baby Suggs eventually loses: the moment when she gets broken, when her 'marrow gets tired' for good, that's when the being able to hold firmly to a belief, a Christian belief or a belief in goodness, becomes impossible. The belief in goodness – its existence in psychic reality – is the only thing that makes it possible to live this absolutely intolerable life.

BYATT: Let's go on to Denver, who is much more at risk than Sethe. Denver's myth is the myth of her own birth against all the odds, which she likes to have told again and again, how she was born and out of the boat into the water, assisted by this matter-of-fact white girl, Amy.
SODRE: Denver only likes the part of the story where she is born; she hates the rest of the story. She is so centred on Sethe that she constantly has to hold on to the beginning of their story.
BYATT: What do you feel is Denver's relationship to Beloved? There is

this extraordinary image – a mythic image – a woman with a murdered child and another child feeding at her breast, and the living child drinking in the blood of the dead child and the milk of the mother at the same time. This is an extraordinary image for us to live with, let alone Sethe and Denver. Do you feel Denver is truly imagined out of that terror?

SODRE: I think Denver's loneliness and possessiveness and jealousy come through as real: there's something moving about her wish to have somebody that belongs only to her. When a relationship becomes triangular – like the moment Paul D appears – she finds it unbearable. She desperately needs an ally – somebody she can feel twinned with – to be blood-sisters with Beloved (she was told she had swallowed some of her murdered sister's blood).

BYATT: Yes, and you feel in a sense it's Denver who calls up the really solid emanation of Beloved. First the dress comes, then the figure comes. When exactly does Beloved appear?

SODRE: After the carnival. Two days after Paul D arrives.

BYATT: And you feel that the house and Sethe and Denver together have caused this avenging ghost to take on human form and flesh and appear with its boots and black dress and its need for water.

SODRE: Since Paul D has driven the ghost out of the house, she has to come back as a physical being; and Denver wants her back.

BYATT: Does it bear any relation at the simple level to people calling up imaginary playmates? Is it the same kind of psychological structure as when children invent somebody they can see who inhabits their bed and their life? Do people do that in order to –

SODRE: – to have an ally to pair up with against the parental couple that excludes the child. The child and the imaginary playmate become, defensively, this new couple. But it's also somebody who is under your control, so it is a very powerful defence against loneliness. It's somebody you create and therefore is exactly what you would like them to be. And the child can have total intimacy with this imaginary friend.

BYATT: So Beloved in a sense is created out of two quite different things. She's created by Sethe's constant need to assure her of her love, and she's created by Denver's need for an ally, and the two together call up the spirit. In all sorts of Western and Greek myths, if you go down to the underworld, you give a beaker of blood to the ghosts and the ghosts are able to absorb energy from the blood, to swell up and rise up and speak.

SODRE: One more thing about Denver: it is very important in terms of hope for some resolution of the racial conflict that Denver's life begins

with help from a white girl, that the couple when Denver comes into the world is made of two women, one black and one white. Amy functions as the other parent.
BYATT: The word Amy is the same as Beloved. *Aimé* in French is beloved. And Toni Morrison must have known that – it's twinning. So in a sense you have one couple followed by another couple. Particularly since Toni Morrison plays a game all the way through of making white people appear to be like dead people or ghosts or people made out of bone, or with no blood in their veins, which is why they're so white. There's a wonderful racial image of the inadequacies of white flesh and blood. And there is Amy who nevertheless transcended these inadequacies and was helpful. Then at the end of the novel there are suddenly several half-white people.
SODRE: Like Miss Lady.
BYATT: Yes, and the white negro, the pale black man who rides on the horse at the end, whom Sethe tries to stab. Denver has relations with white people. This matters. Here he is. Yes. 'The "bleached nigger" was what his enemies called him' (p. 260). And Miss Lady is kind.

> Lady Jones smiled. 'What can you do?'
> 'I can't do anything, but I would learn it for you if you have a little extra.'
> 'Extra?'
> 'Food. My ma'am, she doesn't feel good.'
> 'Oh, baby,' said Mrs. Jones. 'Oh, baby.'
> Denver looked up at her. She did not know it then, but it was the word 'baby,' said softly and with such kindness, that inaugurated her life in the world as a woman. (p. 248)

It is partly-white people who make it possible for Denver to go into the world.
SODRE: It's the word 'baby' that launches her into adulthoood.

BYATT: About Paul D. We were saying earlier, one of the really interesting things about Paul D is that of all the male characters in all the books we've talked about he is the most grown-up, most responsible, most male, most lovable, and yet he is presented as somebody damaged almost beyond repair in all those areas by the life he has had to live. Two questions about that: one, do you find him credible? and two, do you as a reader want to marry him?
SODRE: I think he is one of the most lovable men in novels; I would most

definitely marry him! There is a particular freshness about his contact with Sethe, as soon as he arrives, which I love: the moment they set eyes on each other they become young. She becomes a girl, hc becomes a young man, and that works very well. The way they talk to each other is entirely believable and often delightful. What he says to her at the end is so perfect and moving: when she is slowly killing herself out of despair because she has lost Beloved, whom she calls her 'best thing', and he says, 'You your best thing, Sethe. You are' (p. 273), and brings her back to life.

Another thing which is deeply moving is Sethe's constant preoccupation with her breasts and her milk. She survived her terrible journey to the North because she knew she had to take her milk to her baby; this happened immediately after suffering the trauma of having Schoolteacher's nephews nursing on her breasts, the sight of which drove Halle, her husband, crazy. So it is very moving that the first thing Paul D does when he has a chance is to hold her breasts, making her feel that finally somebody else is taking responsibility for them.

BYATT: In Morrison's earlier novel, *Song of Solomon*, there is a woman who keeps her milk going all the way through her son's boyhood and adult life. Her son's name, or nickname, is Milkman, and she is the mother who can't give up mothering. But here Paul D transfigures this into the image of a desirable woman. There's this wonderful sentence about how he stands behind her and cups her two breasts, as though they were the best part of himself, which both takes them into him and takes away from them the painfulness of being an endless source of nourishment to children.

> Behind her, bending down, his body an arc of kindness, he held her breasts in the palms of his hands. He rubbed his cheek on her back and learned that way her sorrow, the roots of it; its wide trunk and intricate branches. (p. 17)

Her breasts become briefly erotic, which Sethe hasn't been allowed to be.

SODRE: It is an erotic experience and simultaneously a sharing of her terrible burden of responsibility. Sethe responds to his awareness of her needs – he is a man who has got used to women crying when he walks into their house. About Milkman in *The Song of Solomon*, I think that is precisely the opposite image; it is disturbing and horrible that his mother goes on feeding Milkman for ever, almost a curse on him. It's interesting how it's completely reversed here.

BYATT: Partly reversed, because I think it's partly a curse on Sethe; there is a sense that the perpetual milk meant a perpetual possibility to go on feeding Beloved. But feeding the dead is a doom; Sethe is filling up death like a bottomless bottle. As you spoke, I thought of another passage in the Song of Solomon:

> Many waters cannot quench love, neither can the floods drown it: if a man would give all the substance of his house for love, it would utterly be contemned.
>
> We have a little sister, and she hath no breasts: what shall we do for our sister in the day when she shall be spoken for?
>
> If she be a wall, we will build upon her a palace of silver: and if she be a door, we will inclose her with boards of cedar.
>
> I am a wall, and my breasts like towers: then was I in his eyes as one that found favour. (Song of Solomon 8: 7–10)

And earlier there is the very beautiful comparison of the 'sister' to a garden: 'A garden inclosed is my sister, my spouse; a spring shut up, a fountain sealed.' I think all these phrases and images – the water, the overflowing, the little sister, the breasts, the identity of the woman with breasts with the building – reverberate in many ways throughout this novel. This imagery was traditionally applied to the Virgin Mary – the closed garden – and to nuns. And Sethe is the ghastly opposite of all this: she has too many breasts, and this has taken from her the capacity to be a woman to men.

SODRE: She has no space for what she desires for herself; but also, she has had the horrible experience of exchanging sex for having the word 'Beloved' chiselled on the headstone:

> Who would have thought that a little old baby could harbor so much rage? Rutting among the stones under the eyes of the engraver's son was not enough. Not only did she have to live out her years in a house palsied by the baby's fury at having its throat cut, but those ten minutes she spent pressed up against dawn-colored stone studded with star chips, her knees wide open as the grave, were longer than life, more alive, more pulsating than the baby blood that soaked her fingers like oil. (p. 5)

Death is more alive than life, her womb has become a grave, the dead baby is 'engraved' in her genitals.

BYATT: Yes, and in this sense this is this novel's vision of the fear of marriage we've found in all our novels, the fear of growing up and becoming an instrument of the next generation, an instrument of the structure rather than the odd brief moment of being yourself. Which Paul D gives back to Sethe. I think the heroes written by women novelists whom we come to love deeply have this mixture of liking the woman's body and understanding her feelings, which is what women really require from men.

SODRE: There is this very good scene where, after they go to bed together for the first time, both then immediately have rather hostile feelings to each other, as if the moment they are 'married' they want to get out of that mutual house. As soon as Paul D makes love to Sethe, he decides he could definitely live without her, he doesn't like her breasts any more, he doesn't like her scarred back. He starts thinking about the men in Sweet Home and the tree called 'Brother' as if he can't tolerate this heterosexual thing. He immediately goes back to the company of men. He even remembers cooking potatoes, as if there is such a fear of being entangled with this woman that he goes back to men who can cook for him and have maternal qualities. Then he remembers Sixo and the thirty-mile woman, as if his mind goes back again to heterosexuality: Sixo was so completely in love with this woman that he walked thirty miles just to see her for a moment. Paul D has walked for years to meet Sethe again.

BYATT: Sixo produced Seveno, that was his moment, when the thirty-mile woman got away containing the unborn Seveno.

SODRE: But Sethe too is feeling ambivalent; she is angry when she realises he has kept his shirt on, 'Dog, she thought, and then remembered that she had not allowed him the time for taking it off'. And 'considering how quickly they had started getting naked, you'd think by now they would be' (p. 22). It's painful and comic. You can see that they are powerfully drawn to each other, desperately want to make love, but once they do, they want to get out of this 'marriage'.

BYATT: This is something that happens to a lot of people, after intense sexual pleasure. At the same time, it's to do with the atmosphere of 124, which turns it sour. When you spoke about Paul D and the male companionship, I thought how one of the characteristics of the American novel as opposed to the European novel is that the major bonded pairs are almost always two men. *Love and Death in the American Novel* is a brilliant book of literary criticism. Its author, Leslie Fiedler, takes you through every major American text and discovers a bonding between two men, often a black man and a white man. Women are peripheral, dangerous and frightening. And the thing about Paul D is that he has the characteristics of the male in an American novel, but in this novel about black women he likes women, and this is very enabling at least for a woman reader – I don't know what male readers make of Paul D, but I find him comforting, thinking in terms of the American novel in general. If you think of Huck Finn and Jim the negro going along the river, or Ishmael and Queequeg chasing Moby Dick, or Fenimore Cooper's Deerslayer, there is always this pair. Toni Morrison does something new: a black man and a black woman make conversation.

SODRE: It's quite explicit, in that Sethe sees him gazing at her with *interest*, not just with love or curiosity. It goes back to what we discussed in *Villette*, in Lucy Snowe and M. Paul: the man who is interested in the woman's mind is the most sexually attractive (think of Freud's discovery of transference love!).

BYATT: And Paul gives her sense of herself back to her at the end when he says 'You your best thing'. The bit-by-bit analysis of the movements of Paul D's thoughts and feelings is so sure-footed. The exact way in which he has suppressed what he has decided to suppress, is described with such dignity. He has his tobacco box in which he's locked up his heart, and he doesn't get it out, and anyway he can't afford any paper for a cigarette.

> He would keep the rest where it belonged: in that tobacco tin buried in his chest where a red heart used to be. Its lid rusted shut. He would not pry it loose now in front of this sweet sturdy woman, for if she got a whiff of the contents it would shame him. (pp. 72–3)

It is so moving – the way in which he doesn't recall what happened to Halle, Sethe's husband, and then, when he does, he tells her what he thinks she can bear, but some of the bits he doesn't tell her, then he tells her another bit when he has to, which means he too has to remember it. He negotiates what his emotions can take with complexity and tact – he does this in order to stay alive, not in order to stay dead. He inhabits just as much space as he dare, and forgets the other things which he knows are there.

SODRE: The 'enemy' they have to deal with inside themselves is not the same: Paul D has locked his red heart in his internal tobacco tin, and he feels he has triumphed over life, he has killed life.

BYATT: And he works in a slaughterhouse perfectly happily killing the pigs that come up the river, because he doesn't mind any more.

SODRE: Whereas Sethe can't do that; her 'red heart' has to be kept alive for her children.
BYATT: Blood makes milk, so you can't freeze your heart or the milk wouldn't come.
SODRE: So he feels he's battling against his heart, and she feels she's battling against her brain.

BYATT: Very beautiful. What about Baby Suggs? – the important thing in many ways is her name.
SODRE: What do you think Suggs is?
BYATT: I've only just thought that it may be to do with sucking – and there is a possible rhyme with 'dugs'. Suggs is an ugly word, and she is a very beautiful woman who is described by these two words, neither of which belongs to her. Except that she chose them. There's this wonderful thing all through about the names that are given to black people which they don't want or choose, and Baby Suggs hangs on to these two rather horrible words because her husband called her Baby and his name was Suggs, although he came and went almost immediately.
SODRE: This is part of the process of keeping a good memory alive to fight against the overwhelmingly bad memories. Holding on to her name keeps her connected to somebody who knows she is a person.
BYATT: And out of that she can make generosity for a whole community. I love the bit when she goes and sings in the clearing, and the way in which she makes a religion in which people can contemplate –
SODRE: In which they are told they must love themselves.
BYATT: They must love all the organs of their bodies. And they must love the colour of their own skin. The world is full of colour because of coloured people. And she can do that as long as she's not wounded to the quick. At the centre of the novel is a Greek tragedy, what is done to Baby Suggs by what Sethe does. Sethe's action destroys Baby Suggs and what she has built up in freedom. Though of course Sethe's act is an ineluctable consequence of the brutality of the whites. You feel that everybody in the book has a point beyond which they can't go on hoping or believing or loving or caring.
SODRE: And they all know at which moment they broke down.
BYATT: Yes. And they are strong, they do marvels to survive. Think of the black men together, getting out of those cages with the chains; if one of them fell they would all drown, but they all get out.

> For one lost, all lost. The chain that held them would save all or none, and Hi Man was the Delivery. They talked through that chain like Sam Morse and, Great God, they all came up. Like the unshriven dead, zombies on the loose, holding the chains in their hands, they trusted the rain and the dark, yes, but mostly Hi Man and each other. (p. 110)

Baby Suggs's religious group of 'coloredpeople' has this cohesion; she tells them they are beautiful, they must love themselves, must love every inch of their own bodies. This idea of loving your own body connects to Sethe's good feelings about her breasts and her belly and her children.

> Slaves not supposed to have pleasurable feelings on their own; their bodies not supposed to be like that, but they have to have as many children as they can to please whoever owned them. Still, they were not supposed to have pleasure deep down. She said for me not to listen to all that. That I should always listen to my body and love it. (p. 209)

And so when Baby Suggs is defeated it's terrible.
SODRE: When she can't function any more because she's lost her trust, the group falls apart. It's interesting that you linked it up with the men coming out of the boxes, I think that is exactly right. The moment she fails, the whole thing collapses.
BYATT: I suppose one of the glories of the novel is the scene near the end where Denver suddenly decides she must save Sethe and goes out and gets help from the outside community. This actually restores Baby Suggs in a mythic form, because all the neighbours who had been shunning them and isolating 124, come back and offer little dishes of food. As you would to a ghost. As you would to a spirit in a tree, to a local god. It's for Baby Suggs they come, and you could argue that Denver has taken on part of being Baby Suggs, as she grows up. When Lady Jones calls Denver 'Baby', it makes it possible for her to become a woman. Though the vague 'Baby' as a term of affection can seem demeaning. Baby Suggs's name comes from that.
SODRE: Garner thought that, he told her: 'Mrs Baby Suggs ain't no name for a freed Negro'.
BYATT: And she thinks this is all she has left of her husband.
SODRE: He wanted her to stick with 'Jenny'.
BYATT: Which was on her papers and she couldn't do that.

BYATT: Don't you think it's an act of genius for a black woman writing a novel about the slave community, to invent a very friendly, kindly white homestead and call it Sweet Home? With all the connotations of 'Home Sweet Home' and 'There's No Place Like Home'. All our novels are equivocal about the idea of 'home', but this one is savage. The dignity of the black people comes from their refusing to accept that this Sweet Home is anything other than a terrible, ghastly whited sepulchre.

SODRE: But they have to struggle to be able to give it up completely; Sethe feels that her mind behaves shamefully, because she keeps remembering the beauty of nature in Sweet Home. Paul D keeps telling himself that he must not love what is not his; he looks at the moon and makes a deliberate decision not to love it because it's not his, it's a white man's moon. The creation of the Garners and Sweet Home is brilliant; the good-natured, liberal Garners, who have a better kind of slavery, represent a real threat to the slaves' freedom of mind, to their capacity to fight for freedom. And yet it is also true that the Garners made it possible for them to keep family ties, which are a source of strength. Sethe hates herself for remembering the beautiful trees in Sweet Home, because she thinks she remembers them more clearly than she remembers the men hanging dead. There is something excruciatingly painful about this. As if her mind attaches itself to something beautiful, and this torments her as an act of betrayal.

BYATT: No, because she isn't repressing the memory of the hanging people, she's suppressing it for purposes of survival, as Paul D suppresses what he knows about what happened to them all. It isn't a state where someone rather hysterically only remembers the good things, it's the opposite, it's remembering (despite your own will) the good things because they *were* good things. The trees were beautiful, the sunshine shone. There's a wonderful scene where Sethe makes love to Halle in the corn and all the other men watch, because they have no privacy; the other men watch the tops of the corn moving.

SODRE: The writing that describes the lovemaking is just extraordinary: Sethe remembers 'that some of the corn stalks broke, folded down over Halle's back, and among the things her fingers clutched were husk and cornsilk hair' (p. 27). Morrison then intertwines the description of Sethe's memories with the description of the left-out men having a feast with the broken corn, so that the imagery of plucking 'those ears too young to eat' becomes a metaphor for this first lovemaking.

BYATT: Yes, the whole of the cornsilk. In a way the cornsilk being taken away from the corn cob is so much more beautiful than the raggedy dress she is able to make for herself. The dress is the world of culture as opposed to the shining cornsilk of the world of nature. I also admire the immense moral subtlety with which Morrison draws distinctions between the good the white people think they're doing, and how this appears in terms of absolute morals. When the master says to Halle, 'Didn't I let you buy your mother?' and he says 'Yes, but it was with my labor I bought her.'

SODRE: And Baby Suggs thinks she has lost 'her last and usually only living child'.

BYATT: And these facts are so clearly put as a matter of actual justice and observation. And you are brought up against how people can possibly get themselves into such a moral twist as to suppose that there was any virtue in letting somebody buy their mother. The same thing happens when Sethe is looking after the dying Mrs Garner. Sethe is in a state of extreme distress about her children's fate, and the beating of her people, yet she bothers about the old lady and the chamber pot. The old lady is fussing away about her death, which is a huge event to her because she's lived in a space where you're allowed to have huge, significant events in your life, whereas Sethe is in a harsher world where people are constantly hanged from trees, or have their feet chopped off, or their backs laid open, so that a tree of life grows out of their wounds. Which again is a Christian image, a deeply Christian image integrated into some quite other, hideously capricious thing. Again this is morally simple, yet it hurts you to the depths of your soul. The mockery of Sweet Home.

SODRE: It's a brilliant idea to create those specially nice whites: it makes the moral point so forcefully, the horrible complacency of the white couple who feel they are being so good; they are not deliberately cruel, but they are blind. When Sethe has chosen Halle as her partner, and asks 'Is there a wedding?', Mrs Garner answers only 'You are one sweet child.' You can see that Mrs Garner does love Sethe, but as if Sethe was a particularly intelligent and endearing pet. She has no conception of Sethe as a young woman.

BYATT: Another form of the Baby. And of course the whole people are mixed up because the black people give their milk to the white children, so the white children have drunk black milk. At the point of Sethe's terrible deed, a structure has been set up whereby you can *judge* how much Sethe is responsible for the death of her child and how much is the product of the institution of slavery, more particularly the peculiar evil of the Fugitive Slave Act, which gave slave-owners from the South the right to retrieve their 'property' from the non-slave-owning States to which the slaves had fled.

Toni Morrison exposes, precisely, the ridiculous debate (amongst whites) about whether black people are animals or people. The black people have so much more human dignity than the white people in this book, and are so much more thoughtful, intelligent, responsible, caring of each other, responsive to each other than any of the white people are to anybody, because the white people are completely marginalised simply as presences, and slightly thin. Then you get Sethe's full horror when Schoolteacher's unpleasant nephews are writing down her animal characteristics and her human characteristics. This is moral fury, but it fits on at a deep psychological level to the image of the 'crawling already' child – because Beloved was a child, and crawling is what the serpent does in the Bible, and beasts do on all fours. If you think in terms of evolution, the human being moves from beast to man as it gets up unnaturally on its hind legs and begins to walk. Beloved was never allowed to become a full human being and stand up and walk, and neither in a sense was Sethe. This idea of human beings as beasts connects to the terrible punishment of being made to wear bits, which Toni Morrison, herself, was horrified to discover, when she was researching into slave documents. And again the courtesy with which her characters treat each other through these humiliating terrors, takes on a mythic magnanimity and goodness.

SODRE: In such humiliating circumstances you can only keep your dignity if somebody treats you with respect; Paul D says that about the time when he was wearing the iron collar: Sethe looked at him in a way that didn't unman him, and this saved him from his own contempt.

BYATT: Yes, she didn't take his masculinity.

SODRE: It is also interesting that Paul D thought that although Halle and Sixo were definitely men, he wasn't entirely convinced about himself and his brothers; he was afraid that maybe they only became men when Garner said they were.

BYATT: Yes, he said he brought them up as men and not as boys.

SODRE: This very subtly shows that by offering the slaves their manhood as a gift, Garner was stealing it at the same time.

BYATT: This is of course why when Halle was unmanned by having seen Sethe having had her milk stolen, he horrified Paul D by sitting by the churn and covering his face with 'butter and clabber' – 'clabber' is the curds produced by the separation of the milk to make butter – in a sense the fresh milk soured. He just sat there, vacant, and covered his face with butterfat and sour milk. In terms of everything we've been saying he reverted to being a baby, he reverted to being an animal, he ceased to be a man. This was his point of no return, as Baby Suggs's going to bed was her point of no return. This image, which in itself is upsetting, becomes terrifying only in the context of the whole structure of the imagery. It adds of course to the terror of Sethe trying to hold on to the milk-giving relationship both with a living and with a dead child. Because they should be beyond milk, and yet they are stuck with milk.

SODRE: Sethe says clearly that if Denver clung to her in the way Beloved did, she'd be horrified, she would see Denver as a freak. But she can't have a normal relationship with Beloved even if Beloved is now nineteen, because she is still the 'crawling already' baby, with baby thoughts and emotions. (I think the story also allows for the existence of a 'real girl' Beloved, but this is a girl who has lost her mind, or was brought up so cruelly that she has not developed one, and who therefore fits in with Sethe's fantasies.)

SODRE: There is a striking scene where we suddenly see what it is like to be Beloved: the scene where her tooth falls out, and she feels as if she's going to fall apart physically: psychologically she has no skin, she is in constant danger of disintegration. This is fascinating, especially in the context of the importance of skin in the novel: 'She can feel her thickness thinning, dissolving into nothing' (p. 123). The sense of self is a psychological skin. The falling apart and the breakdown is becoming skinless, like the white people connected to death.

BYATT: Yes, which of course is wonderful, because if you see white people skinless you see white people dead. And this novel does. It's Death on a Pale Horse, from the Apocalypse, it's the pale figure. This is why Sethe reacts with such violence against the 'bleached nigger', the good white-haired Bodwin. Every time the white people come riding on a horse they carry with them this archetype. I know it's the horse that's pale, in the Bible, but there is a tradition of the image of the pale rider on the pale horse. And this is Death. Clint Eastwood used it, in *Pale Rider*.

SODRE: To recap a little: this novel is essentially about memory, about characters who don't want to remember, written by an author who is powerfully making the point that we must never, ever forget. Memory and remembering are connected to keeping alive in the mind those who have died, and therefore with the whole process of mourning, which implies both keeping an internal relationship with the dead, but also working through the loss and allowing some degree of separation. This is, of course, what Sethe can't do: she is so occupied by the ghost of this baby, who is greedy for reassurance that it is loved, that a normal mourning process can't take place. Mourning is necessary so life can continue in the present, but the wish of every character to obliterate the past in fact disrupts this process; when remembering is so unbearable, there can be no gradual distancing from the past.

BYATT: They can't afford to mourn Paul A or Sixo or any of the other people who have died because they can't afford to remember how they died. Sethe has taken Beloved's death into her own hands out of love because she wants to make her safe for ever, and the only place she can be safe is on the other side, where Sethe's mother is, but she hasn't made her safe, she's released her into a timeless limbo. I think constantly about what Freud says quoting Frazer, about how ancestors who are recently dead are seen as vengeful and demanding ghosts. There's a wonderful bit in Brian Aldiss's *Helliconia* trilogy, where one of the characters goes on a journey into the underworld in order to meet their parents, and finds that the dead are just terribly angry. This seems to be an experience everybody has of mourning; the dead are felt to be both impotent and furious at being dead. Human beings in various cultures have made this observation and various structures of the spirit world have been made to correspond with this. And what Freud says that Frazer says is that after a time these very angry ghosts become commuted into benign ancestors who can be worshipped and asked for advice. And that in a way is what happens to Baby Suggs: she becomes a benign ancestor, but Beloved doesn't.

SODRE: And, as Freud said, it's the ghosts who cause most guilt that won't go away. These ghosts hate you because they feel you've murdered them; this is relevant to a story in which the dead person has actually been murdered, even if murdered out of love. Of course the baby wouldn't know that, she is very angry and jealous of the other babies who are allowed to be alive. Sethe has to live a sane, ordinary life for Denver's sake, yet she can't because she's so wrapped up with Beloved. And Beloved, the vengeful baby, takes the man away from her mother; she is jealous of Paul D, but also envious of Sethe's connection to life through her sexuality.

BYATT: Yes, mourning and the Oedipus complex become more muddled up with each other.

SODRE: Miranda in *An Unofficial Rose* does exactly that – she separates her mother from the man as if she loved the man, but at a deeper level she wants to be able to entirely occupy her mother's mind.
BYATT: And in many ways you could take it back to Gwendolen, who obviously hated either her father or her stepfather, and tried to annihilate them and bond with her mother, whom she then persecuted.
SODRE: Gwendolen is constantly haunted by a ghost, by the dead face. She hasn't been able to mourn her father and stepfather, so she's haunted by this ghost for ever; she marries the man with the dead face and then has to kill him.
BYATT: It's wonderful how in a novel you can do something quite different from what you can do in life, which is embody the dead, or the phantom, or the vengeful figure, on an equal footing with the other characters in the book, which is of course how you read a book. When you're reading a book, you might fall in love with Paul D or you might feel you were Sethe, and you can move in and out of the characters, but they are all equally real in the book. When in real life you are mourning somebody, the mourners are present to each other, and all differently and intensely aware of a presence of an absence, something angry or in pain or vanishing, who isn't there. In a book all the characters are ambivalently there and not there, and Toni Morrison has exploited this wonderfully. What I love about Beloved is the way she swells and swells and swallows Sethe's life into her own, becoming more and more solid, which is what a phantom creature does in your mind, or a baby does when it grows, inside you and outside you. Beloved is and isn't a real person. Sethe and Beloved are equally real, in the book, as presumably imagined people are in the world of your inner objects and attachments, or in dreams. So she's used both the conventions of the realist novel and the conventions of dream reality to embody mourning in this terribly bloated way.
SODRE: Yes, and the power of imagination is conveyed through the creation of alive and dead characters who all have exactly the same quality of reality, of concreteness. The ghost baby has exactly the same intensity of emotions as a real baby; and Beloved is exactly like a giant baby who has been totally neglected. The baby's fierce possessiveness is compounded of love and hatred: hatred of the mother who is a separate being. The relationship between Sethe and Beloved becomes bad and mad, they are almost murdering each other. Sethe is forever having to placate this gigantic baby who attacks her more and more, so Beloved eats up Sethe's life and increases her guilt constantly. All Sethe wants is

to be forgiven, but Beloved is entirely unforgiving. Only those who are alive, and properly grown up, like Paul D, can bring her forgiveness.
BYATT: And does by saying 'You your best thing'. To go back to Beloved's skin holding her together, what Paul D does is put Sethe back into her own skin. And she can stop pouring herself out in all directions. Another idea that comes to mind is the idea of the bloodsucker, because Beloved is like a leech or tick or bloodsucking vampire, which takes the life out of you. And what might be thought to be milk is actually blood.
SODRE: She takes her life blood, and Paul D can sense this. Beloved's sexual relationship with Paul D takes his life, his manhood away and is completely to do with controlling him and devouring him.

> 'Well, ah, this is not the, a man can't, see, but aw listen here, it ain't that, it really ain't, Ole Garner, what I mean is, it ain't a weakness, the kind of weakness I can fight 'cause 'cause something is happening to me, that girl is doing it, I know you think I never liked her nohow, but she is doing it to me. Fixing me. Sethe, she's fixed me and I can't break it.'
>
> What? A grown man fixed by a girl? But what if the girl was not a girl, but something in disguise? A lowdown something that looked like a sweet young girl and fucking her or not was not the point, it was not being able to stay or go where he wished in 124, and the danger was in losing Sethe because he was not man enough to break out, so he needed her, Sethe, to help him, to know about it, and it shamed him to have to ask the woman he wanted to protect to help him do it, God damn it to hell. (pp. 126–7)

BYATT: Yes, the surprising and interesting thing about it is that what Beloved is trying to achieve through it apart from power over Paul D is that she wants to cease to be a baby and become a woman. Of course she can't because she's dead.
SODRE: In the other, implied, version of the story, Beloved is a real girl who has always lived in a dark room, the prisoner of a white man who used her for sex. In this version of events, Beloved is repeating the past situation, but with herself in the role of the sexual abuser: she sexually exploits and abuses Paul D, and imprisons him in a hateful situation. Paul D is trapped in the cold room, and Beloved acts the part of the white man who comes to visit, just for sex.
BYATT: That again slithers over the boundary of one story, one dream into another – here we move into the area of memories and race

memories. One of the things about black novels, if you can talk about all of them at once, certainly about African novels, is that the writers have said they're rejecting a Christian framework, and there is a great deal of writing about negritude which claims that Africans believe in an animist world and that Western colonialists then tell them that the Western vision is the true vision of reason and religion, whereas what they feel is quite different. I feel that Toni Morrison, with her intensely Christian background, has played with this idea: that there is a spirit world and you might treat it as real as opposed to treating it simply as literary prop. Her attempt to create a spirit world didn't work in *Tar Baby*, as she herself has said. But it works here. It works beautifully. I think one of the wonderful moments is when Sixo goes to the secret place to wait for the thirty-mile woman, and finds that it was a place used by the Red Indians, that the spirits that are in there don't mind him being there. And he says this purely practically. But what this does in terms of the novel is make it purely practically a world in which spirits do rise up and can be accepted as being part of the normal run of things, so that when you read that wonderful first paragraph you think right, we're in a world in which babies haunt houses, this is this world, this is not a world in which you ask 'was there a baby, wasn't there a baby?' There is a baby and it is haunting the house. And Sixo did meet Red Indian spirits and they didn't mind him being there. And you can't call it a metaphor as you might if it was a white ghost story, you can't say that Beloved is a projection of Sethe or a metaphor for her state of mind. She is what she is, she is Beloved in a terrible rage. And this is why the book is so powerful. It's the concreteness.

SODRE: If there wasn't a real, if it was only a psychological ghost, a lot of the power would have been lost.

BYATT: Yes, it isn't psychological, it is a story of things.

SODRE: The other thing about memory is that Beloved has such fragmentary memory. She only has little bits which come either from the other world or from some dimly remembered psychotic-making childhood. Having almost no memory, she can't be felt to be a real person: she is strange, she can't communicate.

BYATT: And because she's got gaps in her memory, she's got gaps in her self, because your self is your memory. She remembers Sethe's earrings which Denver doesn't remember, because by the time Denver was born the earrings were sewed into Sethe's skirt and had gone to Baby Suggs. But her memories have that fragmentary quality that one's own memories of one's babyhood have. You remember certain little bright things. That fits with that scene you mentioned where Beloved feels she's coming to pieces.

> Beloved, inserting a thumb in her mouth along with the forefinger, pulled out a back tooth. There was hardly any blood, but Denver said, 'Ooooh, didn't that hurt you?'
>
> Beloved looked at the tooth and thought, This is it. Next would be her arm, her hand, a toe. Pieces of her would drop maybe one at a time, maybe all at once. Or on one of those mornings before Denver woke and after Sethe left she would fly apart. It is difficult keeping her head on her neck, her legs attached to her hips when she is by herself. Among the things she could not remember was when she first knew that she could wake up any day and find herself in pieces. She had two dreams: exploding, and being swallowed. When her tooth came out – an odd fragment, last in the row – she thought it was starting. (p. 133)

The brilliance of that is, anybody might feel that because teeth do come out, and any dream you have about teeth coming out is a dream of disintegration and flying apart. I don't know what you think about that dream, but I find it a death dream.

SODRE: I agree, but I wanted to read this. This is a scene where they go into the cold room to get cider, and Beloved suddenly disappears, and Denver feels absolutely desperate, panic is creeping over her like hairs, there is no sight or sound of Beloved. What Denver most feared is happening. Then Denver has the same kind of depersonalising experience that Beloved suffers from:

> If she stumbles, she is not aware of it because she does not know where her body stops, which part of her is an arm, a foot or a knee. She feels like an ice cake torn away from the solid surface of the stream, floating on darkness, thick and crashing against the edges of things around it. Breakable, meltable and cold. (pp. 122–3)

Then further down, she says,

> This is worse than when Paul D came to 124 and she cried helplessly into the stove. This is worse. Then it was for herself. Now she is crying because she has no self. Death is a skipped meal compared to this. She can feel her thickness thinning, dissolving into nothing. She grabs the hair at her temples to get enough to

> uproot it and halt the melting for a while. Teeth clamped shut, Denver brakes her sobs. She doesn't move to open the door because there is no world out there. (p. 123)

Gradually, bit by bit, we begin to be able to imagine Beloved's experience, when she was locked in the hold of a ship or locked in the white man's dark room, or living in the world of the dead. The experience that causes this psychological going to pieces starts like that, and Denver has to go through something similar. This is perhaps Beloved's only way of communicating her experiences – in her mindless driven way she gets other people to repeat them. As with the sexual abuse of Paul D, Denver here goes through Beloved's catastrophic experience of being totally abandoned and losing her sense of self.

BYATT: And you can read that all sorts of ways. You could either say that Beloved has called up Denver's experience of exploding apart, or you could say that the ghost Beloved has put a hand on Denver and caused her to feel she's exploding apart, or you could say that they are both a function of Sethe's almost incapacity to hold herself together inside her skin. This brings us back to the question of whether all the characters in a novel are always aspects of one consciousness. When we first meet the anonymous lyric voice which is Beloved but which isn't, which is all black women, Toni Morrison is doing something with her prose which says 'We're all parts of the same stream, we're all ice cakes off the same water.' I think we should say that when we first read it we both found it difficult to deal with, and I think a lot of critics felt it was a bit of an excrescence, a bit too much. But I've now come to the conclusion it's completely necessary to the book; every time you read it it seems more austere and intelligently put together.

SODRE: But also put together in such a way that it works at every possible level.

BYATT: Exactly. And even the loose teeth are in one aspect part of the dead man on the face of the figure of Beloved, or whoever it is. And we don't know really, because the first line of this piece of lyric is

> I am Beloved and she is mine. I see her take flowers away from leaves she puts them in a round basket the leaves are not for her she fills the basket she opens the grass (p. 210)

'I am Beloved and she is mine' is an echo of the Song of Solomon. My beloved is mine and I am his. And here somebody is saying 'I am Beloved, and therefore *she is mine*', but it could be Denver talking, it could be Beloved talking, could be Sethe talking. It is all black women who have lost. It is all dead people, too, I think, saying, 'although I am under the grass I am beloved'. Then the speaking voice moves into the slave ship whilst still being also the voice of Beloved in the grave – that's how I understand it.

SODRE: This emphasises our point of the importance of the book *not* making sense on the first reading: what happened in the past is so unbearable that it can only be apprehended in a fragmentary way. Sethe hates the fact that she has no conscious control over her memory. For example, when Paul D tells her what happened to Halle:

> She shook her head from side to side, resigned to her rebellious brain. Why was there nothing it refused? No misery, no regret, no hateful picture too rotten to accept? Like a greedy child it snatched up everything. Just once, could it say, No thank you? I just ate and can't hold another bite? I am full God damn it of two boys with mossy teeth, one sucking on my breast the other holding me down, their book-reading teacher watching and writing it up. I am still full of that, God damn it, I can't go back and add more. Add my husband to it, watching, above me in the loft – hiding close by – the one place he thought no one would look for him, looking down on what I couldn't look at at all. And not stopping them – looking and letting it happen. But my greedy brain says, Oh thanks, I'd love more – so I add more. And no sooner than I do, there is no stopping. (p. 70)

And then she just goes on adding all the bits. Again she says, 'No thank you, I don't want to know it, to have to remember.' Her memory is an abhorrence to her, like a beast that has got into her head. The reader has to feel that the story can only be told slowly in tiny morsels, otherwise it would be impossible to digest.

BYATT: Morrison describes Sethe's memory as a greedy child, which of course means that in some sense the phantom Beloved is identified with her memory which won't let go. But this brings us to a great ambivalence in the story, because in both Paul D and Sethe their strength is their capacity to remember and not be destroyed.

Immediately after the passage you have just quoted Sethe considers going crazy, like Halle.

> Other people's brains stopped, turned around and went on to something new, which is what must have happened to Halle. And how sweet that would have been: the two of them back by the milk shed, squatting by the churn, smashing cold, lumpy butter into their faces with not a care in the world. (p. 70)

But in fact she stays human; whether she likes it or not she has the intelligence to continue to look at her memories, and more or less see them for what they are. It is her nature; she can't abdicate. And this is partly what drives her to kill her child, but it is what also drives her to be able to save her child. And to save Denver.

Perhaps this is the moment to think about Toni Morrison's original planning of the structure of the narrative and the structure of the family. It was quite possible for Toni Morrison to give Sethe simply the two boys and a baby – and then to let Sethe kill the baby. She didn't have to give her two boys and a baby, *and* a baby born on the journey, a baby she kills *and* one she saves. The complex invention of the family makes a complex moral structure, beautiful and full of surprises. As fast as you think this is all leading to death, you see that it is all equally leading to life and preservation and hope, and to Denver's capacity to move out into the future.

SODRE: Sethe feels betrayed by her memory, but it is the capacity not to forget that keeps her alive.

BYATT: Does this have anything to say to psychoanalysis, which in a sense works on the assumption that if you can really remember clearly you can live?

SODRE: Yes, I think so. Psychoanalysis would say the same thing as Toni Morrison, that however horrible the past, you can only live and be sane and integrated if you are in contact with it. The connection with beauty is important – the sense of hope and the will to create a better life are deeply connected to the ability to preserve beauty and goodness in the internal world. One of the fundamental ideas in Kleinian psychoanalytic theory is that sanity depends on the capacity to retain a good, trusting link with good figures in the internal world – the capacity to survive loss through the internalisation of the good experience. The presence of the sycamores in Sethe's mind, for example, means that cruelty and destructiveness are not totally omnipotent, evil cannot destroy all goodness and all beauty. And, as you said, psychoanalysis at its most fundamental is based on the belief that remembering what has been forgotten for defensive purposes is what cures psychological disturbances; what is forgotten doesn't disappear, only becomes an invisible, and therefore more powerful, enemy within.

BYATT: And this applies to the race as to the individual: the black people must remember the past clearly and what was done, in order to be able to mourn, to go on, to live. And the white people who read this book (who are very secondary people) must be able to be put through a history they didn't go through but ought to know. Which is where a novel is different from your own memories. Because once you've read this, you have acquired memories you might not like to have, but because the book is so strong you now have them and they are part of you. I said once in a television interview that I felt this book was so good that it did enable me to feel the experience of being a black person. Later various people in student audiences asked Toni Morrison about this. They felt I had no right to say that. Toni Morrison herself wasn't quite sure I had. What I was trying to say was that the imaginative power of her writing is Tolstoyan – she gives you no option but to *inhabit her world*. You can't read it as though you were looking on. In that sense you have to acquire, imaginatively, the terrible memories and history you haven't experienced or inherited, and in that sense haven't a 'right' to, but have access to, through the power of art. The novel haunts you as the ghost haunts the novel, exacting imaginative life blood. It's a form of moral *power*, good and terrifying. We were going to talk about what this book sets out to do to the reader.

SODRE: To use Sethe's imagery, I would say that this novel keeps your mind greedily wanting to know, but simultaneously gives you information in such a way that your mind is constantly jogged from one side to the other and you know and don't know simultaneously. There is something very interesting about the way in which the author gives you information that can misinform, and information that's incomplete, and how you are constantly surprised by patterns changing and stories becoming different. The book is also like Baby Suggs's quilt: there are all these different patches and occasionally one patch absolutely screams at you: a red patch of such violence that it creates a wave of disturbance, so that you almost want to stop reading. There is something interesting, too, about the fact that by the end of the book you realise that there's a lot you didn't understand; you want to read it differently, with the knowledge of what actually happened.

BYATT: And in a way this is achieved again by making all the characters so agreeable. You might argue that Denver was an intensely disagreeable person, the way she's treating her mother at the beginning, but she could be treating her a lot worse. There is a kind of dignity between Baby Suggs and Sethe and Paul D and Denver, a kind of making-do, almost comedy, which we've picked up several times in the kitchen scenes, the feeding scenes. These let you think as a reader that you're in a civilised world with warm, friendly people who are doing their best to make life bearable. Then suddenly the writer and the characters drop you off into real depths of horror which you are made to experience all the more because you have trustingly entered this world of vigorous language, good-natured comedy, and apparently comic ghost story. And Morrison doesn't let you off the horror of the moment when Sethe kills Beloved. You get various tellings of it, and you think: well thank God she's told this, now. Then she tells it a bit later again, and you can't quite bear reading it. Then you get covered with the blood of it. And there is a point at which the reader's consciousness goes along with Paul D's, who is completely repelled by what Sethe has done, and indeed says to her, 'Do you go on four legs or do you go on two?' He's actually saying, what you did was what an animal would do, and she more or less replies 'No, I did what a human being would do, I wanted to save my child.' Toni Morrison allows you to stop with Paul D and feel horror, and therefore when she chooses to take you onwards, to the point where you feel immense love and admiration, she has got you in the palm of her hand and you have to go with her. It's all so clear, and at the same time so mysterious.

I'd like to add something about the relation of this novel to American novels from the period when this novel is set. Novels by Hawthorne, Melville, Edgar Allan Poe. Harry Levin wrote a book called *The Power of Blackness*, about the fiction of this time. Melville and Hawthorne and Poe think in black and white, about demons and angels. On the realist level there is the white hero frontiersman who somehow has managed to make friends with a black person. There is Huck Finn and Jim, there is Deerslayer and the Indians, there is the symbiotic tying up of Ishmael and Queequeg on board the *Pequod* where the 'savage' harpooner who is tattooed with the map of the world is the closest friend and the saviour of the white man. There are also other images like Edgar Allan Poe's image of the South, in 'The Narrative of Arthur Gordon Pym'. The characters sail to the Antarctic, where what they find is an evil world of snow-white hell, and blackness becomes lively. And there are all the black people in Melville's 'Benito Cereno'. In all these writers the black and white imagery embodies a deep guilt, and there is a sense in which whiteness and blankness are much more evil and terrifying than blackness and the night. Consider the marvellous chapter in *Moby Dick* on 'The Whiteness of the Whale', for instance. What Toni Morrison has done, I think, is pick up all that imagery, and marginalise the whites almost entirely, destroy all their own metaphors for themselves, one after the other, so that they're not there at all except as bone and teeth. White things are bone and teeth – and milk, of course.

Human beings are black.

BYATT: The Song of Solomon links sisters and water. There is the virginal sister: 'A garden inclosed is my sister, my spouse; a spring shut up, a fountain sealed' (4: 12). Then in the last chapter:

> O that thou wert as my brother, that sucked the breasts of my mother! when I should find thee without, I would kiss thee; yea, I should not be despised.
>
> I would lead thee, and bring thee into my mother's house, who would instruct me: I would cause thee to drink of spiced wine of the juice of my pomegranate.
>
> His left hand should be under my head, and his right hand should embrace me. (8: 1–3)

In a sense, those become the words of Denver, bringing Beloved into the house, and so Beloved becomes everybody's beloved which is why I feel that in some sense she also is Christ, she is either the demon or the saviour, she is, if you like, the suffering, sacrificial lamb who has been killed on behalf of the people. 'Many waters cannot quench love neither can the floods drown it' – I'm sure that image sustains and empowers the image of Beloved under the river.

SODRE: But also her being so thirsty.

BYATT: There is a passage which is spoken by a composite voice of Beloved and all the drowned slaves thrown from the slave ships. It is full of liquids and water, of thirst and drowning. Beloved swallows all the liquid that could possibly be provided; many waters cannot quench love. And Sethe's love has to survive despite all this water. There is an extraordinary scene where Sethe squats down and pees more and more water when she first sees Beloved.

SODRE: And when she finally realises Beloved is the baby she then equates that with her water breaking when she had Denver. Amy thought she was going to create a flood.

BYATT: And Denver is born into the river water, of course. Again I think one needs to think in terms of the Christian imagery of the River Jordan which you cross over to die. The Song of Solomon is an extraordinary mixture of sexual imagery and of religious love, sacrificial love, and parental love – and the word 'sister', used in apposition to 'spouse'. It partly suggests a kind of incest, I suppose, a sort of closeness closer than husband and wife.

SODRE: Sethe says that Halle was like a brother to her. This closeness is necessary, not because of the incestuous implication, but because they had no other family.

BYATT: The black people of Sweet Home make themselves into a kind of artificial family, although they don't even have real names, nobody is anybody's mother and nobody is anybody's father. Some of them have the same names, so one is Paul A and one is Paul D.

SODRE: Three Pauls.

BYATT: They nevertheless somehow connect themselves together into such family as can be managed for the time they are together. And when Paul D comes back, I suppose he is therefore coming back to his sister, his spouse, he's coming in through the gate into the house. But there is Beloved the ghost, who won't be placated, taking up the space of being beloved, so there's no room for Paul D to be beloved, because the space is eaten by the child.

SODRE: Which means there's no space for Sethe to have a life with plans, as she says.

BYATT: And in a sense this does connect back (though I think it's much more moving) to the situation of Ann in *An Unofficial Rose* – a woman trying to make her own life with a lover but being eaten up by the past and by her sex, by the responsibilities that being a woman has put upon her.

SODRE: And by a very possessive child.

SODRE: The great monologue, towards the end of the book, has meaning within all the different versions of the story. Including history, the racial story.

BYATT: If we look at the language of its first paragraph, 'I am beloved and she is mine' we can see how it twists the syntax and the meaning and makes it rather threatening, because it's not going both ways. It's not 'I am beloved and you are beloved', it is 'I am beloved' and therefore the person who loves me is mine, I'm eating everything up.

> I am not separate from her there is no place where I stop her face is my own and I want to be there in the place where her face is and to be looking at it too (p. 210)

SODRE: It's because of her terrible loss that she is so possessive, she's got to eat up her mother because she hasn't got one, she saw her mother dying in the sea.

BYATT: I think this is the original bit, this is also simply the baby in the grave, Sethe's baby. Don't you think?

SODRE: Yes; I think what is difficult to understand on the first reading, and afterwards becomes complex in the most interesting way, is that the monologue can be understood from the point of view of each of the different versions of the story: Sethe's dead baby and her experience of dying and of living in the other world; Beloved the girl imprisoned by the white man who separated her from her mother and used her for sex, the girl who went mad; and the girl captured with her mother and father, who watches her father die and her mother commit suicide by throwing herself in the sea. Everything can be read as referring to all the different stories.

BYATT: Which is a very ambitious thing to try to do. The 'hot thing', which keeps recurring like a punctuation mark, I always took to be the knife coming across the throat of the baby and the blood spurting, but it could be the slave being branded.

SODRE: It could be both – all the different stories are woven into one.

BYATT: That's what I think. Then the voice moves into the grave, in the sense that the dead man is buried on her face, but it might be moving into the hold of the slave ship, because we know that the slaves were packed so tightly that they came across with dead men on top of them. I love it that it says in the beginning.

> in the beginning we could vomit now we do not now we cannot his teeth are pretty white points someone is trembling I can feel it over here he is fighting hard to leave his body which is a small bird trembling there is no room to tremble so he is not able to die my own dead man is pulled away from my face I miss his pretty white points (pp. 210–11)

He obviously had filed teeth, but equally it's her teeth that start going when she starts disintegrating.

SODRE: But it's also like a very small child in this place of death having to be attached to something, anything that seems to contain some life; whatever shines in the darkness, for instance.
BYATT: Then you get the bread that's the colour of the sea and the men without skin pushing people through with poles, and it's clear enough what you're seeing, the sea, the bread, the drowning woman: 'the woman with my face is in the sea   a hot thing' (p. 211).
SODRE: I think what she says is that her woman actively threw herself in the sea, wasn't thrown in the sea, and this is why she feels abandoned by her. 'The men without skin are making loud noises   they push my own man through   they do not push the woman with my face through' (p. 212). They do not push her, she throws herself in. There is this hill made of people, this pile of corpses, which later appears in the last scene, where Sethe tries to kill Bodwin with the ice pick – in her disturbed state of mind she thinks that Bodwin, the white man who is coming to take Denver to work, is the Schoolteacher coming back for her, confusing the past with the present. Here Beloved does the same, because she sees the crowd of black people at the gate as the hill of corpses on the ship, and she sees Sethe running towards it as her mother throwing herself in the sea with the corpses; she thinks it has happened again, and she runs away. In the monologue she constantly refers to being abandoned, and losing her personality – her 'face' when her mother disappears.

> the woman is there with the face I want   the face that is mine   they fall into the sea which is the color of the bread   she has nothing in her ears   if I had the teeth of the man who died on my face I would bite the circle around her neck   bite it away   I know she does not like it   now there is room to crouch and to watch the crouching others   it is the crouching that is now always now   inside   the woman with my face is in the sea   a hot thing (p. 211)

She keeps saying to Sethe that Sethe went away from her, because she has seen her mother dying, and taking her face and her smile away – and Beloved's sense of self as well. And Sethe believes she is talking about the murder.
BYATT: And here is the picture of a whole people which was not allowed to be a mother or to have a child. Or to be a child or to have a mother. They were treated as a commodity. And then later you get the images:

> I am in the water and she is coming there is no round basket (p. 213)

And of course they're Sethe's earrings which she remembers.

> I follow her we are in the diamonds which are her earrings now my face is coming I have to have it I am looking for the join I am loving my face so much (ibid.)

And this is also part of what Baby Suggs said, telling her people they must love their bodies:

> my dark face is close to me I want to join she whispers to me she whispers I reach for her chewing and swallowing she touches me she knows I want to join she chews and swallows me (ibid.)

It moves from being beautiful to being terrifying, all sorts of shapes shifting:

> I am gone now I am her face my own face has left me I see me swim away a hot thing (ibid.)

It is actually very beautiful. Then you start getting the name right in the very end:

> I am not dead I am not there is a house there is what she whispered to me I am where she told me I am not dead I sit the sun closes my eyes when I open them I see the face I lost Sethe's is the face that left me Sethe sees me see her and I see the smile her smiling face is the place for me it is the face I lost she is my face smiling at me doing it at last a hot thing now we can join a hot thing (ibid.)

It is very daring, and at first you think perhaps it doesn't come off. But in fact, if you analyse the construction of the experience of immersion, it becomes a very powerful, very clear emotion like the whole of the rest of the book. Intellectual understanding makes the experience more profound and more direct.

SODRE: But you can only analyse this after you have the book so much in your brain that you can relate to every single bit in all the different levels, of the different stories together. Like the diamonds, the minnows of light reflected in the water, and the cold room where Beloved and Denver go, in which there is the same play of light. You have to see it –

it only makes sense in fact if you think about all the stories at the same time, including history.

BYATT: One of the glorious things about writing a book is that you discover very late what are the key images round which the whole book clusters, which are the knots in the fishing net with which you draw up what it is you're writing about. Reading *Beloved*, for instance, and thinking about the earrings, I am excited by the way in which they work both as images of light and of something shining, and also purely in the plot as the thing which Beloved remembers. And then they permeate all these images of light in water, and somehow at that point the earrings begin to hold the book together. But there are so many images which hold the book together, including water itself.

SODRE: And that holds the reader together. When Denver is telling Beloved stories about the past, stories that Beloved is so hungry for, because she has so little past, Denver is consciously aware that she's making a net with the telling of the stories, to hold Beloved. So in the text itself the function of the writer is spelt out by Denver, who is holding this child with almost no past and no mind, with a net made of the past.

BYATT: And this of course is what Toni Morrison is doing for the descendants of the people she is reimagining and for herself and by extension for us.

Chapter 7

Dreams and Fictions

SODRE: The most striking proof, from the point of view of the psychoanalyst, that the human mind needs 'fictions', is the existence of dreaming, the unconscious capacity to create narratives which represent aspects of the internal world in symbolic form. Freud thought that dreams were needed for fulfilling wishes that couldn't be fulfilled by ordinary external reality, but a dream is never only the fulfilment of a particular desire; it is a form of unconscious communication with oneself. When we dream, we use 'fictional' representations of events that take place in psychic reality to help us to work through conflicts and anxieties. A dream is very different from a work of art – it emerges spontaneously, its meaning is intensely personal, it tends to disappear almost instantly; and yet, at the most basic level, it must come from the same 'place' in the mind.

BYATT: Dreams construct many kinds of narrative, and I believe I remember many kinds from my very early days of dreaming. There are archetypal, or mythic dreams, of the kind that excited Jung – dreams of forests, or mountains, or caves, or suns and moons and stars. Jung encouraged his patients to make drawings of the trees and lakes they met in these dreams. Cecil Day Lewis once told me that he had again and again a dream of walking through a forest and finding a clearing in which stood a cup, or vessel, full of perfect clean water. He said he had this dream over and over again, throughout his whole life. This is like meeting a myth or a fairytale, which appears to have both a 'universal' and perhaps a private significance. I don't know whether he had the dream before he knew the Arthurian legends about the Grail or not. But he gave me the impression that he was very little when it began, and I have similar memories of secret gardens, or orchards, of rivers and waste lands.

This is very different from the kind of dream in which the dreamer is wrestling with family relationships or relationships amongst people known, or half-known. Such dreams are almost hypotheses, or explorations of hidden feelings or judgements. They say: 'If I said this to them what would they do?' A struggle goes on, which is a kind of narrative exploration of possibilities, or hopes, or fears.

And then there is a dream which appears to come from nowhere. There is one that I had about a fortnight ago now which I see as I speak is connected to this book that we are writing: I was in a village which had a big pond and a little bridge from the pond, which crossed a road. It was a very nice, clean, somehow southern English village, almost bare in its cleanness. From the other side of the pond I could see a school building and a library; I was and was not the librarian – sometimes I felt 'librarian' feelings and responsibility, and sometimes I was an observing reader or narrator. I was terribly distressed about the paucity of the provision of children's books in this library – the library was attached to the school, and it all looked terribly nice and clean, and well made. But inside, the books were not there, there was an emptiness, and I didn't know what to do because I was in the small village and no traffic appeared to be coming through it and nothing was happening.

I could offer you a modern social interpretation – that I feel somehow that our children's lives are impoverished by the absence of complicated books in their libraries. Or you might say to me that my unconscious felt suddenly empty of stories but it's interesting that that dream bothered me because I couldn't *place* it. I still have no idea where that place was. It doesn't belong to my life yet I could tell you where the windows were on the library and what the duck pond looked like, and where the pavement went. In fact it also fades into nothing at the edges as though I have imagined just as much space as I needed to imagine to get the two buildings and the pond in. That's a dream with a meaning – it is telling me something about libraries with the wrong books in. It is experienced at the time as a dream with a meaning.

And then you have very, very frightening dreams which are almost physical which I think are primarily to do with your body, so that all you feel is that you are being squashed or pulled, or afraid of being battered. There are two more things I would like to say about dreams and their relation to narrative. As a novelist I am interested in the dreamer's capacity to stand back and analyse a dream while it is happening. You say to yourself, 'Now I *know* this is a story'; sometimes I even think you can push or control the events. You say to yourself, 'You ought to be able to see the so-and-so if you really try' and then you find you can see it. That is not so different from inventing rooms or landscapes in fictions.

The other thing I want to describe is a kind of dream I have which is most deeply to do with myself as a writer – a dream which is experienced more like a poem – where all the images fuse into a kind of intense symbolic knot or painting. In such dreams you can see everything you were worrying about laid out in beautiful objects, solid metaphors you can see and touch, and the relationships between the things for which the dream objects are symbols are much more complex than they could ever be if you described them in a linear narrative. All these kinds of dreams, it seems to me, find their way out into novels.

SODRE: It is very interesting that, among all the different types of dream you describe, there are some which you feel are particularly related to yourself as a writer, and that you find something is 'given' to you in intricate visual imagery that can then be translated into words. You are obviously interested in your dreams because you know they are 'truthful fictions', not 'lies'.

BYATT: And this deals in some deep way with the accusation that has perennially been levelled at fiction, that it is something trivial or false. There was a novelist in the 1960s called B. S. Johnson who attempted to write what he called novels which described nothing that hadn't actually happened. He was obsessed by the possible truth of a phrase from his childhood: 'Telling stories is telling lies.'

This depends on treating 'stories' as a synonym for 'lies'. His mother and my mother would say 'Don't tell me such stories.' I don't know if it works in Portuguese. And he really began to believe that fiction was wicked because it was some kind of untruth, unreality – it got connected in his mind with the fashionable idea that 'reality' was random and chaotic and undescribable. (This led him, which it need not logically have done, to believe that the non-narrative forms of Joyce and Beckett were closer to 'reality' than storytelling.)

Whereas what you're saying is that these stories are simply another form of reality, another part of our world – another kind of truth. What about daydreams which are narratives that you have much more control over?

SODRE: Daydreams are much more controlled, less spontaneous than real dreams, and therefore more easily used for defensive purposes, against knowledge of internal reality. In Hanna Segal's words, 'Where the daydreamer avoids conflict by a phantasy of omnipotent wishfulfilment and a denial of external and psychic realities, the artist seeks to locate his conflict and resolve it in his creation.'

Although we all have a daydream subtext, as it were, going on in our minds, which can be useful for trying things out in fantasy, what we have been mostly interested in when discussing these novels are the daydreams that are used solely for defensive purposes; they can appear to be 'realistic' but they are essentially wish-fulfilling fantasies, consoling lies; people like Gwendolen use them in order *not to know* themselves. When rereading what we said in these conversations, I noticed how often we discussed whether we believed in a character or in a part of a story, or didn't believe it – 'truthful' fictions and 'lying' fictions (or, to use Britton's more elegant phrase, truth-seeking and truth-evading fictions).

BYATT: I was about to say that a great deal of popular romantic fiction is popular in the way that a really good daydream is, and unsatisfying in exactly that way also. Like the daydream we all have when we buy our National Lottery tickets and we sit down for ten minutes and think exactly what we will do when our figures come up on the shimmering balls in the whirly sphere – and then they don't. If you are Barbara Cartland you offer a people a daydream – which they can comfortably recognise as a daydream. The kind that runs: if a very beautiful man were to appear in the place where I work he would immediately see that I am the most attractive and interesting woman there, although to anybody's normal eyes I don't appear to be. This is a game anyone can play, and everyone does play from time to time. Gwendolen's great daydream gets snarled up in reality when she tells herself: 'I am going *now* to become a great actress or a great singer because now it is clearly necessary for me financially to have what this particular daydream has from time to time offered me.' But Klesmer exposes the daydream when he tells her that she hasn't the voice, and above all hasn't *done the work*. But this also educates her.

SODRE: The daydream dis-educates her because it prevents her from engaging in something productive, and especially because it works against self-knowledge.

BYATT: Yes it does, but George Eliot is a very remorseless moralist, and Gwendolen pays for her lack of self-knowledge. I think sometimes that daydreams – like certain frivolous fictions – can give you a bit of time off from terrible reality so that you can better go back to deal with life.

The image of the drowned face in *Daniel Deronda* is like a real dream – the kind that is experienced as a kind of symbolic warning from another world over which you have little control – and yet if you can in some way gather it into your consciousness and know why it so frightens you, you aren't so helpless.

SODRE: Which is what happens at the end of the novel: there is hope for Gwendolen, if she faces her nightmare. George Eliot is profoundly knowledgeable about unconscious defence mechanisms, and through Gwendolen she shows her belief that the only chance one has of achieving psychological balance is through facing one's worst nightmares. Gwendolen doesn't choose to face what she dreads: she feels assaulted by her unconscious.

BYATT: Yes. And the same applies in many ways to Lucy Snowe, who is assaulted by bad dreams and nightmare visions and things in herself that have become uncontrollable and huge. In many ways her account (or Charlotte Brontë's account) of Vashti is experienced by the reader as a bad dream. This may be because Lucy conveys a feeling of being frozen and powerless when she describes dreams and visions – though she also always conveys a feeling of great forces of destruction or possibly creation suppressed and exploding. And this pulls the reader, or at least this reader, into the state of mind of a paralysed dreamer, assaulted by a dream.

It's clear that George Eliot understood the unconscious before Freud connected the unconscious life and the dream life into his kind of narrative. How new was his thinking?

SODRE: Trilling quotes Freud saying: 'The poets and philosophers before me discovered the unconscious. What I discovered was the scientific method by which the unconscious can be studied.' Freud felt greatly indebted to literature, as we know. One particularly beautiful example of a literary dream, in which dreaming is felt to be a grappling of the mind with the most extreme conflict, is in *War and Peace*, when Prince Andrei dreams that he dies, just before he really dies:

> Something not human – death – is breaking in through the door and he must hold the door to. He grapples with the door, straining every ounce of his strength – to lock it is no longer possible – but his efforts are feeble and awkward, and the door, under the pressure of that awful thing, opens and shuts again.
>
> Once more *It* pushes on the door from without. His last superhuman struggles are vain and both leaves of the door are

> noiselessly opened. *It* comes in and it is *death*. And Prince Andrei died. But at the very instant when in his dream he died Prince Andrei remembered that he was asleep, and at the very instant when he died he exerted himself and was awake.
>
> 'Yes, that was death. I died – and woke up. Yes, death is an awakening!' His soul was suddenly flooded with light, and the veil which till then had concealed the unknown was lifted from his spiritual vision. He felt as if powers hitherto confined within him had been set free, and was aware of that strange lightness of being which had not left him since. (Book XII, Ch. 16)

You couldn't get a better example of a dream that is both wish-fulfilling (death is an 'awakening') and a working through of unbearable anxieties toward acceptance of the inevitable.

SODRE: I would be really interested in hearing you talk about how something gets transformed in a writer's mind from the raw material, the basic stuff that's inside you – emotional experience, unconscious processes and things you think and know about – into producing a creative work of art.

BYATT: I think I have always worked very close to my dream imagery, and I've always been very unsatisfied with a reductive social realist image of what a novel is doing, because I have had this strong sense that poetic images and visionary images and dream-structured narratives are of equal importance – without ever being tempted towards surrealism, which doesn't interest me greatly. There are writers and pieces of writing that have excited me, particularly Coleridge, who recorded his own dreams vividly in his notebooks, and clearly felt that his greatest poems derived from dream images. When he wrote 'Kubla Khan', he said that the images rose as vivid spectra before his eyes. The dreams that interest me both in my own work and as I read, are where by looking away from what you're thinking about, you can actually experience it much more intensely in images, or in vivid spectra.

Another very interesting example is the dreams of Descartes. He recorded three dreams on the night of 10 November 1619, which he afterwards saw as a turning-point in his intellectual life. One of these was about struggling up a hill against a terrible wind trying to get to a church – which he himself said was partly to do with having had a set of thoughts that might be against Christianity. In another he dreamed that he found two books: a dictionary, and a collection of poems, entitled

Corpus Poetarum. An unknown man appeared in the dream and told him to look for a poem by Ausonius called 'Est et Non', and another 'Quod vitae sectabor iter'. I read an account published in 1929, by a French scholar, Maxime Leroy, trying to analyse this dream, who said he had sent them to Dr Freud in Vienna, and published Dr Freud's reply. And Dr Freud replied that this was what he called a great dream, in which you really are thinking at full pitch but with dream images, and in this case he said, you may trust the dreamer.

> Les rêves de notre philosophe sont ce que l'on appelle des 'rêves d'en haut' (Träume von oben), c'est-à-dire des formations d'idées qui auraient pu être créées aussi bien pendant l'état de veille que pendant l'état de sommeil et qui, en certaines parties seulement, ont tiré leur substance d'états d'âme assez profonds. Aussi ces rêves présentent-ils le plus souvent un contenu à forme abstraite, poétique ou symbolique.
>
> L'analyse de ces sortes de rêves nous amène communément à ceci: nous ne pouvons pas comprendre le rêve; mais le rêveur – ou le patient – sait le traduire immédiatement et sans difficulté, étant donné que le contenu du rêve est très proche de sa pensée consciente. Il reste alors quelques parties du rêve au sujet desquelles le sujet ne sait que dire: ce sont précisément, les parties qui appartiennent a l'inconscient et qui, sous bien des rapports, sont les plus intéressantes.*

And this, I think, is not an aspect of Freud's thought that is usually discussed, at least by literary critics. It is exciting that Freud said you may sometimes trust the dreamer to be using the dream images to think with, more intensely than they could with flat language. It is also interesting that he discerns parts of these historical dreams that he feels sure he can say the dreamer did not wholly understand – for instance the appearance of the melon, offered by a figure at the side of the path, which Descartes

* Our philosopher's dreams are what are known as 'dreams from above' ('*Träume von oben*'). That is to say, they are formulations of ideas which could have been created just as well in a waking state as during the state of sleep, and which have derived their content only in certain parts from mental states at a comparatively deep level. That is why these dreams offer for the most part a content which has an abstract, poetic or symbolic form.

The analysis of dreams of this kind usually leads us to the following position: we cannot understand the dream, but the dreamer – or the patient – can translate it immediately and without difficulty, given that the content of the dream is very close to his conscious thoughts. There then remain certain parts of the dream about which the dreamer does not know what to say: and these are precisely the parts which belong to the unconscious and which are in many respects the most interesting.

had what Freud called the 'original' idea of interpreting as 'les charmes de la solitude, mais présentés par des sollicitations purement humaines'. Freud comments that the explanation is 'certainly not exact' but might lead to an exact explanation, with a sexual content.

I do have very clear symbolic dreams like that in which figures and landscapes are experienced entirely sensuously; yet the moment I wake up I remember the whole thing and can say what it means. But the dream forms have an intensity and complexity beyond the 'meaning' and affect my work deeply and permanently.

There's a much quieter version of that process, where you think as hard as you can about where your characters are in a novel you are writing, why you have brought them there, where they might go, what the problems are – and then, I've learned increasingly, it is necessary to turn away and trust my unconscious to solve the problem I've set myself. I go to bed, I even go into an intensely deep sleep for half an hour – and when I wake up I have a set of very clear images, much closer to dream than to worrying thought. This must be not unlike being in analysis and offering your dreams to somebody and suddenly seeing what it was you were trying to say, to understand.

Freud does connect private dream imagery out to the imagery of the whole of the human race. His wolves are wolves and they are mythical wolves and the Wolf Man connects to all the wolves in all the fairy stories . . .

SODRE: I would like to go back to Descartes's dream, which we assume must have its roots in his particular unconscious fantasies (which of course we know nothing about) and which has been transformed by him into a different object, a fascinating tool for understanding his mind: we know only some of his *ideas about his dream*, about the two books, the dictionary and the collection of poems, which seem to indicate a sense of different aspects of his mind coming together in integrated ways; we are told that he was 'bold enough to persuade himself that it was the Spirit of Truth which had chosen to open all the treasures of science to him by this dream'. Descartes seems to have experienced his dream very much like, in *The Professor's House*, Tom Outland experiences his vision of the Mesa (and the 'charms of solitude') where he is, he feels, in possession of all the treasures of the universe. ('The moon was up, though the sun hadn't set, and it had the glittering silverness the early stars have in high altitude.')

BYATT: You have written about Freud's own dreams.

SODRE: In a paper called '*Non Vixit* – A Ghost Story' I used one of

Freud's dreams (which is fundamentally about his irrational guilt feelings in relation to the death of his friend Fleischl), in which the dreaming Freud changes the phrase 'non vivit' (he is not alive) to 'non vixit' (he has not lived), to examine the question of dealing with unbearable events in the past by omnipotently obliterating their existence (the dream thought is, 'if somebody has never lived, I cannot have killed him'). The past cannot be obliterated because it remains alive for ever in memory – this is what Toni Morrison illustrates so powerfully in Sethe's fierce battle with her brain to dis-remember. And even Fanny Price refers to this in her 'memory speech', as 'wonderful' memory sometimes becoming horribly tyrannical – she would like to forget Portsmouth. Gwendolen is also engaged in a fierce battle against her past; the opening of the panel door represents also the mind assaulted by a horrible memory: the dead are forever alive in a persecuting way. In these novels many of the characters would like to make aspects of the past 'non vixit'.

SODRE: The richness of every symbolical communication is that thinking is stimulated at many different levels. Every dream – and every myth – has a basic simple structure which is universal and simultaneously has an infinitude of meanings which are particular not just to different people but to different aspects of your psychic life. A work of fiction at its best can be related to many different levels.

BYATT: Yes, and every particular narrative situation in which people might find themselves. I thought both when I read your article on that dream of Freud's, and when you were just talking: Freud teaches his reader to be an analyst, and presumably also taught his patients to be analysts. A patient tells his or her life to an analyst, including his or her symbolic or dreaming life, and an analyst tells back the same story in a different form. It's as though every story has endless, multifarious forms, as you were just saying, and the literary critic can also read into a novel things that the writer might not know they had put in, although they can be as wonderfully obvious as Freud's attempt to come to grips with his own guilt. I think particularly in *Villette*, and possibly also in *Beloved*, there are things which the novelist knew, and knew she had to write, and couldn't have said in any discursive form to anybody. Yet there they are presented in a narrative for us to see and know and read and feel and understand.

We do have to feel it as well. You wrote, in your article about dreaming, that a dream-image wolf in an analysis is an image which exists as a dream image, a picture you said, in the mind of the patient, and is then offered by the patient to the analyst who, if he or she is listening properly, makes her own or his own picture, which is not the same, and yet these two pictures must communicate. This reminded me of things I've written in my own novels again and again and again, of a kind of image hovering between two people, shared, as you always share somebody's image if you read properly, but you know you're not visualising the same scene. Just as much as you can't dream somebody's dream, you don't visualise the room that George Eliot visualised when she wrote her novels. When Toni Morrison writes, 'the sideboard took a step forward' you know, at a ridiculous level, every single one of us will see a different sideboard, and yet because of the nature of narrative and sharing images, it is possible to know exactly what was going on. In this way analysis is and is not the same as reading and writing, and dreaming.

SODRE: When reading a great novel, one has the gratifying experience of being capable simultaneously of sharing a particular experience with the writer, and knowing that you are also creating in your mind something which is particular to you, as what you take in becomes integrated with your own experiences, and as you have your own private imagery for what is being described. One of the painful things about watching a loved novel on the television is that you feel robbed of a piece of your internal world, which you may feel quite possessive of.

BYATT: I can give you a beautiful example of that: I had a friend who watched a television dramatisation of a novel by Rosamond Lehmann and she kept saying over and over again that the actress was all wrong, her shoulders were too broad, the actress was all wrong. And I looked at my friend, who had tiny little delicate thin shoulders, and it was quite clear that until she had seen this actress she had been able to identify bodily with the character, and now she couldn't, because actually the actress was extremely good in the part, but was physically incompatible with my friend. That observation does lead technically into something very interesting for novelists: if you want somebody to share properly, you must be specific. If, for instance, I wanted you to share properly my dream about the school and the library, I would have to tell you that the library was a very tall high building, almost like a mill building, almost like the buildings in Aldeburgh – the converted oasthouses where Benjamin Britten's operas are performed. The buildings towered above me – or they seemed to tower as big buildings do to the eyes of a child.

As I speak, I see my dream library had some connection with those, but were you to visualise Aldeburgh you would be misled, because it would be too specific. But I suddenly felt a need to tell you that the building was tall, in case you'd been imagining a little one. If I went on and described every window to you, I think a point would come when I would be excluding you rather than sharing images.

When I was a young novelist, I always told everybody too much because I was so excited by the richness of what I could see. If I did visualise a room I could see every little thing in it glittering and glittering, and I wanted to share the whole thing. An editor once said to me about another novelist: 'she leaves no room for other people's imagination', and I suddenly realised she was actually saying it to me about me and that there are places where you must leave a space.

SODRE: Yes, there must be the right balance, telling enough but not too much. Patients in analysis can use dreams defensively (unconsciously), by including such an enormous amount of obsessional detail that the analyst feels invaded and unable to think. But your telling me details of your dream makes me curious; and yet, I cannot know what it meant when you dreamt it. You said there weren't enough books for children in the dream library, which you thought must be connected to writing this book. One of the reasons why we chose to write this book in this form is that discussing these novels together constantly enriches the original reading experience, so that in our 'internal library' we feel that we have, in fact, more books now than we started with. On the other hand, the idea 'no books for children', together with the idea 'mill', reminds me of our first conversation about George Eliot, and how painful we felt was the episode in *The Mill on the Floss* when all Maggie Tulliver's books are sold.

BYATT: Yes, she must in fact have been almost the first intellectual heroine who lived for books.

SODRE: This is our last 'official' conversation for this book, and therefore there is a way in which today we are parting from 'our' six books.

BYATT: The workings of the mind are uncanny. I associate Aldeburgh with my parents' last home in Suffolk – where they went when I was quite grown-up, a place which has no childhood associations for me. But when you spoke of our parting from 'our' six books, I remembered the last time I was in the house in Suffolk, when both my parents were dead, and there was in fact a huge heap of books on the floor of my father's bedroom, books I remembered from my childhood, books that had always been there, and I wandered around distractedly 'saving' old favourites, *Leaves from the Golden Bough*, which had belonged to my mother, which I read as a small child, the actual edition of *The Pickwick Papers* I read as a very little girl, the Waverley Novels that had belonged to my paternal grandfather. At once a farewell and an attempt to salvage the most important part of my childhood.

But the school and the library in my dream had a feeling of being a cardboard set for a conventional 'children's story' in which any characters who appeared would be two-dimensional and brightly smiling. It was *too clean*. Desolate and *too clean*.

SODRE: I find it very interesting to see you making new connections to your dream – this links to what you have said about the way in which you write, allowing space for a more unconscious process to take place that can then be consciously integrated and elaborated. Your different thoughts are not part of your original dream and what it meant when you dreamed it; the dream can be used as a springboard for other meaningful memories and thoughts. I think, for instance, that your memory about Aldeburgh now is the opposite from Sethe's dis-remembering; remembering that particularly precious books belonged to particular people also salvages, symbolically, good aspects of your relationship with them. Whereas emphasising the two-dimensionality brings to mind the subject of 'falseness' in literature, which we have discussed all along; and this links in a complex way with childhood experiences of emotional isolation (which every child goes through, even if only momentarily) and the need for emotional contact through books (where the author becomes an imaginary parent telling a meaningful story).

Novels are important for children because they allow them wonderful adventures, creating interesting new worlds they otherwise would have no access to. My first 'grown-up' book was *Treasure Island*; the memory of my aunt translating it aloud to me, and, in her enthusiasm, suddenly leaping up and 'becoming' Long John Silver (with a 'Yo, ho ho and a bottle of rum!') is extraordinarily vivid. I have never dared to reread it as an adult, for fear of losing this experience. I think reading novels may also help children to work through complicated internal situations by presenting them with different symbolic resolutions of unconscious conflicts.

BYATT: That's very interesting. Could you say a little about what *Treasure Island* meant to you as a child? Or expand a little on what kind of situations a child might work through? Are we saying that a child works through things in reading them, differently from an adult? I know as I get older I need different problems, as a reader, and am bored by all but the very greatest presentations of, for instance, choice of partners. Whereas as a girl, I hunted out more and more alternative versions of these.

SODRE: I think the most important thing of all is that hearing the story *is* going out on an adventurous, mysterious journey, like the hero, Jim – in search of a treasure which, for the child reader, is the story itself. Jim is a child, which makes it possible for an immediate identification to happen; and he is telling the story in the past tense, so the child knows that, however frightening the story may become, Jim will survive in the end. Jim's 'history' has become a story even from Jim's point of view. It also occurs to me that this is a story dominated by terrible villains, some of which turn out to be either not as powerful or not as evil as they appear to be . . . so mastery over some fantasised version of the threatening grown-up world must be part of the pleasure of this kind of adventure.

BYATT: We have been talking about books, and also, particularly, talking about sharing. Dream imagery is intensely private and yet also in some curious way intensely general. Everybody has, to a certain extent, the same dreams, and yet they are completely individual. We seem to have linked this to the fact that reading is intensely private, and writing is intensely private, yet the reader shares the story with the writer, and with the characters too. Every reading is a different act of sharing. But if you talk to each other about books as we have been doing, this is yet another form of sharing. We confirm that there are things that both see, but also we are able to tell each other things that the other might not have seen. I was particularly moved by your psychoanalytic description of Christianity when we were talking about *Mansfield Park*: you pointed out so justly how terribly Fanny needed good internal objects, which isn't a way Jane Austen would have thought of it, or even Lionel Trilling when he said that she was 'pure in heart'. Yet in terms of the way we had read the book together, it made complete sense. That is exactly what Fanny needed, she couldn't live without good internal objects and she hadn't really been given any, and this is something I have learned. I could have said that her upbringing was very bad and very inadequate; I could have murmured that there was a terrible lot of noise at Portsmouth, but I wouldn't have been describing the state of affairs so accurately, I wouldn't have *understood* it in the same way.

SODRE: Thinking about the internal world brings to mind the fact that, of the six novels we chose, three have houses explicitly at their centre:

Mansfield Park, *The Professor's House* and *Beloved*, which starts with '124 was spiteful'. The world of these novels is enclosed in a particular place which is, in itself, intensely invested in meaning.

BYATT: In *The Professor's House* the house itself comes to represent fear of marriage, which in this case is primarily a fear of failure of energy.

SODRE: Randall in *An Unofficial Rose* feels, like St Peter, that marriage is life-threatening. He chooses to live moving from one hotel to another; he can't bear permanence.

BYATT: For these men, entering a woman's house is a kind of death. Though in *Daniel Deronda* of course the woman has gone into the man's dead house. The man is death. Which is interesting. And in *Mansfield Park,* despite feminist attempts to say that Sir Thomas Bertram's patriarchy is a form of death, it is actually Mrs Norris who exerts the greater negative power. The two women in *Mansfield Park* again are either inert or destructive. Lady Bertram and Mrs Norris together represent entropy proceeding at vast speed.

SODRE: And the action takes place mostly in the absence of the man, when Mansfield is a woman's house.

BYATT: It's interesting that so many women novelists should have produced this image – I can see, it's quite clear in the case of Lucy Snowe too, that a woman's house is something a woman is afraid of.

SODRE: M. Paul is also a prisoner of a woman's house (Madame Beck's).

BYATT: M. Paul in fact builds a house in which Lucy can be happy, but Lucy is obviously going to have to be happy in it on her own. Which is possible. But readers can also share the fantasy that she might be happy in it if married.

SODRE: But we don't have the means to know if they would have been happy building a home together. I think what you're saying is that these novelists are all saying that the happy marriage is a fantasy, a daydream about a house shared by two; and that there is much more often a reality in which the house is felt to belong to one and to imprison the other. The married couple is locked up in something that is felt to be claustrophobic and even deadly.

BYATT: It's interesting that the major European novels – European as distinguished from British – have an adulterous woman at the centre. Somebody said rather cleverly that all the nineteenth-century stories were about finding out 'who is the father'. But these English novels don't seem to be that, really. They seem to have fear of a house, and love of a house, at the centre. And the house represents continuity.

SODRE: But also the internal world.

BYATT: Can you say a bit more about that – about the way in which houses represent internal worlds?

SODRE: I think the three novels which are centrally about houses are good examples; what happens inside the houses stands symbolically for what happens in the central characters' minds. For instance, '124' is both an enemy – it attacks its inhabitants, it is in a way a horrible parent, whose function ought to be to protect and contain, but which does the opposite; a cruel parent who furiously shakes its children, rather than holding them. But also, 124 is haunted just like Sethe's mind is haunted. Jane Austen deliberately portrays 'Mansfield' as a particular state of mind, not just a place.

Our inner world is populated by lots of characters which are personifications of aspects of one's relationships: one doesn't have only one mother in one's psyche, but several versions of her (generous, neglectful, excited, idealised, withdrawn, etc.). These inner characters also relate to each other; for instance, a conflict within one's personality can be portrayed in fantasy as a battle between a father and a mother who inhabit the 'house' inside one's head.

The 'dangerous' houses in these novels are usually felt to be the *other person's mind*. If St Peter moves to their new house, he will become entirely his wife's creature, he won't have a mind of his own.

BYATT: I associate these images of houses as energy-traps with what Freud said about the death wish. The death wish isn't evil, he says, it's perfectly natural. It proceeds in us *pari passu* with the libido, the life force. We might get overtaken by it too early, but as he describes it, in 'Beyond the Pleasure Principle', it is in one way deeply pleasurable to become nothing. He says every organism wishes only to die after its own fashion. To return to the inorganic state from which it came.

SODRE: We were thinking about the difference between narrative in analysis and narrative in fiction; about the 'text' as something that comes from the patient to the analyst with the analyst as the 'reader'. The first thing that occurred to me is that Freud, when he published his first studies in hysteria, apologised for his case histories reading like short stories; when in fact what makes them so great is that they *do* read like short stories, which makes it possible for the reader to take them in in a way that is lively and interesting; they create a meaningful whole. Whereas if he were going to describe, as it were 'scientifically', every single bit of the patient with great objectivity you wouldn't ever be able to capture the essence of this person who is being described. When I wrote my first clinical paper I had this terrible feeling that if I didn't include every single aspect of my patient, I was not being truthful. It took me a long while to realise that I wasn't communicating anything more truthful by this fragmented accumulation of endless amounts of aspects, whereas if I could convey realistically, but imaginatively, one particular aspect that made sense to me, one of many pictures of the internal reality of the patient, in such a way that it created just the right image in the reader's mind, then something would be communicated which would allow the reader both to connect meaningfully and to think in different directions.

An analyst is trained to listen to stories and to try to think of different versions of the same story. Everybody has many different life histories, and, of course, biographies change as the analysis proceeds – there are different versions of the past, so that the analyst is the 'reader' of these particular texts, whose function is not to discover real events of the past, but to discover different, richer, more truthful versions of the same story. The analyst has to abstract patterns, and think about different relationships, and build up pictures of the internal world. In a helpful analysis the patient wouldn't be left with one single rigid fixed picture of the past, but would be able to play around imaginatively with different possibilities of different relationships; this is achieved mainly by being able to integrate different aspects of oneself, to ackowledge the multiplicity of complex and often painful and frightening feelings. The analyst as 'story-teller' offers the patient different versions of himself.

BYATT: There are one or two things I'd like to pick up there. One is that at one point you were almost saying that the truthfulness of the Freudian short story, or the analyst's story for the patient, depends on a kind of coherence, a kind of *aesthetic* arrangement almost. Then you said that the analyst isn't offering one meaningful story, but the possibility of several meaningful variants in a playful way. It was wonderful to hear psychoanalysis described as a playful form; it brought me back to my belief that literature ought to speak to the pleasure principle, or it is nothing. Because psychoanalysis has no obvious responsibility to the pleasure principle. It is concerned with discovering reality.

SODRE: These two are linked, of course, since the profound pleasure in literature comes from the writer's capacity to apprehend and communicate aspects of reality (including psychic reality) in original and complex ways. There isn't such a thing as one reality only; several versions of reality exist, which need not be contradictory, and can play upon our mind simultaneously, enriching one's capacity to think and to imagine.

BYATT: A writer has an odd sense of what is real and unreal, true and untrue, in the fiction that is being constructed. When I was writing my second novel I felt for a long time that there would come a point, about three-quarters of the way along the narrative, where two of the characters would perhaps make love to each other. When I got there I saw that the whole nature of the novel, and the nature of the people, was such that this could not possibly have happened. The scene up to which the whole of my narrative had, I thought, been leading, didn't happen, it wasn't there. I felt that this was a sort of truthfulness, that I knew it didn't happen. But of course none of that story ever happened, it was a fiction. I could have *made* it happen by just *writing* that scene. One thing I know, both as writer and reader, is that it is possible to deaden a narrative for a very long time by writing something that isn't 'true', in terms of coherence and strength and integrity. Integrity isn't a bad word. Narratives have integrity in both senses of the word. Freud said to his patients that they should tell him the truth as best they could as fully as they could, and that was the only requirement. And of course it is impossible to tell the whole truth. It's curious that when you first fall in love, you have a compulsion to tell the beloved the whole of your life story and they tell you theirs. Later you almost never do this in quite the same way again, as though a kind of storytelling that makes you coherent is part of falling in love. As it is also part of an analytic relationship.

SODRE: In the 'falling in love' situation the wish to know and to be known becomes intertwined with sexuality (and, of course, before Freud worked out the meaning of transference, and could begin to use it productively to understand his patients, he found himself up against his hysterical patients' eroticisation of their relationship with him). But I suspect that in the telling of one's own story there might also be, in addition to the need to be entirely contained in the other person's mind, an unconscious need to comunicate rather idealised versions of oneself.

BYATT: And this desire to be wholly contained in another mind, wholly present in a relationship, can be experienced as *dangerously* close.

SODRE: In many of the novels we discussed there is a profound ambivalence about closeness – as there is about knowledge. The intense desire for closeness creates claustrophobic anxieties. The patient in analysis may wish to be entirely understood, in the sense of accepted and held in mind, but also doesn't want too much known about destructive, not lovable, aspects. The wish for close contact runs together with the wish for independence and privacy. Or perhaps it would be better to describe it as an ebb and flow, towards meeting the other and back into the privacy of the self. Think of Lucy and Paul Emanuel – how intense is this ebb and flow of closeness and distance in their relationship, how desperately they want to be together, and how fiercely they struggle to keep their psychological independence! From the reader's point of view, one of the compelling motives to be engaged in taking in, and to some extent living with, the characters and story in the novel, is, via identification, the becoming involved in such conflicts. One part of us is engaged in the wish to obtain gratification through the gratification of the 'hero' 's wishes; for instance you want Lucy and Paul to get married and live happily ever after. But this would result in a superficial, ultimately boring experience; a 'happy ending', to be satisfying, has to be earned, a fairytale wouldn't exist if it weren't for the witches and dragons. In other words, the experience of conflict – within parts of the self, and between people – and its psychologically truthful resolution is what makes something gripping, what makes 'what happens in the story' really matter.

SODRE: I wanted to ask you something, going back to what you were saying about suddenly finding that a part of the story you are writing is wrong, untrue. You think you are moving towards a particular scene or denouement, and you find that you don't get there; I would like to hear more about the difference between 'inventing' and 'discovering', if I can put it this way. If you 'invent' something false, your reader won't believe you. Is that right?

BYATT: I think that is absolutely right. It's interesting etymologically, because *invenire* in Latin is to find, to discover. Virginia Woolf, in her notebooks, usually uses the verb 'making up' to describe her invention of her characters. I've always been slightly suspicious of that verb – it has associations either of dressmaking, or of childhood invention of imaginary playmates. I think I prefer to think of observing, or discovering, characters, making my way into a previously unknown world, which feels as though it was always there. 'Making up' is daydream, whereas inventing, discovering, has an element of dreaming. One difference between good books and bad books is that with a really good book you do have the sense of discovering a kind of order in the world – or a frightening disorder which somebody has nevertheless had the courage or the power to order for you. Whereas bad books indulge in daydreams or fantasy. As Iris Murdoch points out from time to time, all art but the very greatest is consolation and fantasy, but really great art is a form of knowledge. And I think all the books we've discussed have revealed the world to me. If you say you've discovered something by writing a novel, you can't say what you've discovered in abstract words, because you've discovered the whole world of that novel – 'world' is the right word. Think how different the worlds of all our novels are.

SODRE: In our conversation we keep coming back to why we can't do without these 'new worlds', why it is psychologically enriching to read a good novel. Reading a novel is not therapy, as you said, and yet there is something that can be enriching to the personality, and not just intellectually stimulating. George Eliot thought she wrote novels so that the reader could imagine and therefore extend his or her sympathy to all kinds of different people with their different predicaments. She thought, if people could imagine the lives and minds and thoughts of others, in all their particularity, they would become better people. This is a moral way of thinking about it, but it clearly brings with it the idea that reading a novel changes you. She has of course been accused of being moralistic and didactic, but I don't think her point was that she would tell you things; rather, she thought that by identifying with the characters you would be able to take in other points of view (you would know that others have 'an equivalent centre of self, whence the lights and shadows must always fall with a certain difference').

BYATT: I was going to say two things at once which appear to be mutually contradictory but aren't: the first is that reading a novel is the human activity which brings the inner world rigorously into play. But as you suggest, a novel is equally useful for imagining a social world, imagining people other than yourself as though you could enter their inner worlds. Of our novelists, Eliot and Murdoch are the two who very deliberately try to extend the number and kind of people you are made to take account of. Both do it for moral reasons, but also out of a kind of glee at being able to do it, being able to imagine these alien beings. Then I think of discoveries I made as a child. I didn't really read George Eliot until I was a grown woman, whereas I read Charlotte Brontë and Jane Austen as a quite small child. When we were talking about *Mansfield Park* I said that, on first meeting Fanny, I realised that women had to be silent, long before it was borne in upon me in life that women had to be silent. In the same way Charlotte Brontë gave me the possibility of contemplating an unfulfilled life when I read *Villette*. *Jane Eyre* doesn't do that for you because it gives you the daydream end so powerfully. But Lucy Snowe sits down and thinks it out: I have no money, I am not very beautiful, I am not very outgoing, I am going to have nothing. And it is actually very good for you to think out, to feel out, these hypothetical situations in depth before you encounter them. Which is why my dream is about people not having books when they were young; not having the books when their consciousness is being formed.

SODRE: You said that George Eliot and Iris Murdoch were the authors who wanted to extend your experience to others – and I was wondering about Toni Morrison, specifically with *Beloved*, where she is writing both for people who feel their history is tied up with that experience, and for people who don't.

BYATT: Toni Morrison gives us a way into that history by her truthfulness – and one keeps coming back to that word truthfulness – you feel that Toni Morrison is truthful in a profoundly imaginative way about what it was to be a nineteeth-century black woman who couldn't keep her children. She's done the work, she's done the imaginative work, she has *thought through* what it was like to be owned, to have children, to have them taken away and sold like piglets, and she's done it with a kind of courage which is almost unbearable to share in the imagination. We also said when we were discussing *Beloved* that in many ways the black characters were almost too good, yet we felt this was right because she had touched some mythic depth at which their goodness was real and necessary. You pointed out that Sethe needed good internal objects and just about had them; you connected this to Christianity and to the way in which biblical language and biblical narrative is used in *Beloved*. I think the experience of discussing the book deepened my understanding of it greatly.

SODRE: Yes, *Beloved* is one of the only novels I can remember in which the rereading had an even greater impact on me than the reading the first time. I didn't get the sort of detachment that comes with the already known, I felt it penetrated deeper layers in my mind; as we have said, this is partly due to the complex and compact way in which she writes, with this tremendous emotional punch, but partly I think it's the rawness of the experience which one defends against, psychologically.

One of the qualities she has as a great writer is precisely that she makes it possible for you to identify not only with an unknown experience but with an abhorrent one; for instance, the experience of a mother who kills her own child.

BYATT: To go back to rereading. Every time you reread one of these novels, you rediscover both the people and the narrative, *and* the mind of the author which is the place in which all these things cohere. There is a sense, I do believe, in which all the characters in any book are always aspects of a central consciousness, like all the people in a dream: your father in your dream is yourself, not your father. You might possibly compare rereading to repeatedly telling the same part of your life to an analyst? Understanding would make that, too, both more coherent and more glittering with meaning . . . I suppose we picked these books because they are books that we revisit and revisit so that they become part of ourselves, which is easy to say but very, very complicated to experience. One is so much richer for being a great number of people. I would like to add that you don't feel on the whole the same way about characters and stories in plays or films. This is because the encounter isn't solitary, like dreaming or daydreaming: it's public, and there is also the question of the actor's relation to the characters and to the audience. Shakespeare had it both ways, of course, with the added power of verse and rhythm . . .

SODRE: We were talking earlier about ownership of your visual images, and the way you lose this once the 'story' is placed outside. You said that when you read you turn to your internal world – in which you now have this other universe, part of the author's internal world, which you suddenly have access to; a great writer allows you to imagine that you are also contributing to the creation of this world. I don't mean that you consciously think that, but you have in your hands a little bundle of pieces of paper with little black things dotted all over them which you call a book, and as you look at it wonderful stories appear in your mind, which must give you (your omnipotent infantile self, presumably!) the gratifying illusion that you are helping to create this.

The author gives you the story, but you may have given Lady Macbeth a purple dress of your own design if you're reading *Macbeth*, whereas if you see it on stage she may be wearing black. On the other hand, if you are entirely absorbed by the play, the boundary between yourself and the world on the stage gets blurred, the distinction between what is you and what is not-you becomes irrelevant, and you may watch in the same state of mind as you watch the story in the novel taking place in the stage inside your head.

BYATT: I think one starts to want to write novels because there is no pleasure in the world greater than creating these brilliantly coloured coherent worlds in your head. But that implies the need to be solitary, which I don't think happens to playwrights because they have to come to grips with actors, directors, sets, other people helping them to make the thing. You can't write a novel if you can't stand being alone for very long periods in your life. My working day now is prolonging the way of life discovered by a lonely child who escaped into books. I spent the first half of my writing life saying dutifully, 'Books are bad because you escape into them' and then I decided, no they're not, they're still more interesting than most of the rest of life. Sometimes I think we live in a world where solitude is increasingly less valued, and even suspected.

SODRE: There are different kinds of solitude. The sort of aloneness where you couldn't imagine a world, through your own creativity or somebody else's, could be unbearable; but what *you* are describing isn't lonely, because in your mind you are either with the author, if you are a reader, or you are the author relating to your own characters as your own creations but also as people. You are not living in a blank. It would be terrible if you were completely on your own with a blank mind. So although it is, of course, true that as a writer you have to bear to be on your own to be able to create, as soon as you are creating, your mind is populated. I think this connects to the question of good internal objects because you can tolerate being on your own – not for ever but for periods of time – if you are supported by your past experiences, which implies that there are people in your mind who hold on to you, who have loved you, who still love you.

BYATT: We noticed that Fanny has a little room to retreat to, to be on her own – and we are required to, we do, love her partly because she has this need – but then we are solitary when we are reading her. Lucy Snowe has an attic to which she retreats and you see that she couldn't survive without it and yet she's afraid of it turning into the other sort of solitude.

SODRE: The attic *chez* Madame Beck I think is rather a frightening place, where M. Paul imprisoned her on the day of the play, and where she sees the nun. Lucy desperately needs privacy in this house of spies, where Madame Beck even steals her letters to read them at her leisure – even her bureau is violated. Lucy's attic is in her mind – in her fiercely guarded mental space where nobody must intrude; thinking for herself, but also keeping secrets – even from the reader! – is for her a matter of survival. In her early letters and journal (quoted in Lyndall Gordon's biography) Charlotte Brontë writes about her despair at having no privacy in her hated job as a teacher; she writes with her eyes shut, thus creating an 'attic' behind her eyelids:

> I am just going to write because I cannot help it. Wiggins [Branwell] might indeed talk of scriblomania if he were to see me

> just now encompassed by the bulls . . . all wondering why I write with my eyes shut – staring, gaping long their astonishment. E. Cook on one side of me E. Lister on the other and Miss W[oole]r in the background. Stupidity the atmosphere, school-books the employment, asses the society. What in all this is there to remind me of the divine, silent, unseen land of thought, dim now and indefinite as the dream of a dream, the shadow of a shade.

But she also feels afraid of being alone, away from home, from her sisters, and she is aware that she uses the Angria world as a kind of escapism, and yet she can't bear to let go; she knows that she has to create a different kind of fiction which isn't defensive and for that she has to bear to be alone.

> When I depart from these [dream-people] I feel almost as if I stood on the threshold of a home and were bidding farewell to its inmates. When I strive to conjure new inmates I feel as if I had got into a distant country where every face was unknown, and the character of all the population an enigma which it would take much study to comprehend and much talent to expound. Still, I long to quit for a while that burning climate where I have sojourned too long – its skies flame, the glow of sunset is always upon it. (ibid.)

BYATT: I've always felt strongly about that aspect of her. Cassandra, the main character in *The Game*, my second novel, is very much in danger of being overwhelmed by a fantasy life or a reading life which has turned into bad daydreams or obsessive image-making of an almost mad kind, which is what happens to Lucy. On the other hand the Professor in *The Professor's House* wants to be entirely alone in order to write history – and his world is more peopled when he is alone, and very impoverished when there are only his wife, daughters and sons-in-law in it. And as you pointed out, Tom Outland has a vision of total solitude as total plenitude. And the wonderful moment at the end of *Beloved* when Paul D gives Sethe to herself and he says 'You your best thing' is surely also to do with solitude and self-containment. Until that moment she's been unable to be alone with herself, or at peace with the beings who inhabit her mind and her memory. It's curious how *An Unofficial Rose* won't fit into the pattern of relations I'm seeing between the texts. It's more like a play, in that sense – as though the characters are caught in a moral drama, like an allegory, rather than in some depth of solitary contemplation of the psyche. It's as though Iris Murdoch chooses to display the psyche by fragmenting it and playing little bits of it against each other in endless little variations on the same theme. A *Psychomachia*, a Battle of the Soul, to use an ancient name for a spiritual personified allegory. She doesn't, at least in that novel, give you a central character with whom to identify, who is alone or has this need to be alone.

BYATT: When we began these conversations, I said that novelists are good gossips, they love noticing little things about people and chattering about them. John Forrester in his excellent book, *Language and the Origins of Psychoanalysis*, begins by quoting Freud's description of his method as a 'talking cure'. I feel we've discovered or reintroduced conversation as a form of shared reading – a pleasure and a way of learning which has almost vanished. We have allowed ourselves to talk about the characters in the novels as though they were real people, which is an almost primitive mode of discourse which literary criticism has eschewed for a long time. We know now so well that they are *not* real. We are constantly told that they are hypotheses, narrative functions. We have lost the capacity to talk about them as their creators must have wanted us to, and as indeed we do in normal, unprofessional conversation. I feel what you and I have had is a sort of conversation which is sophisticated at one level and very deliberately primitive and naive at another, which has brought the worlds of the books, at least for us, back together, briefly. Do you think gossip is a good way of putting it?
SODRE: Yes. We wanted to have the freedom to imagine these characters and talk about them as if they were people we knew – as if we had just met round the corner; to be imaginative and exchange ideas about them, and to suspend for a moment – as one does when one is reading alone – the knowledge that we are talking about something that isn't true. We can pretend, which I think is intensely pleasurable, that we are talking about people who are real, because that's how we feel about them. We chose books that were deeply meaningful to both of us because we knew we could do our 'gossiping' with ease. This links to storytelling, originally oral rather than written, and also to childhood, being told stories before one could read. When you learn how to read, a process of internalisation takes place: the person who tells you the story becomes a person in your mind. One of the pleasures of doing this book is that we are talking about them, our characters, and we are also talking about each other, and how we react to these different experiences – learning different ways of reading, and therefore different 'stories within

the story' – the differences in our thinking as much as the similarities and identifications.

BYATT: I think we have found more similarities than differences, but I think we began on our dialogue because we both felt that that was true. As you said earlier on in this conversation, we began on that dialogue because we both instinctively responded to George Eliot and her wisdom in very much the same way. I feel that during our talks I have been given all sorts of new information and understanding – not only because you have a professionalism that I don't have, but because you have pointed out little things I hadn't noticed and should have done, and shall remember. When we were talking about *An Unofficial Rose* you remarked quite casually that of course the quarrel between the siblings about the German knife refers back to the quarrel between the siblings about the little silver knife in *Mansfield Park*. I'd never thought of that – although the moment you'd said it it seemed obvious, and I had thought of the general analogy with *Mansfield Park*, which I hadn't seen as a suggestion before I myself said it. It's wonderful how just talking can go on adding, apparently endlessly, to understanding.

SODRE: But I would never have thought that *An Unofficial Rose* had anything at all to do with *Mansfield Park*, if you hadn't told me that. Once you told me, I went back and reread it, looking for clues. It came as a complete surprise that I told you something you had not thought of, since I had the impression that I'd learned that from you.

BYATT: That's the best way of talking. One of the things that seems to be happening in modern universities is that owing to the pressure of students and the absence of staff, students are being taught increasingly by lecture and not by conversation: conversational teaching is being diminished or abandoned. Yet when I was a teacher – and teaching, like novel-writing, is a gossiping structure – what I learned most from was dialogues with students: students telling me something I didn't know; students understanding something I was saying, but understanding slightly differently. Writing lectures was one way of acquiring and ordering knowledge, but actually working something out with somebody, in conversation, was quite another thing, and equally valid. If I could change the universities now, I would abolish all the lectures, put them on video once and for all, and reinstitute seminars. If you don't discuss, you don't understand.

SODRE: Perhaps we should talk about endings, before the end of our last conversation. It has been said that endings are for the novelist the most difficult thing to do. Could you comment?

BYATT: I think this is partly because endings are felt to be more artificial than the flow of the narrative. There is no *reason* why any story should come to an end, unless it is a tragedy and the end is death, or a fairytale comedy, where the end is marriage. The ending, as you are suggesting, is negotiated with the narrative expectations of the reader, who has certain needs, purely *as a reader* – a need for happiness and satisfaction, and an equally strong need for *closure* – a need to feel that the end of the story has been arrived at and is known. This is an aesthetic need, to do with wholeness, which runs counter to many modern aesthetic theories which insist on denying the reader both emotional and aesthetic satisfaction. Several of our novels seem to solve this with a double ending – one happy and closed, one open and uncertain.

SODRE: Yes; we discussed this in *Villette*, in relation to the 'happy ending' for Paulina and Graham, which is sarcastically repeated by Brontë at the end, when she offers the false happy ending for Lucy and Paul for those weak readers who couldn't bear the tragedy; and we also thought that on rereading the novel, one finds Lucy's experience of Paul's drowning in the imagery of the (untold) disaster that happened in the years after 'Bretton'. This led me to wonder if such a need (for tragedy and comedy, as it were) is present in the other novels; and *Daniel Deronda* comes to mind immediately, with Gwendolen's tragedy and Deronda's and Mirah's rather sentimental finale. In *Mansfield Park*, which is more a 'comedy', everybody (almost) comes to a tragic end except for Fanny and Edmund – who have a blissful, fairytale-ish happy ending . . . except that the author puts some doubt in your mind as to the veracity of it! I think Cather provides a deeply satisfying end, which is simultaneously open and closed: the Professor has suffered a 'small death', as you said: he is facing, and mourning, a part of himself – and yet the last words are: 'He thought he knew where he was, and that he could face with fortitude the *Berengaria* and the future.' This is an example of Cather's brilliant craftsmanship: something has closed down – and this is also contained in the tragic death of Tom Outland – and opened in a different way towards the new stage in the future (and one is reminded of George Eliot's first words in the Finale of *Middlemarch*: 'Every limit is a beginning as well as an ending'). And yet . . . Cather has also provided the reader with one word that unsettles everything: 'He *thought* he knew . . .' This word opens a gap for the possibility of tragic closure; moments ago, after all, St Peter had felt suicidal.

The last page of *An Unofficial Rose* contains the happy ending and the tragic one: Hugh sails with Mildred towards a blissful future, and on his way delivers the *coup de grâce* to the failed romance between Felix and Ann, when he complacently and obtusely tells Felix that Ann is 'Gay, rather, in her own little way. She's quite a bouncy little person, really' (Ch. 36). Murdoch shows in Hugh's internal monologue his capacity to erase from his mind all painful experience, all sense of guilt and responsibility:

> Hugh got up when Felix was gone and wandered out of the now empty bar on to the deck. He walked to the rail. Behind the ship the pale road of the wake stretched away back into the night. The black empty water surrounded them, the old eternal preoccupied ruthless sea. Hugh worshipped its darkness, its vastness, its utter indifference. He felt lighter and happier than at any time since Fanny became ill; perhaps, he suddenly thought, lighter and happier than ever before. Yet how did one know? One forgot, one forgot. What hold had one on the past? The present moment was a little light travelling in darkness. Penn Graham would forget, and think that he enjoyed his time in England. Ann had forgotten the real Randall, Randall had forgotten the real Ann, probably by now. Hugh had rejected Emma for reasons, and forgotten the reasons. His consciousness was a tenuous and dim receptacle and it would soon be extinct. But meanwhile there was now, the wind and the starry night and the great erasing sea. And ahead there was India and the unknown future, however brief. And there was comfortable, cosy Mildred and gay enamoured Felix. Perhaps he had been confused, perhaps he had understood nothing, but he had certainly survived. He was free. (Ch. 36)

Hugh's perception of Felix as 'gay, enamoured' gives the reader a pang, for his tragic fate. Murdoch describes Hugh's amazing capacity to undo the past both by the detailed way she follows his trend of thought, but also, more strikingly, by the way he thinks about the sea: the double meaning of 'wake' he is leaving behind himself, followed by the change in his perception of the sea, which moves from 'eternal preoccupied ruthless' to 'utter indifference', to 'great erasing sea'. Hugh is a champion 'dis-rememberer'! The ending is happy, but the reader is not allowed to forget the tragedy left in its 'wake'.

BYATT: You are suggesting that as well as the happy, or unhappy, fairytale or tragic, conventional endings the reader expects from novels, there is a subtler 'casting off' going on – a releasing of both reader and writer – and in Hugh's case, comically and ironically, the characters – from the burden of *remembering* the stories, their events and their form. Hugh's ship and the *Berengaria*'s approach are part perhaps of an ancient image of the sea as the boundary of human consciousness, out of which we come, and into which we disappear. The different descriptions of it that succeed each other in Hugh's – or Murdoch's reader's – mind move from the anthropomorphic, with human emotions – 'ruthless preoccupied' – through an intermediate *half*-anthropomorphic 'indifferent' to the inhuman 'great erasing', where the sea becomes both separate from our readings of our fates and an instrument of forgetting. Iris Murdoch is attached to images of the sea, both as swallowing fate to be fought (many of her characters nearly die while swimming), and as the inhuman which transcends us. Both in *The Sea, The Sea* and in *Time of the Angels* she refers to Valéry's beautiful and mysterious line in 'Le Cimetière marin', where the horizon and the shore are 'La mer, la mer, toujours recommencée', which is beautiful in a poem about the finality of death, and the possibility of endurance in memory.

SODRE: The wish to forget tragedy is tremendously powerful, as I have just discovered in a very striking way: when I was rereading the end of *Beloved* I found out that I had, in fact, forgotten something of crucial importance: that the novel, which has a deeply satisfying happy ending – the only one in these six novels that feels entirely earned, the very beautiful, moving words 'You your best thing, Sethe. You are' (p. 273) – *does not end there*! The last, short, chapter is about Beloved, 'disremembered and unaccounted for'. Forgetting her is the price Sethe has to pay to be able to survive, and I am amazed that I, too, 'disremembered' her. In fact, I think we never discussed this last chapter!

BYATT: I am as delighted and shocked and satisfied as you are that we both with one accord *forgot* that last chapter of *Beloved*. In fact, as Toni Morrison might have suspected we would, I have always read it too fast, with half-averted eyes. I think this is because *Beloved* the novel is a story that breaks a taboo, tells us about a thing we don't want to know, infanticide, and we hurry to unknow it – and its author is lying in wait for us.

Morrison too uses water as an image of erasure and forgetting, though ambiguously. The phrase that comes after 'It was not a story to pass on' – 'They forgot her like a bad dream' – fits so well on to what we have been saying to each other about how narratives and memory and dreams and telling go together – as do, perhaps, bad dreams, disremembering, and *not* telling.

Source Notes

A Note on the Texts

The texts used are: Jane Austen, *Mansfield Park* (1814), ed. Tony Tanner (1966; Penguin Classics, 1985); Charlotte Brontë, *Villette* (1853), ed. Mark Lilley (1979; Penguin Classics, 1985); George Eliot, *Daniel Deronda* (1876), ed. Barbara Hardy; (Penguin English Library, 1967); Willa Cather, *The Professor's House* (1925), introduced by A. S. Byatt (Virago, 1981); Iris Murdoch, *An Unofficial Rose* (Penguin, 1962); Toni Morrison, *Beloved* (Chatto & Windus, 1987). For ease of reference, sources are given by chapter rather than page, except for *Beloved*.

Chapter One: MANSFIELD PARK

The critical and biographical studies mentioned include Lionel Trilling's 'Mansfield Park', in *The Opposing Self: Nine Essays in Criticism* (London, Secker & Warburg, 1955); Tony Tanner, Introduction to the Penguin *Mansfield Park* (Harmondsworth, 1985); Marilyn Butler, *Jane Austen: The War of Ideas* (Oxford University Press, 1988), and Park Honan, *Jane Austen: Her Life* (London, Weidenfeld & Nicolson, 1987); Elizabeth Jenkins, *Jane Austen: A Biography* (1938; new edition, London, Gollancz, 1986). The letter to Cassandra can be found in *Jane Austen's Letters*, ed. Deirdre Le Faye (Oxford University Press, 1995); see also *Jane Austen: 'My Dear Cassandra'. The Illustrated Letters*, selected by Penelope Hughes-Hallett (London, Collins & Brown, 1990). The little prayer comes from Jane Austen, *Catharine and Other Writings*, ed. Margaret Anne Doody and Douglas Murray (Oxford University Press, World's Classics, 1993).

Relevant psychoanalytic writings on the Oedipus complex include: R. Britton, M. Feldman, and E. O'Shaughnessy, *The Oedipus Complex Today*, ed. J. Steiner (London, Karnac, 1989); Sigmund Freud, 'The Interpretation of

Dreams' in the *Standard Edition of the Complete Psychological Works of Sigmund Freud* (London, The Hogarth Press, 1950). For a psychoanalytic view of Sophocles' Oedipus plays see J. Steiner, 'Two Types of Pathological Organization in *Oedipus the King* and *Oedipus at Colonus*', in *Psychic Retreats* (London, Routledge, 1993). And for fairytales, see Bruno Bettelheim, *The Uses of Enchantment* (London, Thames & Hudson, 1976), and Marina Warner, *From the Beast to the Blonde* (London, Chatto & Windus, 1994).

Chapter Two: VILLETTE

The most useful source is still *The Brontës: Their Lives, Friendships and Correspondence* 4 vols, ed. A. Symington and J. Wise (Oxford, Blackwell, 1933, repr. 1980). A revised edition is in process, beginning with *The Letters of Charlotte Brontë: Volume One, 1827–47*, ed. Margaret Smith (Oxford University Press, 1995). Among the numerous biographies, we have generally referred to the following: Elizabeth Gaskell, *The Life of Charlotte Brontë* (1857); Winifred Gérin, *Charlotte Brontë: The Evolution of Genius* (Oxford University Press, 1967, repr. 1971); Lyndall Gordon, *Charlotte Brontë: A Passionate Life* (London, Chatto & Windus, 1994); and Juliet Barker, *The Brontës* (London, Weidenfeld & Nicolson, 1995). Studies of the juvenilia are *An Edition of the Early Writings of Charlotte Brontë*, vol. i, ed. Christine Alexander (Oxford, Blackwell, 1987); and *The Juvenilia of Jane Austen and Charlotte Brontë*, ed. Francis Beer (Harmondsworth, Penguin, 1986).

The essay by F. R. Leavis on *Othello*, 'Diabolic Intellect and the Noble Hero' (1952), is reprinted in his *The Common Pursuit* (Harmondsworth, Penguin, 1993 edn).

The work by Melanie Klein referred to is 'Mourning and its relation to manic depressive states', in *Love, Guilt and Reparation* (London, The Hogarth Press, 1940). For the differentiation of dreaming, daydreaming and creative thinking, see Hanna Segal, *Delusion and Artistic Creativity and Other Psychoanalytic Essays* (London, Karnac and Free Association Books, 1981) and *Dream, Phantasy and Art* (London, Tavistock/Routledge, 1991); and D. Winnicott, 'Dreaming, Fantasying, and Living' in *Playing and Reality* (London, Tavistock, 1971).

Chapter Three: DANIEL DERONDA

For George Eliot's essays and poems, see *George Eliot: Selected Essays, Poems and Other Writings*, ed. A. S. Byatt (Harmondsworth, Penguin, 1990). The best biographical information remains Gordon Haight, *George Eliot: A Biography* (Oxford University Press, 1968; Penguin 1991), and his edition of *The George*

Eliot Letters (9 vols, New Haven, Yale University Press, 1955, 1978). Critical studies include Gillian Beer, *Darwin's Plots* (London, Routledge, 1983) and *George Eliot* (Brighton, Harvester Press, 1986); Barbara Hardy, *The Appropriate Form; Ritual and Feeling in the Novels of George Eliot* (Swansea, University College of Swansea Press, 1973); *Particularities: Readings in George Eliot* (London, Peter Owen, 1985); *The Novels of George Eliot* (London, Athlone Press, 1994); Jenny Uglow, *George Eliot* (London, Virago, 1987).

Elinor Shaffer's point about Daniel Deronda and Renan's Christ can be found in *'Kubla Khan' and The Fall of Jerusalem: The Mythological School in Biblical Criticism and Secular Literature, 1770–1880* (Cambridge University Press, 1985). Edward Dowden's essay 'George Eliot' can be found in *George Eliot: The Critical Heritage*, ed. David Carroll (London, Routledge, 1971). The work by Jean Michelet referred to is *L'Insecte* (Paris, Librairie Hachette, 1858). A. C. Bradley's essay on *Hamlet* appears in *Shakespearian Tragedy* (1904; Penguin, 1991).

Psychoanalytic studies interesting in connection with *Deronda* include W. Bion, *Learning From Experience* (London, Karnac, 1962) and *Elements of Psychoanalysis* (London, Karnac, 1963); and more specifically, Margot Waddell, 'George Eliot: The Unmapped Country' in M. H. Williams and M. Waddell, *The Chamber of Maiden Thought* (London, Routledge, 1991) and 'Concepts of the Inner World in George Eliot's Work' in *Journal of Child Psychotherapy*, vol. 12, n. 2 (1986).

Chapter Four: THE PROFESSOR'S HOUSE

The most recent critical biography of Willa Cather is Hermione Lee, *Willa Cather: A Life Saved Up* (London, Virago, 1989). Cather's essay, 'The Kingdom of Art' is included in *The Kingdom of Art: Willa Cather, First Principles and Critical Statements 1893–96*, ed. Bernice Slote (Nebraska, University of Nebraska Press, 1967). Her story 'The Enchanted Bluff' can be found in *The Short Stories of Willa Cather*, ed. Hermione Lee (London, Virago, 1989). *Death Comes to the Archbishop* is also reprinted by Virago, introduced by A. S. Byatt (1984).

Chapter Five: AN UNOFFICIAL ROSE

A. S. Byatt's study of Iris Murdoch is *Degrees of Freedom: The Early Novels of Iris Murdoch* (London, Chatto & Windus, 1965, revised edn. Vintage, 1994). 'Against Dryness' was published in *Encounter* No. 88 (January 1961) and is included in *The Novel Today: Contemporary Writers on Modern Fiction*, ed. Malcolm Bradbury (London, Fontana, 1990); 'On "God" and "Good" ' and

'The Idea of Perfection' are included in *The Sovereignty of Good* (London, Routledge, 1991); *Sartre, Romantic Rationalist* (1953) was reissued with a new introduction in 1989 (Harmondsworth Penguin).

Other works mentioned include Simone Weil's *Gravity and Grace* (1952; repr., London, Routledge, 1972). And see also S. Freud, 'Mourning and Melancholia' in *Standard Edition*, vol. XIV. For George Eliot's scorn of compensation, in 'Silly Novels by Lady Novelists,' see *George Eliot: Selected Essays, Poems and Other Writings*, ed. A. S. Byatt (Harmondsworth, Penguin, 1990). John Bayley's study of Henry James's *The Golden Bowl* appears in *The Characters of Love: A Study on the Literature of Personality* (London, Constable, 1960).

Chapter Six: BELOVED

The other novels by Toni Morrison referred to are *Song of Solomon* and *Tar Baby* (London, Chatto & Windus, 1978, 1981). Her views on writing and religious belief can be found in *Playing in the Dark: Whiteness and the Literary Imagination* (Cambridge, Mass., Harvard University Press, 1992).

For the themes raised in connection with earlier American novels, see Leslie Fiedler, *Love and Death in the American Novel* (Harmondsworth, Penguin, 1984) and Harry Levin, *The Power of Blackness* (Ohio University Press, 1987); and for the underworld journey see Brian Aldiss, *Helliconia* trilogy (London, Jonathan Cape, 1982–5). Freud quotes Frazer on ancestors in *Totem and Taboo* (1912–13), (Harmondsworth, the Pelican Freud Library XIII, 1985). For a discussion of this in relation to other modern novels, see 'The Omnipotence of Thought' in A. S. Byatt, *Passions of the Mind* (London, Chatto & Windus, 1991).

Chapter Seven: DREAMS AND FICTIONS

On psychoanalysis and creativity see R. Britton, 'Wordsworth's Best Conjecture: A Theory of Psychic Development' and 'Reality and Unreality in Phantasy and Fiction: a Comment on Freud's "Creative Writers and Day-Dreaming" ' in *Love, Hate and Knowledge* (London, Routledge, forthcoming), and also Hanna Segal, 'A Psychoanalytic Approach to Aesthetics' (1952) and 'Delusion and Artistic Creativity' (1974) in her selected essays (1981; listed in notes to *Villette*). For narrative in psychoanalysis see R. Schaffer, *The Analytic Attitude* (London, Karnac and The Institute of Psychoanalysis, 1983); for language see John Forrester, *Language and the Origins of Psychoanalysis* (London, Macmillan, 1980).

Descartes's dream is quoted from Maxime Leroy, *Descartes: le philosophie au masque* (Paris, 1929); see also Freud, 'Some Dreams of Descartes', *Standard Edition*, vol. XXI. For Charlotte Brontë on dreams, see Lyndall Gordon's biography (listed in notes to *Villette*). And for Klein theory in general, see Hanna Segal, *Introduction to the Work of Melanie Klein* (London, The Hogarth Press, 1978) and E. Spillius, *Melanie Klein Today, Developments in Theory and Practice* (London, Routledge, 1988).

Index